CHARTERS OF BURTON ABBEY

ANGLO-SAXON CHARTERS · II

CHARTERS OF BURTON ABBEY

EDITED BY

P. H. SAWYER

Published for THE BRITISH ACADEMY
by THE OXFORD UNIVERSITY PRESS
1979

Oxford University Press, Walton Street, Oxford OX2 6DP

OXFORD LONDON GLASGOW
NEW YORK TORONTO MELBOURNE WELLINGTON
KUALA LUMPUR SINGAPORE JAKARTA HONG KONG TOKYO
DELHI BOMBAY CALCUTTA MADRAS KARACHI
NAIROBI DAR ES SALAAM CAPE TOWN

ISBN 0 19 725940 5

Printed in Great Britain
at the University Press, Oxford
by Eric Buckley
Printer to the University

TO

CHRISTOPHER CHENEY

FOREWORD

PROFESSOR PETER SAWYER's edition of the charters of the Benedictine abbey of Burton upon Trent in Staffordshire forms the second volume in the series sponsored by the British Academy and the Royal Historical Society which is intended to provide a critical edition of all surviving written title-deeds of the Anglo-Saxon period. The first fascicule, *Charters of Rochester*, edited by the late Professor Alistair Campbell, appeared in 1973. In his Foreword to that work, Professor C. R. Cheney, Chairman of the joint committee responsible for the series, gave a full account of the origins of the project and of its progress to that date. In addition, he outlined the principles on which the editorial work was to be based. Readers are referred to that earlier Foreword for information on these general points. While the broad editorial plan laid down by the committee has been adhered to in the present volume, a small number of modifications have been introduced. Most notably, some plates have been included to illustrate original charters in the William Salt Library, Stafford. Dr Michael Lapidge has provided a Glossary of Latin words, and there is also a list of vernacular words occurring in boundary clauses. It seems especially valuable that the rich collection of Burton charters should be edited so soon in the series of fascicules, for the vast majority of pre-Conquest title-deeds relate to southern England, which has become a relatively familiar field through the work of generations of scholars. In this volume we have the opportunity to study a great landed estate of the north midlands at an exceptionally early period.

Since 1973 the joint committee has suffered a sad loss by the death in 1976 of Vivian Galbraith, who had been an enthusiastic inspirer and friend of the project since its inception. Professor Cheney, having steered the committee's work wisely and tolerantly from its first meeting, demitted office as Chairman in 1978, and Professor G. W. S. Barrow was appointed in his stead. Professor Sawyer continues as Honorary Secretary. Fortunately, Professor Cheney remains a member of the committee, and the remaining membership consists of Mr T. A. M. Bishop, Professor Julian Brown, Dr Pierre Chaplais, Dr Margaret Gelling, Dr N. R. Ker, and Professor Eric Stanley. The publishing rate of one fascicule a year which had been hoped for at the outset of the project has not been attained and must now seem somewhat un-realistic. Nevertheless, the fascicules for Sherborne and Selsey are well advanced, and the respective editors are actively at work on the charters of Abingdon, Canterbury, Exeter, Winchester, and Worcester.

G. W. S. BARROW

ACKNOWLEDGEMENTS

THANKS are due in the first place to the owners and custodians of the manuscripts on which this edition is based; in particular to the Marquess of Anglesey and the Trustees of the William Salt Library, and to Mr K. H. Stanesby and Mr F. B. Stitt, librarians respectively of Burton upon Trent Public Library and the William Salt Library. I am also glad to acknowledge the willing help given by the staffs of the British and Bodleian Libraries and the National Library of Wales, especially by Mr David Huws and Mr B. G. Owen of the latter institution.

Many scholars have, by their advice and criticism, saved me from errors and greatly increased the usefulness of this book. My main obligation is to Professor Dorothy Whitelock who generously devoted much time and effort to this work, and whose comments have been of the greatest value. Help that she and others have given on some specific points is acknowledged in notes, but I should here like to express more general thanks to the members of the committee responsible for this corpus of Anglo-Saxon charters, all of whom read the complete type-script, and in particular to Professor Julian Brown, Dr Pierre Chaplais, and Dr Neil Ker, and, on linguistic matters, Professor Eric Stanley. The editing of the texts has been much improved thanks to the help generously given by Dr David Dumville and Dr Michael Lapidge, who also passed on some valuable suggestions made by Dr Michael Winterbottom. Dr Lapidge has put me further in his debt by compiling the Latin glossary. I have also benefited from the advice of Dr Gillian Fellows Jensen, Dr Margaret Gelling, Mr Simon Keynes, Professor Harold Mattingly, and Mr Ian Moxon. Of the many people who have helped in the production of this book I am particularly indebted to Miss Sheona Ferguson, who typed it all.

CONTENTS

INTRODUCTION

1. THE ARCHIVES OF BURTON ABBEY

THE thirty-eight charters in this fascicule come from the archives of the abbey of Burton upon Trent. All were copied, at least in part, in the thirteenth century by a scribe of that abbey into a quire of *carte antique* that now forms part of the miscellaneous Burton collection, MS. Peniarth 390 in the National Library of Wales at Aberystwyth. Four of the charters (**28, 29, 31, 35**) were copied in the thirteenth-century Burton cartulary deposited by the Marquess of Anglesey in the British Library as MS. Loans 30. Eight are also preserved on seven single sheets of parchment, written in various hands of the tenth and eleventh centuries.[1]

Only six of these charters should be condemned as spurious (**10, 18, 21, 26, 35, 37**), one is suspicious (**6** or **7**), while two are later copies that pretend to be originals but may derive from authentic charters (**14, 17**). No more than half the collection concerns estates owned or claimed by Burton Abbey: twelve (**5, 6, 7, 17, 18, 26, 27, 28, 29, 31, 34, 35**) were certainly and five (**1, 8, 15, 16, 23**) were possibly title-deeds of abbey estates. One is a charter for an estate that Wulfric owned but did not bequeath to the abbey (**11**) and two others (**12, 22**) may be of the same kind. These and most of the others, several of which may have belonged to members of the founder's family, may have been deposited with the abbey. **20** is a grant to Wulfgeat of land that was apparently held later by Wulfric's mother, and three are grants to Morcar (**32, 34, 37**), only one of which concerned an estate later owned by the abbey. It may also be suggested, but cannot be proved, that several of the charters belonged to Wulfric's brother, Ælfhelm (**2, 3, 9, 13, 19, 21**).

2. THE MANUSCRIPTS

Apart from Burton Muniment 1, which contains **28** and **29**, there are six single-sheet versions of Burton charters, three of which (**23, 27, 32**) have some claim to be considered originals. The others were written some time after their purported dates. **14** is a clumsy early-eleventh-century version of a possibly authentic charter of 956, **17** is an elaborate attempt made in the late eleventh century to reproduce the forms of a mid-tenth-century charter and, in marked contrast, the manifestly spurious **26**, although bearing the date 996, is closely modelled on the text of **17** and the witness-list of **27**. **17** and **26** were probably produced

[1] **14, 17, 23, 26, 27, 28, 29, 32.**

at Burton Abbey, as was the elaborate copy of the foundation charter
and the founder's will, now Burton Muniment 1 **(28, 29)**, and these
are good examples of the script of the abbey after the Norman Conquest.
The origin of the other charters is unknown. Burton Muniments 1 and 2
(14) were, until their deposit in Burton upon Trent Museum, in the
possession of the Marquess of Anglesey, whose ancestor, Sir William
Paget, acquired the estates of Burton Abbey at the Dissolution. The
other five charters were presented to the William Salt Library at Stafford
in 1941 by Mr R. H. Landor, who was apparently the descendant of an
agent of the Paget estates early in the nineteenth century.[1]

All these charters were in the archives of Burton Abbey in the thirteenth century when they were copied into Peniarth 390. Most of the
surviving originals have numbers endorsed in a medieval hand which
are the same as the numbers assigned to these texts in the present edition **(14, 17, 26, 27)** which like Peniarth 390 is arranged chronologically
and therefore follows the same order, with the exception of **4** which
was copied in the wrong place because of its incorrect date. **32** is
endorsed *XXXI* suggesting that **28** and **29** were counted as one document in the archive but, as Burton Muniment 1 has no numerical
endorsement, the number was probably on the other version from which
the thirteenth-century copies of these texts were taken.[2]

Peniarth 390 is a manuscript of 220 leaves, measuring 240 × 165 mm.[3]
The leaves have been both paginated and more recently (April 1972)
foliated. The main part of the manuscript, fos 1–184, was written
between *c*. 1240 and 1264, largely by one scribe who may have also been
responsible for the Burton Annals, now British Library MS. Cotton
Vespasian E iii, fos 4–100ᵛ. It contains a variety of texts, including
a version of Glanvill, but some, like the documents concerning the
election of John de Stafford as abbot of Burton in 1260 (fos 171ᵛ–172),
are clearly connected with the abbey. The charters, on fos 173–184ᵛ
which form one quire, are written by the main scribe. This manuscript
was owned in the seventeenth century by Robert Vaughan of Hengwrt
and was numbered 150 in his library. When it was used by Birch for
his *Cartularium Saxonicum* it was owned by Mr W. E. W. Wynne of
Peniarth and in 1909 it was presented to the National Library of Wales.
Five charters in Peniarth 390 appear to have been copied, sometimes
rather carelessly, from the surviving single-sheet versions **(17, 23, 26,
27, 32)**. The text of **14** in Peniarth 390 is significantly better than the
single-sheet version, suggesting that the scribe had another source, now
lost, for he does not elsewhere show much competence and in many
places clearly had no idea what the charters meant. He abbreviated most

[1] Information supplied by Mr F. B. Stitt, Librarian of the William Salt Library.
[2] See below, pp. xxxvii–viii.
[3] G. R. C. Davis, *Medieval Cartularies of Great Britain* (1958), no. 93; the following
account of Peniarth 390 is based on a typescript description prepared for N.L.W. by
Mr D. Huws and supplied by Mr B. G. Owens, formerly Keeper of MSS.

of the texts by omitting in the boundaries all but three (11, 17, 27) and shortening most of the witness-lists, an economy that hampers discussion of authenticity and sometimes makes identification of the estates impossible. Bounds are only preserved for nine of the charters (11, 14, 17, 23, 26, 27, 31, 32, 35) and with one exception (23) these can be positively identified, if not completely worked out. Many other estates can be identified for reasons that are fully explained in the notes, the most common being that places have distinctive names (e.g. 9, 21, 33) or occur in recognizable combinations (e.g. 3, 5, 6, 7, 19, 22, 24, 31). There are, however, seven charters concerning places that cannot be identified (4, 10, 12, 16, 25, 36, 38) and five for which only tentative identifications can be offered (1, 2, 8, 15, 23). It is some compensation for the omissions in Peniarth 390 that the scribe copied the chrismons and these are reproduced on Pl. I.

Apart from the extract from 28 that occurs at the start of the Burton Annals the only other medieval copies of the pre-Conquest charters of Burton are in the Burton Cartulary deposited by the Marquess of Anglesey in the British Library as MS. Loans 30.[1] The original part of this cartulary was compiled in the decade before 1241 and begins at fo. 8 with the four charters 28, 29, 31, and 35. This cartulary was the only version of the Burton charters known, directly or indirectly, to most scholars from the sixteenth century to the nineteenth and Kemble only included two of them in his edition.

3. THE WILL OF WULFRIC (no. 29)

Burton Abbey was founded by Wulfric. His will, carefully preserved at Burton, shows that he was a landowner on a vast scale, with estates in many parts of England, and that he was a member of one of the leading tenth-century English families. He bequeathed a large part of his property to his abbey, and many of the charters in its archives were title-deeds to these estates; some other charters kept there appear to have been concerned with estates to which the abbey never had any claim but which had been held by Wulfric or members of his family. Wulfric's will is, therefore, the key to the collection. The following translation is based on that published by Professor Whitelock with some changes that have been made with her approval. To facilitate discussion the place-names, which are given in the form in which they occur in Burton Muniment 1, are numbered and those that can be identified with confidence are marked on the map on p. xvi.

TRANSLATION OF WULFRIC'S WILL

In nomine domini. Wulfric here declares his will to his dear lord and to all his friends. First I grant to my lord two hundred mancuses of gold,

[1] Davis, op. cit., no. 91.

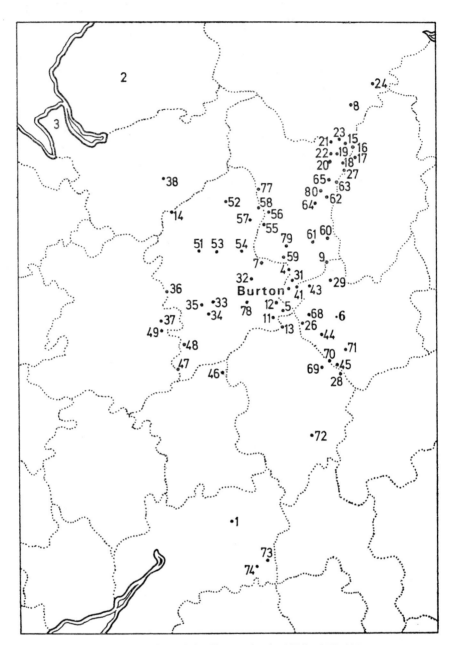

FIGURE 1. Map of the Estates in the Will of Wulfric

The estates are numbered in the order in which they occur in the will. In the key on the facing page, unidentified names are given in the form in which they occur in Burton Muniment 1. For further details see pp. xxiii–xxxiv.

1. Dumbleton
2. Between Ribble and Mersey
3. Wirral
4. Rolleston
5. Harlaston
6. Barlestone
7. Marchington
8. Conisborough
9. Alvaston
10. *æt Northtune*
11. Elford
12. Oakley
13. Tamworth
14. Balterley
15. Wales
16. Thorpe Salvin
17. Whitwell
18. Clowne
19. Barlborough
20. Duckmanton
21. Mosbrough
22. Eckington
23. Beighton
24. Doncaster
25. *æt Morlingtune*
26. Austrey
27. Palterton
28. Wibtoft
29. Tonge
30. Burton upon Trent
31. Stretton
32. Bromley
33. *Bedintun*, now Pillaton
34. Gailey
35. Whiston
36. Longford
37. Stirchley
38. Newton by Middlewich
39. *Wædedun*
40. *Niwantun*
41. Winshill
42. *Suttun*
43. Ticknall
44. Shenton
45. Wigston Parva
46. Halesowen
47. Romsley
48. Shipley
49. Sutton Maddock
50. *æt Actune*
51. Darlaston
52. Rudyard
53. Cotwalton
54. Church Leigh
55. Okeover
56. Ilam
57. Cauldon
58. Castern
59. Sutton on the Hill
60. Morley
61. Breadsall
62. Morton
63. Pilsley
64. Ogston
65. North Wingfield
66. *Snodeswic*
67. Tathwell, Lincs. (not marked)
68. Appleby Magna
69. Weston in Arden
70. Burton Hastings
71. Sharnford
72. Harbury
73. Aldsworth
74. Arlington
75. *Eccleshale*
76. *æt Waddune*
77. Sheen
78. Longdon
79. Bupton
80. Stretton

KEY TO FIGURE 1

and two silver-hilted swords and four horses, two saddled and two unsaddled, and the weapons which are due with them. And I grant to every bishop five mancuses of gold and to each of the two archbishops ten mancuses of gold. And I grant to every monastic house (*into ælcum munucregole*) one pound and to every abbot and every abbess five mancuses of gold. And I grant to Archbishop Ælfric the land *æt Dumeltan* (1) along with the other, for my soul, in the hope that he may be a better friend and supporter of the monastery which I have founded.

And I grant to Ælfhelm and Wulfheah the lands *betwux Ribbel 7 Mærse* (2) and *on Wirhalum* (3), that they may share them between them as evenly as they can—unless either of them wishes to have his own— on condition that when it is the shad season, each of them shall pay three thousand shad to the monastery at Burton. And I grant to Ælfhelm *Rolfestun* (4) and *Heorlfestun* (5). And I grant to Wulfheah the estates *æt Beorelfestune* (6) and *æt Mærchamtune* (7). And I grant to Ælfhelm the estate *æt Cunugesburh* (8), on condition that he arrange that the monks shall have each year a third of the fish, and he two-thirds. And I grant Wulfheah the estate *æt Alewaldestune* (9), and I grant Ufegeat the estate *æt Northtune* (10) in the hope that he may be a better friend and supporter of the monastery.

And I grant to my wretched daughter (*earman dehter*) the estate *æt Elleforda* (11) and that *æt Acclea* (12), with all that now belongs there as long as her life lasts, and after her death the land is to go to the monastery at Burton. And she shall not possess it on such terms that she can forfeit it for any reason, but she is to have the use of it as long as she can perform the services due from it, and afterwards it is to go to the monastery at Burton because it was my godfather's gift. And I desire that Ælfhelm may be the protector of her and of the land. And the land *æt Tamwurthin* (13) is not to be subject to any service nor to any man born, but she is to have the lordship.

And I grant to my retainer Wulfgar the estate *æt Baltrytheleage* (14) just as his father acquired it for him (or for himself). And I bequeath to Morcar the estates *æt Walesho* (15), *æt Theogendethorpe* (16), *æt Hwitewylle* (17), *æt Clune* (18), *æt Barleburh* (19), *æt Ducemannestune* (20), *æt Moresburh* (21), *æt Eccingtune* (22), *æt Bectune* (23), *æt Doneceastre* (24), and *æt Morlingtune* (25). And to his wife I grant *Aldulfestreo* (26) just as it now stands with the produce and the men. And I grant to my kinsman Ælfhelm the estate *æt Paltertune* (27), and that which Scegth bequeathed to me. And I grant to Æthelric for his day the estate *æt Wibbetofte* (28), and that *æt Twongan* (29), and after his day it is to go to Burton for my soul and for his (or my) mother's and for his.

And these are the estates which I grant to Burton: first *Byrtun* (30) on which the monastery stands, and *Strættun* (31) and *Bromleage* (32) and *Bedintun* (33) and *Gageleage* (34) and *Witestan* (35) and *Laganford*

(36) and *Styrcleage* (37) and *Niwantun æt thære wic* (38) and *Wædedun* (39) and the little estate which I have in the other *Niwantun* (40) and *Wineshylle* (41) and *Suttun* (42) and *Ticenheale* (43) and that *æt Scenctune* (44) and that *æt Wicgestane* (45) and that *æt Halen* (46) and *Hremesleage* (47) and that *æt Sciplea* (48) and that *æt Suthtune* (49) and that *æt Actune* (50) for two lives as the terms state; and *Deorlafestun* (51) and what belongs to it, namely *Rudegeard* (52) and my little estate in *Cotewaltune* (53); and *Lege* (54) with all that belongs to it; *Acofre* (55) with what belongs to it, that is *Hilum* (56) and *Celfdun* (57) and *Cætesthyrne* (58); and the heriot-land *æt Suthtune* (59) and *Morlege* (60) and *Brægdeshale* (61) and *Mortun* (62) and all the soke (*socna*) that belongs to it and the land included in it *æt Pillesleage* (63) and *Oggodestun* (64) and *Wynnefeld* (65) and *Snodeswic* (66) with *Mortune* and that *æt Tathawyllan* (67) and the estate *æt Æppebbyg* (68) which I bought with my money, and that *æt Westune* (69) and *Burhtun* (70) and the hide *æt Scearnforda* (71) along with *Wiggestane* (45) and that *æt Hereburgebyrig* (72) and *Ealdeswyrthe* (73) and *Ælfredingtune* (74) and *Eccleshale* (75) and *æt Waddune* (76) and one hide *æt Sceon* (77).

And I grant to the community at Tamworth the estate *æt Langandune* (78) just as they have let it to me, and they are to have half the usufruct and the monks of Burton half of the produce, and of the men and the stock, and of all things.

And the bishop is to take possession of his estate *æt Bubbandune* (79) and the monks at Burton are to take what is on the land, both produce and men, and all things; and the land at the mire is to go to the bishop.

And I desire that the king be lord of the monastery which I built and the estates which I have bequeathed to it to the glory of God and the honour of my lord and for my soul; and that Archbishop Ælfric and my brother Ælfhelm be protectors and friends and advocates of that foundation against any man born, not as their own possession, but as belonging to St Benedict's order.

And I grant to my god-daughter, the daughter of Morcar and Ealdgyth, the estate *æt Strættune* (80) and the brooch (*būle*) which was her grandmother's. And to the monastery at Burton a hundred wild horses, and sixteen tame geldings, and besides this all that I possess in livestock and other goods except those which I have bequeathed.

And whoever perverts this, may God Almighty remove him from all God's joy and from the communion of all Christians, unless it be my royal lord alone, and I believe him to be so good and gracious that he will not himself do it, nor permit any other man to do it. *Valete in Cristo. Amen.*

The will was drawn up before the confirmation charter of 1004, and the reference to Dumbleton (1) shows that this happened after Archbishop Ælfric acquired his interest there in 1002. The earliest manuscript is, however, a copy on a single sheet, now Burton Muniment 1, on which it follows Æthelred's confirmation charter (28), both texts being written by one scribe towards the end of the eleventh century. The thirteenth-century versions of these texts had a common source that differed significantly from the surviving single sheet.[1] As they agree in placing the will after the charter, and the charter's endorsement *þis is seo freols boc to þam mynstre æt Byrtune . . .* after the will, it is reasonable to suggest that their common source was a single sheet similar to Burton Muniment 1. As explained above (p. xiv), when the Burton charters were numbered, probably in the thirteenth century, the number XXVIII seems to have covered both will and charter. Burton Muniment 1 is the only single sheet from this archive without such numerical endorsement and it is therefore likely that the number was endorsed on the lost version.

Wills were sometimes issued in more than one exemplar but there is no evidence that this was done in the case of Wulfric's. Some of its provisions were known at Abingdon Abbey, the later owner of Dumbleton, and a note made at Abingdon specifically mentions the bequest of land there to Archbishop Ælfric. It also reports the bequests made generally to bishops, archbishops, monasteries, abbots, and abbesses, the construction of Burton Abbey and its endowment with Wulfric's entire paternal inheritance, worth 700 pounds, a detail that is found in neither will nor charter, although it is also reported in the thirteenth-century Burton Annals.[2]

The verbal invocation with which the will begins is familiar in charters but unusual in wills, the only other examples being the mid-tenth-century wills of Bishop Theodred and Ealdorman Ælfgar.[3] The same function is normally served symbolically by the cross with which most wills begin; sixteen of the nineteen wills that survive on single sheets begin in this way, the exceptions being Stowe Charter 36, the bottom portion of a chirograph, and the pair of wills on Harley Charter 43 C 4. The valediction *Valete in Cristo*, to which Burton Muniment 1 apparently added *Amen*, is unique; the only parallels being two wills that end *Amen*.[4] The English text begins with a notification similar to that found in the wills of Ealdorman Æthelmær and Æthelgifu.[5] The first bequest, made to his lord, is shown by the laws of Cnut (II Cnut 71) to have combined the money due as heriot from an earl with the horses and equipment due from a king's thegn, which is perhaps consistent with his description in the confirmation charter as a *minister* of noble lineage.

[1] See below, pp. xxxvii–viii.
[2] Luard, *Annales Monastici*, i. 183; Stevenson, *Chron. Abingdon*, i. 411.
[3] Sawyer 1526, 1483.
[4] Sawyer 1488, 1523.
[5] Sawyer 1498, 1497; on the latter see now Whitelock 1968.

4. THE BENEFICIARIES OF THE WILL

Wulfric bequeathed five mancuses, gold coins each worth thirty pence, to every bishop, abbot, abbess, and twice that sum to each archbishop. He also gave one pound to each *munucregole*, a word that literally meant 'monastic rule or order'. The Latin note of the will made at Abingdon supports this interpretation: *dedit . . . unicuique abbatiæ librum auri et unicuique* [? *abbati*] *et abbatissæ v mancas.*[1] The assumption that the pound was of gold was probably made because the other payments were in gold coins but, as the will is careful to specify that the mancuses were of gold, it seems more likely that the pound, which is not so described, was the normal pound of silver. Bequests to one or more religious communities were commonly made in wills but such generosity towards monasteries in general was unusual. Wulfric seems, in fact, to have had great enthusiasm for reformed monasticism, and his greatest generosity was reserved for his own foundation at Burton which according to Æthelred's charter (28) was to follow the rule of St Benedict and which had as its first abbot Wulfgeat, who probably came from Winchester, the leading centre of reformed monasticism.[2] Wulfric placed his monastery under the lordship of the king, who was alone excluded from the concluding anathema. Wulfric hoped that Burton Abbey would be protected by Archbishop Ælfric and his own brother Ælfhelm, who were both given bequests, the archbishop's being expressly to gain his support for the monastery. There were several religious communities in the area but the only one mentioned in the will, apart from Burton, was Tamworth, with which his daughter may have been associated and of which the patron saint was Eadgyth.[3] It was not very generously treated, only receiving back an estate (78) that Wulfric had leased, and it was expected to share the produce, stock, and men with his new foundation. A similar arrangement was made over the estate at Bupton (79) that Wulfric had leased from the bishop of Lichfield, but in that case all the men and produce were to go to Burton.

Almost all the other bequests were to people who are either explicitly described as, or can be shown to be, members of Wulfric's family. The exceptions are Wulfgar and Æthelric. Wulfgar is described as Wulfric's *cniht*, a word normally used for the higher officials of a household and the position of this bequest in the will, between those made to Wulfric's close relations, suggests a very close relationship, possibly kinship. The clause *ealswa his fæder hit him begeat* is ambiguous; if it is rendered 'just as his father acquired it for him' it could imply that the father had acquired from Wulfric a life interest on his son's behalf in the estate of Balterley (14) when Wulfgar entered his service, but the meaning may be 'just as his father acquired it for himself' The bequest to Æthelric

---

[1] Stevenson, *Chron. Abingdon*, i. 411.
[2] *Chronicon Abbatum* in *Mon. Angl.* iii. 47.
[3] *V.C.H. Staffordshire*, iii. 309–15.

of two estates (28, 29) with reversion to Burton Abbey was made, according to Burton Muniment 1, 'for my soul and for my mother's and for his' but the thirteenth-century versions agree on the reading *for his modor* which was a correct genitival form in Old English and is to be preferred, making the reversion 'for my soul and for his mother's and for his'. It would in any case be strange to have such an incidental reference to a bequest for the soul of Wulfric's mother but, whichever reading is taken, the implication is that Æthelric was a kinsman.

The Ælfhelm to whom a number of important bequests were made (2–5, 8) may be identified as the brother who Wulfric hoped would protect the abbey. His association in the will with Wulfheah (2, 3, 6, 7, 9) and Ufegeat (10) shows that he was the ealdorman who was killed in 1006 when Wulfheah and Ufegeat, said by Florence of Worcester to be his sons, were blinded.[1] His daughter Ælfgifu is not mentioned, probably because she was very young. Wulfric's own daughter is unnamed and the adjective used to describe her, *earm*, is more likely to have the meaning of 'wretched or unhappy' than poor in the sense of 'destitute' and may possibly mean that she was an invalid. Any explanation of what Professor Whitelock described as the mysterious references to this daughter is necessarily speculative. Professor Whitelock herself suggested that they imply that Wulfric feared she might forfeit her estates.[2] The fact that she was only given a life interest in two small estates that in DB had a total assessment of 5 hides (11, 12) may mean that she was a member of a religious community and would not be expected to marry or have legitimate heirs. The strange reference to the highly privileged status of Tamworth (13) and the apparent bequest to her of the lordship of land at Tamworth can hardly refer to the former royal *vicus* with its *burh* and is perhaps better understood as referring to the community at Tamworth. It would not be surprising if a religious community there had a highly privileged position[3] and it is possible that Wulfric had the lordship of it in much the same sense that he made the king lord of Burton Abbey. His remark about his wretched, possibly invalid, daughter, and the gift of something, if very little, to the community at Tamworth could perhaps have resulted from his daughter's connection with that community and its unwillingness to adopt a reformed rule.

After the endowment of the abbey and the gifts to Ælfhelm and his sons, the most important bequests were to Morcar, his wife Ealdgyth, and their daughter, who was also Wulfric's god-daughter. The bequest to this god-daughter of a piece of jewellery that had belonged to her grandmother suggests that she was the granddaughter of Wulfric's only

---

[1] *ASC*; *Fl. Wig.*, s.a. 1006.
[2] Whitelock, *Wills*, p. 155.
[3] The omission from DB of any account of either Tamworth or the community at Tamworth may be significant.

sister. Morcar was the thegn of the Seven Boroughs who, with his brother Sigeferth, was murdered in 1015, an event described in some detail in the *Anglo-Saxon Chronicle* which also reports that the ætheling Edmund married Sigeferth's widow against the king's will and then went 'to the Five Boroughs, and at once took possession of all Sigeferth's estates and Morcar's, and the people all submitted to him'. Florence of Worcester names Sigeferth's widow Aldgyth which the will shows was also the name of Morcar's wife. As the evidence of the *Anglo-Saxon Chronicle* that Edmund married Sigeferth's widow is clear, either both brothers married women with the same name, or Florence confused their names. Apart from the estates he received from Wulfric, Morcar was the beneficiary of three Burton charters (**32, 34, 37**) and may be identified as the witness who subscribes irregularly between 1001 and 1013 in charters concerning Warwickshire, Huntingdonshire, and Northamptonshire,[1] as well as the foundation charters of Burton and Eynsham Abbeys.[2] Sigeferth only witnesses four charters between 1009 and 1013, two in company with Morcar concerning land in Huntingdonshire and Northamptonshire[3] and **32** is a grant to Morcar in which, significantly, Sigeferth's name is in capital letters.[4] Morcar and Sigeferth also occur in the will of the ætheling Athelstan.[5] The Ælfhelm who is described as a kinsman of Wulfric and was given Palterton (27) was probably also a descendant of Wulfric's sister, for the bequest to him follows that to Ealdgyth, and in 1065 it was held by Leofnoth who also held several of Morcar's estates as well as Stretton (80) which Wulfric bequeathed to Morcar's daughter.

5. THE ESTATES IN THE WILL[6]

1 *æt Dumeltan.* In 995 King Æthelred granted Wulfric, son of Wulfrun, an estate of 2½ hides at Dumbleton, Gloucs., which had been confiscated from Æthelsige and granted to Hawas from whom Wulfric obtained it by exchange (Sawyer 886). In 1002 the king granted 24 hides at Dumbleton to Archbishop Ælfric (Sawyer 901) which must be 'the other' mentioned in the will, thus providing a date limit for it. Archbishop Ælfric died on 16 November, probably in 1005, having bequeathed Dumbleton to Abingdon Abbey (Sawyer 1488) who held it at the Norman Conquest when it was assessed at 7½ hides, a reduction that may have been due to beneficial hidation (DB, i. 166a, *Dubentone*).

[1] Sawyer 898, 926, 931.
[2] **28** and Sawyer 911.
[3] Sawyer 926, 931.
[4] He also subscribes Sawyer 933. I am indebted to Mr Simon Keynes for drawing my attention to this subscription of Sigeferth, omitted by Kemble from his edition; cf. *Remarks and Collections of Thomas Hearne*, vol. iii, ed. C. E. Doble (Oxford Historical Society, 1889), pp. 444–5.
[5] Sawyer 1503.
[6] Earlier discussions of identifications, etc., are Bridgeman 1916/1, Stevenson 1911/1 and Whitelock, *Wills*, pp. 151–60.

2 *betwux Ribbel 7 Mærse*. The southern part of Lancashire was described in DB as *inter Ripam et Mersham* (DB, i. 269b, cf. 262b) and was *Terra Regis* before the Conquest with the King holding the six chief estates to which the whole territory was tributary. The area must have been brought under the control of the English king soon after the fortification of Manchester in 919, possibly in 920 when the rulers of Northumbria and Strathclyde submitted to Edward the Elder.[1] Athelstan's grant of Amounderness, north of the Ribble, in 934 to the archbishop of York (Sawyer 407) shows that this frontier region was being granted out in large blocks and it may be that the area between the Ribble and the Mersey had been the subject of a similar grant.[2] The will shows that it was not under direct royal control in the early eleventh century and it probably became royal demesne after the death of Ælfhelm.

3 *on Wirhalum*. Wirral may similarly have been treated as a unit in the tenth century but on the eve of the Conquest it was held by a number of different landowners, among whom Earl Edwin and the church of St Werburgh at Chester were prominent (DB, i. 263a–7b, *Wilaveston* Hundred). Some fisheries are mentioned in the DB account of both these areas but there is no evidence that Burton Abbey retained any rights to fish from either Wirral or South Lancashire.

4 *Rolfestun*. Rolleston, Staffs., three miles north of Burton, was one of the places granted to Wulfsige in 942 (5) and is also the subject of 31, a grant dated 1008 by Æthelred to Abbot Wulfgeat and Burton Abbey of 2½ hides at *Rolfestun* in exchange for two estates in Gloucs. that had been part of the abbey's original endowment (73, 74). Rolleston was presumably confiscated after Ælfhelm's death and was an appropriate exchange for these inconveniently distant estates because it was close to the abbey and had belonged to its founder. The bounds in 31 describe a larger area than the modern parish of Rolleston. The abbey did not long own it and T.R.E. it was held by Earl Morcar with an assessment of 2½ hides (DB, i. 248b, *Rolvestune*).

5 *Heorlfestun* or *Heorelfestun*. Probably Harlaston, Staffs., which was held T.R.E. by Earl Ælfgar and assessed at 4 hides (DB, i. 246b, *Horulvestone*).

6 *æt Beorelfestune* has been identified as Barlaston, Staffs., held T.R.E. by a free man called Augustinus (DB, i. 249a, *Bernulvestone*) but as there is no reason to assume that it lay in Staffs., Barlestone, Leics., is also possible and, to judge by the form of the name in DB, seems more likely (DB, i. 232b, 234, *Berulvestone*). The T.R.E. holder of this Leics. estate, then assessed at 4 hides, is unknown.

7 *æt Mærchamtune*. Marchington, Staffs. According to 11 land here was granted in 951 by King Eadred to Wulfhelm, *miles*, from whom

---

[1] *ASC*, s.a.   [2] Sawyer 1975.

Wulfric may have inherited it. T.R.E. it was assessed at 2 hides and, together with a virgate at Agardsley, was held by Wulfric, a free man (DB, i. 248b, *Merchametone*).

8 *æt Cunugesburh*. Conisborough, Yorks. W.R., was held T.R.E. by Earl Harold and assessed at 5 carucates although with its sokeland in twenty-eight places the total assessment was over 90 carucates (DB, i. 321a, *Coningesburg*). Wulfric's estate probably included the whole DB manor with sokeland stretching over a wide area of south Yorks. from Thorne and Fishlake, 14 miles north-east of Conisborough, to Kiveton and Harthill, 10 miles to the south. Bridgeman[1] objected that the will does not specify any 'other subordinate manors, as there are in some of the other gifts, e.g. Darlaston, Leigh, Okeover and Morton', but additional care might be expected in the description of these bequests to the abbey. The name 'the king's stronghold' shows that it had been a place of importance and it is unlikely that many, if any, of the soke-lands were added to the manor in the eleventh century. Sir Charles Clay accepts that the estate had been consolidated long before the Norman Conquest.[2] He follows Hunter in arguing that the mention of fisheries, which cannot have been important at Conisborough itself, shows that Wulfric's estate extended as far as Hatfield, Thorne, and Fishlake. The only fisheries mentioned at Conisborough in DB were the 20 *piscinae* at Tudworth which is not ideally suited as a fishery centre, causing Dr Maxwell to suggest that they were the fisheries for the whole estate.[3] Burton Abbey did not retain any right to fish from this manor.

9 *æt Alewaldestune* is probably Alvaston, Derbys. The early forms of this name, although very similar to those of Elvaston, about a mile to the east, point clearly to the personal name Alwald, which was fairly common in the eleventh century and derived from both *Ælfweald* and *Æthelweald*, while Elvaston apparently comes directly from *Æthelweald*.[4] It is unlikely that two places so close together would have had the same name, and the formal distinction between them, preserved in the modern spellings and pronunciation, suggests that they were always distin-guishable and that the form in the will refers to Alvaston. A sixteenth-century English translation of the will has the form *Æthelwaldeston* but, as all other manuscripts agree on *Alewaldestun*, this form appears to be an interpretation of the translator. Alvaston and Elvaston were both held T.R.E. by Toki and, together with Ambaston and Thulston, in Elvaston parish, had a total assessment of 10 carucates (DB, i. 276b, *Ælvvoldestvn*, *Aleuuoldestune*).

---

[1] Bridgeman 1916/1, p. 26.

[2] C. T. Clay, *Early Yorkshire Charters*, viii, *The Honour of Warenne* (Yorkshire Archaeological Society, 1949), pp. 137–8.

[3] The *Domesday Geography of Northern England*, ed. H. C. Darby and I. S. Maxwell (Cambridge, 1962), p. 59.

[4] *PN Derbys.*, pp. 461–2.

10 *æt Northtune.* This is such a common place-name that it cannot be identified with any confidence. As the only bequest to Ufegeat, made to ensure his support for Burton Abbey, it is likely to have been a substantial estate and was possibly the 8 hides *æt Northtune* which were the subject of **12**, a charter that may have been, like **11**, one of Wulfric's title-deeds. The reasons for thinking that this may have been Norton juxta Twycross, Leics., held T.R.E. by Godgifu and assessed at 6 carucates (DB, i. 231b), are explained in the notes on that charter.

11 *æt Elleforda* has generally, and reasonably, been identified as Elford, Staffs., held T.R.E. by Earl Ælfgar and assessed at 3 hides (DB, i. 246b, *Eleford*).

12 *æt Acclea* or *Aclea* is probably Oakley, Staffs., about two miles north of Elford, held T.R.E. by Wulfwine and assessed at 2 hides (DB, i. 249, *Acle*).

13 *æt Tamworthin* or *Tomwurthin.* Tamworth, Staffs., see above, p. xxii.

14 *æt Baltrytheleage.* Probably Balterley, Staffs., held T.R.E. by two king's thegns, Godwine and Wulfric, each with ½ virgate (DB, i. 250b, *Baltredelege*).

The next eleven estates were bequeathed to Morcar. The eight that can be identified with some confidence lie in south Yorks. or north Derbys., most of them close to the county border, and they are named in a clockwise order from Whitwell (17) to Beighton (23), a regularity that helps the identification of the first two estates (15, 16).

15 *æt Walesho* was probably associated with Wales, Yorks. W.R., which was assessed at 3½ carucates T.R.E. and was sokeland of Earl Edwin's manor of Laughton and Throapham (DB, i. 319a, 379a, *Wales*).

16 *æt Theogendethorpe.* Thorpe Salvin, Yorks. W.R., lies between Wales and Whitwell and is a possible identification (DB, i. 319a, *Torp*).

The next seven places were all held T.R.E., at least in part, by Leofnoth, who was probably, as Sir Frank Stenton suggested, the brother of the Leofric who also had large holdings in the same area, some of which were held jointly by the two men.[1]

17 *æt Hwitewylle.* Whitwell, Derbys. Leofnoth held 6 carucates there and in Barlborough (DB, i. 277a, *Barleburg* and *Witeuuelle*).

18 *æt Clune.* Clowne, Derbys. 2 bovates at *Clvne* were appurtenant to Leofnoth's estate at Barlborough and Whitwell. Another 6 bovates were held T.R.E. and in 1086 by Earnwig, a king's thegn (DB, i. 278b).

19 *æt Barleburh.* Barlborough, Derbys., see 17.

20 *æt Ducemannestune.* Duckmanton, Derbys. Leofnoth held 4 carucates 2 bovates there (DB, i. 277a, *Dochemanestun*).

21 *æt Moresburh.* Mosbrough, Derbys. 2 carucates at *Moresburg* were sokeland of Eckington, see 22.

22 *æt Eccingtune.* Eckington, Derbys. 4 carucates were held there by

[1] *V.C.H. Derbyshire*, i. 305–6.

Leofnoth with sokeland at Mosbrough and Beighton, see 21, 23 (DB, i. 277a, *Echintvne*). In the account of the royal estate of Newbold, Eckington is described as a berewick (DB, i. 272a, *Echintune*). **37** purports to be a grant of 2 hides at *Ecgintune* to Morcar in 1012. This has been identified as Egginton, Derbys., but is more likely to be Eckington.

23 *æt Bectune*. Beighton, Derbys. DB describes three holdings in *Bectune*; 4 bovates were sokeland of Leofnoth's estate at Eckington (DB, i. 277a), $5\frac{1}{2}$ bovates were sokeland of Sutton Scarsdale, held T.R.E. by Steinulf (DB, i. 273b) and $6\frac{1}{2}$ bovates were held T.R.E. by Swein (DB, i. 278a).

24 *æt Doneceastre*. Doncaster, Yorks. W.R. 2 carucates were sokeland of Earl Tostig's manor of Hexthorpe (DB, i. 307b, *Donecastre*), 3 bovates were sokeland of Wheatley, held T.R.E. as two manors by Wulfsige and Ragnald (DB, i. 308a) and 5 or 6 bovates were a berewick of Edlington which had been held by Norman (DB, i. 321b).

25 *æt Morlingtune* cannot be identified. Bridgeman thought it was probably in the same district as the other gifts to Morcar but, as the regular order of estates is broken by Doncaster, it may be in another area altogether.

26 *Adulfestreo*. Austrey, Warwicks. In 1086 this was held by three tenants in chief; Burton Abbey had $2\frac{1}{2}$ hides which had been given by Earl Leofric (DB, i. 239a, *Advlvestrev*), Nigel de Albini held $5\frac{1}{2}$ hides and 1 virgate which had been held T.R.E. by eight thegns (DB, i. 244a), and Henry de Ferrers held $2\frac{1}{4}$ hides for which no T.R.E. holder is named, and which were held of him by Nigel, probably de Albini (DB, i. 242a). **18** is a spurious charter granting 5 hides at Austrey to Wulfric *minister* in 958.

27 *æt Paltertune*. Palterton, Derbys., held T.R.E. by Leofnoth and, with berewicks at Scarcliffe and Tunstall, was assessed at 6 carucates 2 bovates (DB, i. 277a, *Paltretvne*).

28 *æt Wibbetofte*. Wibtoft, Warwicks. DB groups Wibtoft together with Willey, jointly assessed at 3 hides, and with Weston in Arden, assessed at 2 hides. All three were held T.R.E. by Saxi (DB, i. 240a, *Wibetot*), an association that supports the identification of both Wibtoft and the Weston bequeathed to Burton Abbey, see 69.

29 *æt Twongan* has been identified as either Tonge, Leics., or Tong, Salop. Ekwall (*DEPN*, s.n. *tang, Tong*) preferred the latter because the other early forms of that name, *Tweongan, Tvange*, point to the same origin as the name in the will, OE *twang*, meaning 'fork of a river'. The early forms of the Leics. Tonge, *Tunge, Tunga*, suggest a different origin, OE *tunge*, meaning 'tongue of land'. The argument is not decisive because, as Dr B. H. Cox has pointed out,[1] there is a lot of

---

[1] In a letter.

Scandinavian influence in the area of Tonge and the name could well have been influenced by ON *tunga*. An additional consideration, to which Professor E. G. Stanley has drawn my attention, is that in this area *-ong-* forms developed into *-ung-*, and that *w* was lost before *u* in all areas. Tong, Salop, was held T.R.E. by Earl Morcar and assessed at 3 hides (DB, i. 253b) and Tonge, Leics., was assessed at 21½ carucates and was held in 1086 by Henry de Ferrers, with no pre-Conquest tenant named (DB, i. 233a). **22** is concerned with lands that formed part of Henry de Ferrers's estate of Tonge and the presence of that charter in the Burton archives would be explained if the *Twongan* of the will could be identified with Tonge, Leics.

The next forty-eight places were bequeathed to Burton Abbey. The places that can be definitely identified show that there is a tendency to list them in a regular geographical order similar to that noted in the bequests to Morcar. There are, in fact, two clockwise sequences in which almost the only irregularities are caused by the listing of berewicks or appurtenant holdings. The first sequence runs from Stretton (31) to Newton by Middlewich (38) and the second from Winshill (41) or possibly Newton Solney (40) to Arlington (74) and possibly to Sheen (77), the last bequest to Burton. These sequences are sufficiently clear to make possible the confirmation of identifications that would otherwise depend solely on the forms of the names. So, for example, the identification of Gailey (34) is confirmed by its position between Pillaton (33) and Whiston (35). In the second sequence the following identifications are strengthened by the way they fit the regular order: 44, 46–50 (although the precise identification of 50 must remain doubtful), 59–61, and 72. It is possible that this sequence continued and that 75 and 76 lay between 74 and 77. The only bequests to Burton that cannot be plotted on the map are: *Wædedun* (39) and *æt Waddune* (76), for neither of which it is possible to make a suggestion; *Snodeswic* (66) which is lost, although its general location is known; *æt Actune* (50) for which there are too many possibilities; *Suttun* (42) which is either a lost place in the vicinity of Winshill and Ticknall or a marked exception to the general regularity of the list; and, finally, two estates for which reasonable suggestions can be made but with such common names that the identifications cannot be considered certain, 40 and 75.

30 *Byrtun*. Burton upon Trent, Staffs., held T.R.E. by the abbey and assessed at 1½ hides (DB, i. 247b). The will clearly implies that the monastery was already built when the will was drawn up.

31 *Strættun*. Stretton, Staffs. Held by Burton Abbey T.R.E. and assessed at 1½ hides (DB, i. 247b, *Stratone*). Stretton was one of the estates granted to Wulfsige in 942 **(5)**.

32 *Bromleage*. Bromley, Staffs. *Bromleg'* was granted to Wulfsige in 942 **(5)** and according to **27** Wulfric was granted 3 hides at *Bromleage*

which had been held by his mother. The bounds of **27** show that the estate was Abbots Bromley, Staffs., which was held T.R.E. by Burton Abbey and assessed at $\frac{1}{2}$ hide. This apparent reduction in the assessment could have been the result of beneficial hidation but as there is no evidence of this on other Burton estates it seems more likely that the 3 hides were the original assessment of both parts of Bromley and included Kings Bromley which was held T.R.E. by Earl Harold and assessed at 3 hides (DB, i. 246a, *Bromelei*). Harold probably held this, his only estate in the county, by right of his wife, Ealdgyth, whose grandfather, Earl Leofric, according to Florence of Worcester, died there in 1057.

33 *Bedintun*, now Pillaton, Staffs. In DB Burton Abbey held $\frac{1}{2}$ hide at *Beddintone* (DB, i. 247b) and in the early-twelfth-century Surveys this was in two equal parts called *Bedintona* and *Pilatehala*.[1] The last reference to *Bedintona* is in a charter that cannot be later than 1135. Later references are always to Pillatonhall or Pillaton, presumably because *Bedintona* was deserted.[2]

34 *Gageleage*. Gailey, Staffs., held T.R.E. by Bodin and assessed at 1 hide (DB, i. 249b, *Gragelie*).

35 *Witestan*. Whiston, Staffs., was held by Burton Abbey in DB and assessed at 1 hide (DB, i. 247b, *Witestone*).

36 *Laganford*. This form appears to have been common to both early versions of the will and was corrected in one cartulary to Langeford. It is a common place-name but may be identified as Longford, Salop, because one of its berewicks was Stirchley, named next in the will. T.R.E. it was held by Earl Edwin and, with four unnamed berewicks, was assessed at 6 hides (DB, i. 257b, *Langeford*).

37 *Styrcleage*. Stirchley, Staffs., was one of the berewicks of Longford but is not named in DB.[3]

38 *Niwantun æt thære wic* is probably Newton by Middlewich, Cheshire, held T.R.E. by Grifin, a free man, and assessed at 1 hide (DB, i. 267a, *Nevtone*).

39 *Wædedun* has not been identified.

40 *Niwantun*. It has been suggested that because the next place in the will is Winshill this is probably Newton Solney, Derbys., about two miles to the north. It was held T.R.E. by Earl Ælfgar and, with its berewick Bretby, was assessed at 7 carucates (DB, i. 272b, *Newetun*). This seems large for 'a little estate' but it is possible that Wulfric only held a small part of it. **16** is a grant of 5 hides at *Niwantune* to Æthelgeard in 956 and this may have been the title-deed of the whole estate. Burton Abbey had no interest in any place of that name at the Conquest.

---

[1] *Surveys*, pp. 228–9.
[2] *V.C.H. Staffordshire*, v. 118.
[3] R. W. Eyton, *Antiquities of Shropshire*, viii (1859), p. 102.

41 *Wineshylle*. Winshill, Staffs., in which Burton Abbey held 2 carucates
T.R.E. (DB, i. 273a, *Wineshalle*).

42 *Sutton*. Three places with this very common name were bequeathed
by Wulfric to Burton Abbey The context of the others suggests that they
were Sutton Maddock, Salop (49) and Sutton on the Hill, Derbys. (59).
There is also a charter (8) granting 4 hides of land at *Suthtone* to
Ulfketel, with licence to buy a fifth, in 949, and this probably referred
to one of the Suttons owned by Wulfric, the assessment agreeing best
with Sutton Maddock, which was 4 hides in DB. It has been suggested
that this first Sutton in the will was Sutton on the Hill, Derbys., where
Burton Abbey had 1 carucate in 1086 as sokeland of its manor of Mickleover (DB, i. 273a), but as this estate was given to the abbey by William I,
its possession of a hide there later is irrelevant to the identification
of any of the places in the will. If the third Sutton is correctly identified
as Sutton on the Hill, this one must be elsewhere. The order of entries
suggests that it should be sought in the neighbourhood of Winshill and
Ticknall, but that would mean it is a lost place. If that possibility is
rejected there is no reason for any identification, unless it is assumed
that it lay near other estates held by Wulfric, in which case Sutton
Cheney, Leics., near Shenton (44), or Sutton in the Elms, Leics., near
Sharnford (71), should be considered. The T.R.E. holders of those
estates are unknown (DB, i. 231a, 231b, 232b, 234b).

43 *Ticenheale*. Ticknall, Derbys., was held by Burton Abbey and
assessed at $5\frac{1}{3}$ bovates in DB (i. 273a, *Tichenballe*).

44 *æt Scenctune*. Ekwall's identification as Shenton, Leics. seems to be
correct (*DEPN*, s.n.). In 1086 it was held by three tenants in chief,
the main estate being Robert de Vesci's, which was assessed at 5 carucates 6 bovates, presumably a 6-carucate estate from which 2 bovates,
held by Henry de Ferrers, had been detached (DB, i. 233a, 234a,
Scentone). Count Alberic held 1 carucate there which had been held by
Harding (DB, i. 231b). The main estate had been held T.R.E. by
Æthelric son of Mærgeat, an important pre-Conquest landowner in
Lincolnshire, Northants., and Warwicks., and a benefactor of West-
minster Abbey.[1]

45 *æt Wicgestane*. Wigston Parva, Leics. The later reference (71)
to Sharnford along with Wigston confirms this identification. In DB
a priest Ælfric held 2 carucates there that were appurtenant to Sharnford
(DB, i. 231a, *Wicestan*).

46 *æt Halen* has been identified, with some hesitation, by Ekwall as
Sheriff Hales, Salop (*DEPN*, s.n.), held T.R.E. by Earl Ælfgar and Earl
Edwin and assessed at 2 hides (DB, i. 248a, *Halas*). Professor Whitelock
suggested that the context made Halesowen, Worcs., likely and this was

[1] Olof von Feilitzen, *The Pre-Conquest Personal Names of Domesday Book* (Uppsala,
1937), p. 186.

assessed at 10 hides and held T.R.E. by Wulfwine (DB, i. 176a, *Hala*). Dr Margaret Gelling has pointed out that the form of the name in the will is preserved in Hawne in Halesowen.[1]

47 *Hremesleage*. Romsley, Salop, is more likely than Romsley, Worcs. The latter is only two miles from Halesowen and is not in DB, but the Salop estate is grouped together with the next bequest, Shipley, in that part of Earl Roger's fief in DB which was, by mistake, included with Warwicks. although then part of Staffs. (DB, i. 239a, *Rameslege*, cf. *V.C.H. Warwicks*. i. 308, *V.C.H. Salop*, i. 286). One hide there had been held T.R.E. by Aki.

48 *æt Sciplea*. Shipley, Salop. One hide there was held T.R.E. by *Alsi* (DB, i. 239a, *Sciplei*).

49 *æt Suthtune*. The geographical sequence suggests that this was Sutton Maddock, Salop, held T.R.E. by Earl Morcar and assessed at 4 hides (DB, i. 259a, *Sudtone*). This may have been the subject of **8**.

50 *æt Actune*. This is a very common name, especially in Salop where there are five examples in DB. Professor Whitelock followed Bridgeman in thinking that it might be Acton Round, held T.R.E. by Wulfgeat and assessed at 4 hides (DB, i. 254a) but Acton Burnell or the nearby Acton Pigot, held T.R.E. by Godric and Geiri respectively and assessed at $3\frac{1}{2}$ and 3 hides, would fit as well (DB, i. 255b, 254b). So too would Acton Reynold held T.R.E. by Siward and assessed at 3 hides (DB, i. 255a).

51 *Deorlafestun*. Darlaston, Staffs., was held T.R.E. by Burton Abbey and assessed at 3 virgates (DB, i. 247b, *Derlavestone*), and is also the subject of **17**.

52 *Rudegeard*. Rudyard, Staffs., is described in DB as *Terra Regis* and was held T.R.E. by Wulfmær and, although no assessment is given, there was said to be land for 1 or 2 ploughs. The omission of this and the following estate from the confirmation charter **(28)** may mean that these two appurtenances of Darlaston did not, in fact, reach the abbey.

53 *Cotewaltun*. Cotwalton, Staffs., was also *Terra Regis* in 1086 and 1 virgate there was held T.R.E. by *Aluuin* and *Rafuuinus* (DB, i. 246b, *Cotewoldestune*). Bridgeman drew attention to the existence about a mile north-east of Cotwalton of a hamlet called Spot or Spot Grange, but this can hardly preserve the memory of an association with Wulfric. It is more likely to be connected with other local names which include The Spot and Spot Acre.

54 *Lege*. Church Leigh, Staffs., was held by Burton Abbey T.R.E. and assessed at 3 virgates (DB, i. 247b, *Lege*). The will mentions, but does not name, dependencies, while DB gives no hint of their existence.

---

[1] In a letter; cf. A. Mawer and F. M. Stenton, *The Place-Names of Worcestershire* (E.P.N.S. iv, 1927), p. 296.

Survey A shows that they included Field and Dodsleigh and that Leigh and Field were jointly assessed at 3 virgates (*Surveys*, pp. 225–7).

55 *Acofre*. Okeover, Derbys., was held by Burton Abbey and, *cum appendiciis*, was assessed at 3 virgates in DB (i. 247b, *Acovre*). The berewicks are not named in DB but the *Surveys* show that the 3 virgates included Ilam (pp. 224–5). Cauldon and Castern were presumably other berewicks, see 57, 58.

56 *Hilum*. Ilam, Derbys., is not named in DB, but the *Surveys* show it was part of the abbey's estate of Okeover; see 55.

57 *Celfdun*. Cauldon, Derbys. One virgate was held there T.R.E. by Godgifu (DB, i. 248b, *Caldone*). There is no other evidence that Burton Abbey had land there as part of its foundation grant. The association is preserved in the chapels of Ilam church, namely Sheen, Okeover, and Cauldon (*Burton Cartulary*, pp. 45, 73).

58 *Cætesthyrne*. Castern, Staffs. Not named in DB but the abbot of Burton had land there in the mid-twelfth century (Jeayes 1937, no. 21 i).

59 *æt Suthtune*. The sequence of estates suggests that this is Sutton on the Hill, Derbys. The alternative, Sutton Scarsdale, is too far north. In DB 1 carucate at Sutton on the Hill is described as sokeland of Mickleover which was given to the abbey by William I (DB, i. 273a, see below, p. xlvi). It is, however, possible that the abbey already had a claim to land in that area. The term heriot-land means either land which Wulfric had received as heriot or land from which heriots were due to him.

60 *Morlege*. This is a very common name but the next place shows that it is Morley, Derbys., and that the regular geographical sequence is maintained. T.R.E. it was apparently held by Siward and assessed at $\frac{2}{3}$ carucate (DB, i. 275b, *Morleia*).

61 *Brægdeshale*. Breadsall, Derbys., was held T.R.E. by Siward and assessed at 5 carucates. The most reasonable interpretation of the curious way DB refers to these places, with *In Morlei* treated as a hundredal rubric and the entry beginning *Ibidem* referring, apparently, to Breadsall (DB, i. 275b, *Braideshale*), is that the name *Morlei* has been mistakenly treated as a hundredal name, possibly because of its connection with Morleystone Hundred. In any case, DB makes the connection between Morley and Breadsall clear.

62 *Mortun*. The places (63–6) associated with *Mortun* show that it is Morton, Derbys. T.R.E. Swein *cilt* held $11\frac{1}{2}$ bovates and 8 acres in Morton, Ogston, and Wessington (DB, i. 276b). 15 may refer to the same place.

63 *æt Pillesleage*. Pilsley, Derbys. T.R.E. Swein *cilt* had 1 carucate 7 bovates in Pilsley, *Caldecotes*, and Williamthorpe (DB, i. 276b).

64 *Oggodestun.* Ogston, Derbys., see 62. Two bovates there were sokeland of Crich which was held T.R.E. by Leofric and Leofnoth (DB,
i. 277a, *Ougedestun*).

65 *Wynnefeld,* probably North Wingfield, Derbys., where there were
2 bovates of sokeland belonging to Pilsley (DB, i. 276b, *Winnefelt*).
This association, and its position, make it more likely than South
Wingfield, Derbys., which was held T.R.E. by Alnoth and assessed at
2 carucates (DB, i. 273b, *Winefeld*).

66 *Snodeswic* cannot be identified but is clearly the *Esnotrewic* in the
Derbys. DB where Halfdan held ½ carucate T.R.E. (DB, i. 276a). The
phrase *Snodeswic into Mortune* means either that it is attached to Morton
or that it is to be so attached in the future.

67 *æt Tathawyllan,* probably Tathwell, Lincolnshire. Ekwall expressed
doubts about this identification (*DEPN,* s.n.) but it fits the geographical
order of the will, and 1 carucate there was held T.R.E. by Siward who
also held several other estates that Wulfric bequeathed to the abbey.
The total assessment of Tathwell was 6 carucates, the other part being
held T.R.E. by Earl Harold (DB, i. 349b, 363b, *Tadewelle*).

68 *æt Æppebbyg* is clearly a misreading for *Æppelbyg* and may be
identified as Appleby Magna, Leics. Burton Abbey had 5 carucates
there T.R.E., one of which had been given by Abbot Leofric to Godgifu
(DB, i. 273a, *Apleby*).

69 *æt Westune.* Weston in Arden, Warwicks., fits the geographical
sequence very well and the identification is supported by its ownership
T.R.E. by Saxi as part of the group of estates that included Wibtoft
(28; DB, i. 240a, *Westone*).

70 *Burhtun.* Burton Hastings, Warwicks., was held T.R.E. by Siward
and assessed at 4 hides. **36** may possibly refer to the same place.

71 *æt Scearnforda.* Sharnford, Leics. The association with Wigston
confirms this identification. Wulfric's hide may have been that held
in DB by Judith which had earlier been held by Waltheof or Asbiorn
(DB, i. 236a, *Scerneford*). The reference in the will to a hide is significant,
for in DB this estate was assessed in carucates.

72 *æt Hereburgebyrig.* Harbury, Warwicks., was held T.R.E. by several
people; Orderic had 4 hides, Leofwine and Alric 4½ hides, Alwine
3 virgates, and Siward 2 hides (DB, i. 239b, 241b, 242a, 243b, *Erebur(ge)-
berie*). As Siward held several estates that Wulfric bequeathed to the
abbey, his holding here may represent Wulfric's estate.

73, 74 *Ealdeswyrthe, Ælfredingtune.* These two estates were exchanged
for Rolleston in 1008 because they were very far from the monastery **(31)**
and they may be identified as Aldsworth and Arlington, Gloucs. Aldsworth, assessed at 2 hides and held by *Balchi* T.R.E., was listed as

Terra Tainorum in DB (i. 170b, *Aldeswrde*). Arlington was *Terra Regis* and was held T.R.E. by Cynewig *chelle*, a thegn of King Edward, and assessed at 5 hides (DB, i. 164a, *Alvredintune*).

75 *Eccleshale*. There are at least four places in England with this name. Two are in Warwicks. and have the modern form Exhall. One of these, near Coventry, is not in DB, but the other, near Alcester, was held T.R.E. by *Leuiet* and assessed at 1½ hides (DB, i. 243a, *Ecleshelle*). Ecclesall, Yorks. W.R., is not in DB, but Eccleshall, Staffs., was held by the bishop of Chester and assessed at 7 hides (DB, i. 247a, *Ecleshelle*). The sequence of estates suggests that the present estate may have been the Staffs. example.

76 *æt Waddune*. Professor Whitelock suggested, very tentatively, that this might be Whaddon, Gloucs., but, although the DB form of that name is *Wadune*, other early forms show that the first element was OE *hwæte*, and the same is true of other places called Whaddon (*DEPN*, s.n.). The form in the will is unlikely to refer to any of these. It is also unlikely to be a repetition of *Wædedun* (39). If the regular geographical sequence is maintained it would lie south and west of Sheen, possibly between that and Eccleshall, Staffs.

77 *æt Sceon*. Sheen, Staffs., is listed under *Terra Regis* and T.R.E. Alward had land there for 1 or 2 ploughs (DB, i. 246b, *Sceon*). It was later a chapelry of Ilam, see 57.

78 *æt Langandune*, probably Longdon, Staffs. This is not in DB, possibly because of exceptional privileges enjoyed by Tamworth.

79 *æt Bubbandune*. Bupton, Derbys., where the bishop of Chester held 5 carucates (DB, i. 273a, *Bubedene*).

80 *æt Strættune*, probably Stretton, Derbys. Leofnoth held 1 carucate in Stretton, Egstow and Handley (DB, i. 277a, *Stratvne*) and 2½ bovates in *alia Stratvne* (ibid.) which has been identified as Little Stretton or Stretton Hall in Stretton.

6. THE ENDORSEMENTS OF THE CONFIRMATION CHARTER AND WILL (28, 29)

Æthelred's charter confirming the endowment of Burton Abbey (28) and Wulfric's will (29) were both copied in the late eleventh century on a sheet of parchment, now Burton Muniment 1, which also has three endorsements. The first, in English, refers to the charter rather than the will. The second, in Latin, is a list of estates of Burton Abbey deriving from a source closely connected with the Domesday inquiry. There is an early-twelfth-century copy of this endorsement in Burton Muniment 1925. The third endorsement, also in English, is a list of estates, with hidages, in Offlow Hundred, Staffordshire. In the Burton cartularies, **28** and **29** are copied consecutively and are followed by the first two endorsements, while Peniarth 390 also has the third.

These endorsements are of particular interest not only because of their close association with **28** and **29,** but also because any explanation of the relationship between the surviving copies of these important texts must also take into account the differences between the copies of the endorsements. In the following edition they are printed from the dorse of Burton Muniment 1 (siglum D) with all significant variants from Peniarth 390 (siglum B) and MS. Loans 30 (siglum C).

Endorsement 1. Written on the dorse of D before folding, by the scribe of the charter.

þis is seo freols boc to þam mynstre æt Byrtune þe Æþelred cyning [æ]fre^a écelice gefreode . gode to lofe . 7 eallon his halgan to peorþunge . spa spa ^{b}Þulfric hit^b geédstaðelode . for hine sylfne^c . 7 [f]or^d his yldrena sapla . 7 hit mid munecon gesette . Þ þær æfre inne þæs hades menn under heora abbude . . gode þeopian . æfter [San]ctus^e Benedictus tæcinge . SIC FIAT^f .

Variants: ^{a} C; efere B; [.]fre D ^{b} ... ^{b} D; hit Þulfric B; hit Þulfric ær C, K ^{c} B, D; sylfne *omitted* C, K ^{d} B, C; [.]or D ^{e} B, C; [...]ctus D ^{f} D; *not in* B, C

Endorsement 2. Written after folding, in a hand of s. xi². Variants are also given from Burton Muniment 1925 (siglum P), a parchment roll of two membranes, 50×750 mm., written s. xii¹. This roll also contains an incomplete copy of an early-twelfth-century survey of the estates of Burton Abbey, known as Survey B. For an edition and discussion see J. F. A. Walmsley, 'Another Domesday Text', *Medieval Studies*, xxxix (1977), pp. 109–20. Where relevant, comparison is also made with the details in DB, i. 239, 247b, 273, 280 (siglum Q).

Ecclesia^a Sanctę Marię de Birtone^b in Stadfordscire .^{c}
In ipsa uilla^d habet unam hidam 7 dimidiam . Terra est .ii. carucis^e. Valet^f .lxx.^{g} solidos.
In Brantestone^h tenet .i. hidam 7 dimidiam . Terra .v. carucis. Valet^f .xl. solidos .
In Witmere^i cum appendiciis .i. hidam 7 dimidiam . Terra .vii. carucis . Valet^k .l. solidos .
In Stratone^l una hida et dimidia . Terra .ii. carucis . Valet^f .xl. solidos .
In Brunlege^m cum appendiciis dimidia hida . Terra . est .i. caruce . Valet^f .xx. solidos .
In Derlavestone^o .iii. uirgatę terrę^p. Terra est .ii. carucis . Valet^f .xxx. solidos^q.
In Lege .iii. uirgate terre . Terra est .iii. carucis . Valet^k .xl. solidos .
In Acóuere cum appendiciis .iii. uirgate terre . Terra [.ii].^{r} carucis . Valet^k .xx. solidos .
In Witestone^s . una^t hida . Terra .i. caruce . Valet^f .v. solidos^u.
In Bedintonæ^w dimidia hida . Terra .ii. carucis . Valet^f .x. solidos^x.
In Derby^y. habet ęcclesia^z de Bertonæ^{a2}. unum molinum^{b2}. 7 unam masuram^{c2} liberam . 7 alias duas de quibus rex [h]abet^{d2} socam .^{e2} In Vfre^{g2} .x. carucate^{h2} terre cum appendiciis . Terra .xv. carucis . Valet^f .x. libras . Ad socam ipsius manerii . pertinent .vi. carucate^{i2}. terre . 7 .ii. bouate . In Apleby^{l2} ^{m2} carucate^{h2} terre .^{n2} Terra . carucis .^{n2} Valet^f .iii. libras^{o2}. In Wineshylle^{p2} .ii. carucate^i.² terre . Terra . iii. carucis^{i2}. Valet^f .iii. libras^{o2}.

In Cotes^{q2} .ii.^{r2} carucate terre . Terra .iii. carucis^{i2}. Valet^f .xxx. solidos .
In . Stapenhylle^{s2} .iiii. carucate^{i2} terre . 7 .ii. bouate . Terra .iiii. carucis^{i2} .
Valet^f .iii. libras^{t2} . In Caldevvelle^{u2} .ii. carucate^{h2} terre . Terra .ii. carucis^{i2}.
Valet^f .xx. solidos . In Tichenhalle^{w2} . v. bouate terre 7 tertiam partem unius
bouate . Valet^f .x. solidos . ^{y2}Caldeuuelle^{y2} dedit rex .W*illelmus* . monachis pro
beneficio suo . ^{x2}
In Warwicescira^{z2} . Aldulvestrev^{a3} .ii. hide . 7 dimidia . Terra .iiii. carucis^{j2} .
Valet^f .xxx. solidos .

Variants: ^{a} Scriptura sicut continetur in Libro Regis *heading in* P; Sic con-
tinetur super Domusday apud Winton'. *rubric in* C
^{b} Bertone P, Q; Burthune B; Burtune C
^{c} Ecclesia . . . Staffordscire . Sic scribitur in Domusday *rubric in* B; Stafford-
sire C; Terra Sanctae Mariae de Bertone . Q 247b
^{d} P *inserts* Bertone; Q *inserts* Stadford
^{e} P *has* carr' *here and throughout, with indicated exceptions.* B, C, Q *normally
read* car'
^{f} valet B
^{g} .xl. C
^{h} D, P; Brantiston' B; Brantistone C
^{i} D, P; Withmer' B; Withmere C
^{k} Valet B, C
^{l} D, P; Stratton' B; Straton' C
^{m} D; Brvnlege P; Broml' B; Bromlege C
^{o} D, P; Derlauestone' B, C
^{p} virgate terre B, C
^{q} solidos *omitted* C; T.R.E. ualebat .xxx. solidos . 7 post .x. solidos . Modo
.xxvii. solidos 7 .iiii. denarios . Q
^{r} B, C, P; D *damaged*
^{s} D, P; Witeston' B, C
^{t} B, D, P; i. C
^{u} Valet .iiii. solidos . Q
^{w} D; Bedintone P; Bedinton' B, C; Beddintone Q
^{x} Valuit .xiii. solidos . modo .vii. solidos . 7 .iiii. denarios . Q
^{y} D, P; Derb' B; Dereby C
^{z} D, P; ecclesia B, C; abbas Q 280
^{a2} D; Burton' B, C; Bertone P, Q
^{b2} B, D, Q; molendinum C, P
^{c2} C, D, P, Q; mansuram B
^{d2} B, C, P; [.]abet D
^{e2} Q *adds* 7 .xiii. acras prati .
^{g2} C, D, P; Vfra B
^{h2} carrucate P
^{i2} car' P
^{l2} D, P, Q; Appelb' B; Appelby C
^{m2} *Blank* C, D; .v. P, Q; .v. *apparently added in another hand* B
^{n2} . . . ^{n2} D; Terra .v. carucis . P, Q *and, with* v *apparently in another hand,* B;
omitted C
^{o2} B, C, D, P; modo .lx. solidos Q
^{p2} D, P; Wineshill' C; Wynesh' B; Wineshalle Q
^{q2} B, C, D, P; Cotvne *deleted with* Cotes *added above the line* Q
^{r2} B, D, P, Q; .iij. C
^{s2} D; Stapenhelle P; Stapeh' B; Stapehill' C; Stapenhille Q
^{t2} lib' D, P; libr' B, C

^{u2} D; Caldwell' B; Caldewalle C; Caldewelle P
^{w2} D, P; Tychenhal' B; Tichenhale C; Tichenballe Q
^{x2} ... ^{x2} *Before* In Tichenhale *in* C; Hoc manerium dedit ... suo . *before* In Tichenballe Q
^{y2} D; Caldwell' B; Caldewelle C, P, Q
^{z2} D, P; Warewicescira C; Warewicesira B
^{a3} B, D, Q 239; Alduluestre C; Aldvlvestrev P

Endorsement 3. Written in a hand of s. xi/xii. Printed with facsimile, *O.S.F.*, iii, Anglesey 2; see also C. G. O. Bridgeman in *Collections for a History of Staffordshire*, 1919 (William Salt Archaeological Society), pp. 131–4.

þus fela hyda sind^a in Offalape^b hundred . In Bromlege .iii. hid' . Alrepæs .iii. hid' . Þicgintu[n 7]^c Hopepæs .v. hid' . Þaleshale^d . 7 Þodnesbyri^e .ii. hid' . Þilinhale^f .ii. hid' . Fulcpipaginel . xviii.hid' . Preostesland of Þulfrenehamtun .viii. hid' . þe bisceop^g .xxv. hid' . Elleford .iii. hid' . Heorlauestun^h .iiii. hid' . þorp .iii. hid' . Cliftun^h .viii. hid' . Siricescotan .ii. hid' . Aclea .ii. hid' . Hþiccenofre .ii. hid' . Ridepare^i . þe uue reste . ðder half hid' . Rodberdes land .jx. hid' . 7^k an half . Se abbud of Byrtun^l .vi. hid' . Scenstan^h .iiii. hid' .

Variants in B: ^{a} synden ^{b} Offalapa ^{c} B; D *damaged* ^{d} Þalesal' ^{e} Þodnesbyr' ^{f} Þilenhal' ^{g} bissop ^{h} -ton ^{i} Rideware ^{k} ant ^{l} on Byrton'

None of the medieval copies of **28** (B, C, D) is derived from any other; they all have a common exemplar which appears to have had some errors and confusions, such as the phrase *lunaticis demoniisque obsensum*,[1] which are, however, insufficient cause to assume that the common exemplar was not the original charter. There are some indications that B and C had a common exemplar that was not the source of D; they share a number of readings that are better than those in D but that is not, of course, decisive for they could well represent errors in D. More significantly they both omit the subscription of Godric *minister* and they both mistranscribe the name Styrr.[2] The spacing of the subscriptions in C suggests that in its source the subscriptions were arranged very much as they appear in D. There are no decisive indications of the history of Endorsement 1, but it probably went with **28**. This interpretation of the textual history of **28** gains support from that of **29**. For the text B and C certainly have a common exemplar which is shown to be different from D by their agreement in the phrase *for his modor* where D has *for minre meder*.[3]

As explained above, p. xiv, when the charters of Burton Abbey were enumerated, probably in the thirteenth century, it appears that only one number, XXVIII, was allocated to **28** and **29** together, suggesting not only that they were on one sheet, like D, but that the originals of these two texts were not then in the archives. The absence of a numerical endorsement from D further suggests that there was another

[1] See **28**, notes *l, z, e* 2.
[2] See **28** notes *u* 4, *c* 5.
[3] See **29** note *y* 2.

sheet which is likely to have been the source of the cartulary versions of
28 and **29**. One good reason for the production of a second copy would
have been the gross incompetence of D's version of **28**.

The probable relationship between the surviving medieval versions
of these texts is therefore best represented by the stemma:

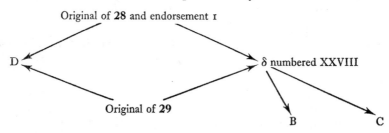

Original of **28** and endorsement 1

D

δ numbered XXVIII

Original of **29**

B

C

There are several indications that the history of Endorsement 2 was
the same as that proposed for **28** and **29**; B and C both have a heading
that cannot have been taken from D, in which the spelling *Domusday*
occurs. C made some corrections, notably by moving the note about the
gift of Cauldwell to a more appropriate place. It is noteworthy that in
the entry about Appleby δ apparently had the same lacunae as D, and
that the missing figures were added to B, possibly from P or from a
version of the relevant part of DB, such as that in MS. Loans 30, fo.
36ᵛ. Endorsement 3 may also have been copied on δ, and omitted by C,
but it appears more likely that B added this endorsement from D after
copying the other endorsements from δ.

7. WULFRIC AND HIS FAMILY

There is no contemporary evidence for the nickname Spot or Spott given
to Wulfric in the thirteenth-century Burton Annals and in a closely
related passage in the History of Abingdon Abbey.[1] In the charter
granting him part of Dumbleton in 995 he is described as Wulfric
Wulfrunesunu and the same man also witnessed Æthelred's confirmation of Æthelric's will shortly afterwards.[2] He was probably the Wulfric
minister who, until 1002, witnessed many of Æthelred's charters. Two
charters of 982 and 988 have two such witnesses[3] but after that there
is only one who occurs in eighteen of the twenty-four possible lists.
The date of his first appearance cannot be determined. Wulfric was
a fairly common name in the middle years of the tenth century and it is
not normally possible to say that different references are to the same
man. One well-documented exception, called Wulfric Cufing in the will

---

[1] Luard, *Annales Monastici*, i. 183; Stevenson, *Chron. Abingdon*, i. 411.
[2] Sawyer 886, 939.
[3] Sawyer 840, 868. In Sawyer 872 two Wulfrics occur in Kemble's edition, but the
first should read Wulfsige, see E. E. Barker, *Sussex Archaeological Collections*, lxxxviii
(1949), p. 108 n. 35. I am indebted to Mr Keynes for drawing my attention to this
correction.

of Bishop Ælfsige, had extensive estates in the south which he forfeited in, or shortly after, 958 but recovered from Edgar in 960, and eight charters survive by which he was granted or confirmed land in several places between 940 and 958.[1] Other charters, including some from Mercia, may have been grants to Wulfric the testator but it is not possible to say which nor to determine how many men are represented by the surviving grants to Wulfric, variously described as *minister, fidelissimus minister, miles, procer, proceriali potencia ditatus, pedisequus,* and *princeps.*[2] In this period two charters, one of doubtful authenticity, were witnessed by three Wulfrics,[3] but normally no more than two occur; but it would be wrong to assume that only two, or at most three, Wulfrics ever attended court; some men of local importance may only have witnessed charters dealing with estates in their own districts. It is, however, clear that the Wulfrics who were active before 960 did not long survive that year. By 965 one of Wulfric Cufing's estates, Denchworth, was confirmed to Abingdon Abbey and in 968 another, Boxford, was granted to Ælfwine.[4] These could have been transferred in his lifetime, but after 960 the name Wulfric rarely occurs as that of either beneficiary or witness. There are, in fact, only seven occurrences of the name Wulfric in five acceptable charters between 960 and 975. Wulfric *minister* was granted land at Plaish and Aston, Salop, in 963 in a charter also witnessed by Wulfric *minister,* and the same witness occurs twice in a charter of 972 and once in charters of 971 and 975, all concerning Mercian estates, and in one dated 973 concerning land in Berkshire.[5] Some of these, and especially those occurring after 970, may well be Wulfric Spot.

He seems to have died between his last subscription in 1002 and 1004. There are no *ministri* in the surviving copy of the one witness-list for 1003[6] and it is possible that he was alive when Æthelred confirmed the privileges and endowment of Burton Abbey. The charter does not explicitly state that he was dead, but Stevenson argued that as it confirmed a bequest he must have been dead;[7] Wulfric may, however, have taken the precaution of obtaining royal confirmation in his lifetime. The abbey was certainly in existence when the will was drawn up. It is noteworthy that Wulfric did not witness the charter of 1004, but neither Ordulf nor Æthelmær witnessed the foundation charters of their abbeys, Tavistock and Eynsham.[8] According to the late *Chronicon Abbatum* of Burton, where Wulfric is called *consul ac comes Merciorum,* he died on 22 October from wounds received in battle at Ipswich in 1010.[9] This

---

[1] Whitelock, *Wills*, pp. 115–16.

[2] Sawyer 472–3, 504, 519–20, 530, 541, 550–2, 634–6; see below p. xlviii.

[3] Sawyer 543, 658.   [4] Sawyer 733, 761.

[5] Sawyer 723, 782, 786, 790, 801. Wulfric *minister* also occurs in the same period in the following charters of doubtful reliability: Sawyer 725, 753, 787, 792, 799.

[6] Sawyer 1664.

[7] Stevenson 1911/1, p. 22.   [8] Sawyer 838, 911.

[9] The battle was, in fact, at *Ringmere*. The compiler of *Chronicon Abbatum* (*Mon. Angl.* iii. 47) was presumably misled by the entry in *ASC* 1010.

led Bridgeman and others to identify him as Wulfric, son of Leofwine, whose death in that battle is reported in the *Anglo-Saxon Chronicle* (1010), but the arguments against that identification advanced by Stevenson and Professor Whitelock are compelling.[1] One decisive point is that two of Wulfric's bequests, Dumbleton and Rolleston (1 and 4), took effect before 1006. It is nevertheless likely that Burton Abbey commemorated the death of the founder on or about the right day.

Wulfric's mother may be identified as the Wulfrun who was captured at Tamworth in 940 by Olaf Guthfrithson and was foundress of Wolverhampton.[2] The name was not common and her association with the area in which Wulfric was a notable landowner makes the identification more than likely. Apart from Wulfric's will, information about her family comes from the confirmation of her endowment of Wolverhampton by Archbishop Sigeric, apparently in 994.[3] This is, unfortunately, known only from seventeenth-century transcripts of a lost manuscript and it has several unusual features, but the statements about her family may be trustworthy; namely that she had an only daughter *Elfthrith*, for Ælfthryth, and a kinsman called Wulfgeat, whose crimes needed expiation. The charter states explicitly that Ælfthryth is dead, but does not make clear whether Wulfgeat and Wulfrun's unnamed husband, who is also mentioned, were alive or not. The statement in **27**, dated 996, that Wulfric had been given Bromley by his mother does not prove that she was then dead, although she does not seem to have been alive when the will was drawn up. Bromley was one of the three estates granted to Wulfsige the Black in 942 **(5)** that were held by Wulfric and, although that cannot prove kinship between them, the reference in **27** to his mother's ownership of Bromley strengthens that possibility. Professor Whitelock has suggested that the reference in the D version of the *Anglo-Saxon Chronicle* to the capture of Wulfrun in 940 may have been due to the interest taken at York, where that version of the *Chronicle* is likely to have been compiled, in the mother of the man who later became ealdorman of Northumbria.[4] It is, however, possible that she was remembered in her own right as a member of perhaps one of the greatest Mercian families, and the chronicler certainly assumes that she was well known.

Nothing is known of Wulfric's father. The names given to his children, Wulfric, Ælfhelm, and Ælfthryth, may possibly indicate that his name began with the element *Ælf-*. He was probably dead when Wolverhampton was founded and the description of Wulfric as the son of Wulfrun in 995 would have been more natural if his father died when

---

[1] Stevenson 1911/1, pp. 21–2; Whitelock, *Wills*, p. 153.

[2] *ASC* 943 D; *V.C.H. Staffordshire*, iii. 321–2.

[3] Sawyer 1380. Spelman's transcript, which is independent of Dugdale's, is in Manchester, John Rylands Library, MS. English 880, fos. 145–8ᵛ. I owe this reference to Mr Keynes.

[4] Whitelock 1959, p. 80.

Wulfric was a child. It may, however, mean that Wulfric *nobilis pro-geniei minister* owed his rank, influence, and wealth more to his mother who may herself have been a sole heiress, than to his father. Wulfrun is unlikely to have married a man of no consequence, and the general distribution of Wulfric's estates as revealed in the will, and the slight knowledge that we have of his brother's estates,[1] suggests that, like his mother, his father was a Mercian landowner. If there is anything in the claim that Wulfric endowed Burton Abbey with the whole of his paternal inheritance, that may provide a clue to the extent of that inheritance.[2]

The beneficiaries of some of the Burton charters were probably Wulfric's kinsmen, a possibility strengthened by the recurrence among the grantees of personal-name elements that seem to have been favoured by that family. The best case is **20**, a grant by Edgar in 963 to Wulfgeat *minister* of land at Upper Arley, Worcs., that formed part of Wulfrun's endowment of Wolverhampton and it is therefore probable that this Wulfgeat was the kinsman specifically mentioned in connection with that foundation. Some other charters granting estates that appear to have been held by Wulfric later—in the absence of bounds it is not possible to be sure—may also have been grants to members of the same family. One example is the Ælfheah *minister* who was, according to **12**, granted land *æt Northtune* in 951. There is no doubt about the identifica-tion of Marchington granted to Wulfhelm *miles* in the same year **(11)**; and he was probably a kinsman of Wulfric who held that estate later. The same man may also have been granted Aston and Great Barr, Staffs., in a charter dated 957[3] that is connected stylistically with **11** and the other alliterative charters that form an important part of the Burton archive. It is more than likely that Wulfric numbered among his family one or more of the Wulfrics who occur in charters of the mid-tenth century, including the grant of Bourton, Gloucs., in 949 and of Wark-ton, Northants., in 946, both also alliterative charters.[4] If, as seems likely, the same family held land outside the area of Wulfric's own estates, the charters to Wulfmær granting land in Wilts. **(19)** and to Ælfwine *scriptor* granting land in Oxon. **(24)** may also have been family archives and the beneficiaries therefore kinsmen of Wulfric. It would be more hazardous to postulate kinship between Wulfric and the beneficiaries of earlier charters in the archive, notably Uhtred, who may have been the son of Eadwulf of Bamburgh **(3, 9)**, and Ealhhelm, probably the man whose grandson Ælfwine fought at Maldon **(1)**. In these and other cases kinship is possible, but the charters are as likely to be title-deeds of estates that were acquired by members of Wulfric's family in one of the many ways that are so well illustrated by Wulfric's will: gift, bequest, lease, and purchase, as well as inheritance.

Wulfric apparently had only one surviving child when he made his

---

[1] Ibid.   [2] See below, p. xlv.
[3] Sawyer 574.   [4] Sawyer 550, 520.

The Family of Wulfric

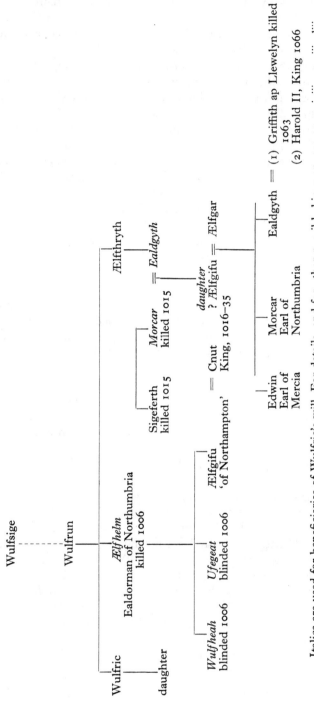

Italics are used for beneficiaries of Wulfric's will. For details, and for other possible kinsmen, see pp. xxi–iii, xxxviii–xliii.

will, an unnamed daughter who was not expected to have an heir. His
brother, Ælfhelm, became ealdorman of Northumbria by 993 but was
killed in 1006.[1] At the same time Ælfhelm's sons, Wulfheah and Ufegeat, were blinded, leaving as the only representative of that branch of
the family Ælfgifu 'of Northampton'. The hostility shown by Æthelred
to that family may give added significance to Cnut's choice of her as his
concubine. The bequests made to Morcar, to his wife Ealdgyth, and to
their daughter suggest that there was close kinship with Wulfric, and
the most likely connection is that Morcar married Wulfric's niece,
daughter of his sister Ælfthryth, a relationship that is also indicated
by the absence of any bequest by Wulfric to Morcar's brother, Sigeferth.
The fact that Earl Ælfgar later chose to call one of his sons Morcar,
itself an unusual name, and that his daughter was called Ealdgyth may
mean that there was some direct relationship between thegn Morcar's
family and Ælfgar's. It is possible that Earl Ælfgar's wife, Ælfgifu,
was the daughter of Morcar and Ealdgyth, but no such relationship can
be proved. That Ælfgar and his family held many of the estates that had
once belonged to Wulfsige the Black, as well as many owned by Wulfric,
would be consistent with some kinship; and the emphasis in the post-
Conquest grant to Burton Abbey of Coton, which had been held by
Wulfsige (6), on the estate's descent from Earl Morcar's mother, may
mean that Ælfgar gained some rights in the area by marriage.[2] If so,
he was only strengthening an association that he inherited from his
father, Earl Leofric, who died at Bromley, presumably Kings Bromley,[3]
and whose widow, Godgifu, held important interests in the area. In this
connection it should also be noted that the abbot of Burton immediately
before the Conquest was Leofric, Earl Leofric's nephew.[4] Whether
Earl Leofric's interest in the area was inherited from the family of Wulfric or derived ultimately from grants made after their fall, or from a
combination of the two, cannot be determined.

The Leofric and Leofnoth, probably brothers,[5] who held many of the
estates of thegn Morcar (as well as Stretton, bequeathed by Wulfric to
Morcar's daughter, and some of the land granted to Morcar in 32), had
such common names that no connection with the family of Earl Leofric
can be claimed; but their landholdings show that they benefited from
thegn Morcar's fall. Whether they did so by inheritance after the death
of Edmund Ironside, who seized Morcar's estates in 1015, or by the
regranting of confiscated estates is uncertain, but the possibility of
inheritance is slightly increased by the facts that Leofric held most of
Silverstone T.R.E. and that that estate had apparently been granted
to Wulfsige in 942 (7).

[1] Whitelock 1959, p. 80.   [2] See below, p. xlvi.
[3] Fl. Wig., s.a. 1057.
[4] Harmer, Writs, p. 565; The Heads of Religious Houses: England and Wales 990–
1216, ed. D. Knowles, C. N. L. Brooke, Vera C. M. London (Cambridge, 1972), p. 31.
[5] See above, p. xxvi.

8. BURTON ABBEY AND ITS ENDOWMENT

The first endorsement of the confirmation charter and will **(28, 29)**
shows that there had been some form of organized religious life at Burton
that Wulfric could claim to re-establish. It was later believed at Burton
that this earlier community was associated with St Modwenna and it has
been assumed that it survived until the ninth century and was de-
stroyed by the Vikings.[1] In the eleventh century there were several
communities, apparently of secular canons, in this area of Mercia, some
of which may be traced back to the seventh century, while others were
founded or possibly refounded in the tenth century, and a few survived
to become the privileged royal free chapels of the later Middle Ages.[2]
Only two of these pre-Conquest communities are mentioned in the
Burton charters: Tamworth **(29)** and Bakewell **(9)**. There is likely to
have been some sort of community in the *vicus regalis* of Tamworth
from a very early date and Bakewell, where Uhtred apparently intended
to establish a *coenubium* at the end of his life, is shown by the presence
of a series of stone crosses, the earliest apparently dating from the
eighth century, to have been a centre of some sort of religious life for
a long time.[3] Wulfric himself clearly favoured the Benedictine rule
rather than communities of this kind; Tamworth received back no more
than its own estate and his attitude may be contrasted with the respect
shown for such communities by his contemporary, Wulfgeat of Don-
nington.[4] The absence of any bequest to his mother's own foundation,
Wolverhampton, is striking. The initial dedication of his abbey to
St Benedict did not, however, long survive. In DB it is the church of
St Mary and the normal dedication later was to SS Mary and Modwenna.

The construction of the abbey had already begun when the will was
made, for the first bequest was Burton 'on which the monastery stands'
and the confirmation charter refers to Wulfric's having built and endowed it. That endowment was large, consisting of forty-six named
places, thirty-four of which can be identified in DB where they have
a total assessment of more than 80 hides or carucates. According to
the thirteenth-century annals of the abbey, Wulfric endowed it with the
whole of his paternal inheritance, worth 700 pounds.[5] Whatever the
source of this information, his gifts included two estates, Bromley and
Stretton, that had once belonged to Wulfsige the Black, who is more

[1] The most recent general account of Burton Abbey is in *V.C.H. Staffordshire*, iii.
199–212.
[2] Dorothy Styles, 'The Early History of the King's Chapels in Staffordshire',
Transactions of the Birmingham Archaeological Society, lx (1940 for 1936), pp. 56–95;
J. H. Denton, *English Royal Free Chapels 1100–1300* (Manchester, 1970).
[3] F. C. Plumtre, 'The Parish Church of Bakewell in Derbyshire', *Archaeological
Journal*, iv (1847), pp. 37–58; T. E. Routh, 'A Corpus of the Pre-Conquest Carved
Stones of Derbyshire', *Journal of the Derbyshire Archaeological and Natural History
Society*, N.S., xi (1937), pp. 1–46, esp. 6–19.
[4] Sawyer 1534.
[5] Luard, *Annales Monastici*, i. 183.

likely to have been a kinsman on his mother's than on his father's side. As explained above,[1] the bequests to the abbey seem to be in two parts in the will, each described in a regular geographical order. The first sequence includes Bromley and Stretton and it may therefore be that the second part, beginning with Newton or Winshill, was his paternal inheritance. The confirmation charter lists almost all the places named in the will, with some changes of order that are probably not significant, but the omission of the dependencies of Darlaston and of the hide at Sheen, all of which are listed as *Terra Regis* in DB, may mean that these bequests never reached the abbey.

The endowment described in DB and in the early-twelfth-century Surveys[2] includes only thirteen places from the original endowment. The losses may have occurred as a consequence of the fall from favour of Wulfric's brother Ælfhelm in 1006, followed nine years later by the fall of Morcar; but, as six of the estates lost by the abbey were held T.R.E. by Earl Ælfgar and his family, the damage could have been done in the time of Abbot Leofric, Ælfgar's cousin, who certainly alienated 1 hide at Appleby to his aunt, Godgifu. Another prominent pre-Conquest owner of land that should have belonged to the abbey was Siward Barn, whose estates passed after the Conquest to Henry de Ferrers.[3] Apart from Æthelric son of Mærgeat nothing is known about the others who T.R.E. held land that should have belonged to the abbey.

The losses were in part balanced by acquisitions in the century after the foundation. Lucius III's confirmation of the abbey's endowment[4] gives the impression that there were only two benefactors, Wulfric and William I, but that bull contains several demonstrable confusions; a surer guide to the progress of the endowment is provided by DB, supplemented by the twelfth-century Surveys and, in one or two cases, by early post-Conquest charters. These show that, in the century after the foundation, Burton Abbey acquired the following estates, listed here in chronological order of acquisition, as far as possible:

Rolleston, Staffs., bequeathed by Wulfric to Ælfhelm and in 1008 granted by the king in exchange for two Gloucs. estates (31). The abbey lost it before the Conquest and T.R.E. it was held by Earl Morcar. It had formed part of the large grant to Wulfsige in 942 (5).

Wetmoor, Staffs., granted to the abbey by Æthelred in 1012 according to the suspect charter, 35, was certainly held by the abbey T.R.E. with an assessment of 1½ hides. The Surveys show that it included Horninglow; and the bounds given in the charter suggest that Anslow was included, as it certainly was later.[5]

---

[1] p. xxviii.

[2] The early-twelfth-century Surveys, distinguished as A and B, have been printed from a thirteenth-century copy, and discussed, by Bridgeman in *Surveys*. An early-twelfth-century copy of Survey B occurs in Burton Muniment 1925, see p. xxxv above.

[3] *V.C.H. Warwickshire*, i. 282–3.

[4] *Mon. Angl.* iii. 42.

[5] *Surveys*, pp. 219–22.

Willington, Derbys., was given, according to the late *Chronicon Abbatum*, by Edward the Confessor in the time of Abbot Brihtric, that is between 1042 and 1050.[1] In the Surveys it was an abbey estate, assessed at 3 carucates, but in DB it was part of Ralph fitzHubert's fief and had been held T.R.E. by Leofric (DB, i. 277a). Bridgeman suggested that Leofric was the abbot of that name, but he was more probably the presumed brother of Leofnoth who, with Leofric, had held a large part of Ralph's fief in Derbys. and Notts.[2]

Stapenhill, Derbys., was also given by Edward the Confessor before 1050, according to the *Chronicon Abbatum*. It was held by the abbey T.R.E. and assessed at 4 carucates 2 bovates (DB, i. 273a). Comparison with the Surveys shows that this estate included Brislingcote and Stanton.[3] The carucate at Stanton by Newhall was probably the subject of **1** and **23**. According to the Surveys it was held of the abbey by Geoffrey de Clinton, who acquired it in exchange for the church of Stapenhill and for the tithes of the other part of Stanton that he held of another fief.[4]

Austrey, Warwicks., is said by DB (i. 239a) to have been given to the abbey by Earl Leofric, who died in 1057. It had been bequeathed by Wulfric to Morcar's wife and is the subject of the spurious charter **18**.

Coton, Derbys., was, according to DB (i. 273a), held T.R.E. by Earl Ælfgar but in 1086 was held by the abbey. A note in the Burton cartulary claims that Coton was given to the abbey by Earl Morcar, was seized by the Conqueror and later restored by him.[5] William's writ granting it to Burton does not mention Morcar's gift but does add the condition that it was to be held as the mother of Earl Morcar had held it.[6] By the beginning of the twelfth century this estate had been alienated, probably by Abbot Geoffrey (expelled in 1094), and it is not described in the Surveys. Coton was one of the estates granted to Wulfsige in 942 **(6)**.

Cauldwell, Derbys., was, according to DB (i. 273a), given to the abbey by William I. It is included in the Surveys and was, like Coton, part of the grant to Wulfsige in 942 **(6)**.

Mickleover, Derbys., with its berewicks, Little Over, Findern, and Potlack, was given by William I, according to the *Chronicon Abbatum*. In DB (i. 273a) it was held T.R.E. by King Edward and by the abbey in 1086. It is also the subject of **34**.

Branston, Staffs., was held by the abbey in 1086 but by Godgifu T.R.E. (DB, i. 247b). It presumably passed to the abbey after the Conquest. It was one of the estates granted to Wulfsige in 942 **(5)**.

---

[1] *Mon. Angl.* iii. 47; cf. *Heads of Religious Houses* (cited p. xliii, note 4), p. 31.
[2] *Surveys*, pp. 293–4.   [3] *Surveys*, pp. 238–40, 294–6.
[4] *Surveys*, pp. 240, 295; Jeayes 1937, no. 4.
[5] *Burton Cartulary*, p. 9.
[6] *Regesta Regum Anglo-Normannorum*, i. ed. H. W. C. Davis (Oxford, 1913), no. 223.

In addition, DB lists holdings in Derby (i. 280a), and the Surveys (p. 247) show that the abbey had also acquired a small interest in Stretton on Dunsmore and Wolston, Warwicks.

The total assessment of the estates held by the abbey in DB that were acquired after the original endowment, excluding the sokeland of Mickleover, was 5½ hides, 18 carucates, 2 bovates. This may be compared with what was left of the original endowment, assessed in DB at 7¾ hides, 7 carucates, 5½ bovates. Many of these added estates were the subject of charters to Wulfsige the Black in 942; Rolleston and Branston **(5)**, Coton and Cauldwell **(6)**, and Stapenhill **(7)**. If either **6** or **7** was forged on the basis of the other, it may have been to provide a title-deed and claim to one or more of these estates.

9. THE ALLITERATIVE CHARTERS

Eight Burton charters **(4, 5, 6, 7, 8, 9, 11, 13)** belong to a group of texts, dated between 930 and 956, that are distinctive in being written, at least in part, in rhythmical and alliterative Latin. The eighteen charters of this type, from Abingdon, Ely, Evesham, Glastonbury, Thorney, and Worcester as well as Burton, have been listed by Professor Whitelock who has also drawn attention to a vernacular version of such a charter from Peterborough, to the occurrence of an identical vernacular passage in a Winchester charter, and to a quotation from an alliterative charter in a St Albans cartulary.[1] The Burton charters of this type illustrate many of the distinctive features of the group, including the elaborate royal titles with their emphasis on the role of *paganorum gubernator* **(4, 8, 9, 13)**, the dating by regnal years, generally expressed in elaborate terms **(5, 8, 9, 11, 13)**, the tendency to vary the titles of witnesses, in particular by using English words **(8, 11, 13)**, and to give them in pairs **(9, 11)**, and the naming of the place of issue in the final paragraph **(5, 8)**. Most of these alliterative charters, including all the Burton examples granting land in identifiable places, were grants of land in the Midlands, although the grants themselves were made at assemblies held in other parts of the country. The royal titles, for example *rex Ængulsæxna ond Norðhymbra imperator paganorum gubernator Brittonumque propugnator* **(8)**, would have been particularly appropriate for the kings who ruled Mercia and claimed to rule the north, and a close parallel is found in one of Edgar's charters when he was king only of Mercia and Northumbria, *rex Merciorum et Nor-thanhymbrorum atque Brettonum.*[2] Professor Whitelock has advanced

[1] Whitelock 1968, p. 42. The texts are Sawyer 404, 472–3, 520, 544, 550, 556, 566, 572, 574, 633, and the eight Burton charters listed above. Sawyer 931, dated 1013, is also of this type and is probably spurious although based on an authentic alliterative charter. For the quotation from St Albans (Sawyer 1497), see Whitelock 1968, pp. 38–9.

[2] Sawyer 677.

convincing reasons for accepting most of these alliterative charters as genuine. The only Burton text about which there need be any doubt is one of the pair **6** or **7**. If these were, as the copyist states, identical except for the places named, there is a strong suspicion that one is a copy of the other, confected to include some estates that were not in the original charter. This suspicion is strengthened by the fact that both these charters include Drakelow and Walton, while none of the places in the very similar, but not identical, charter **5** is included in either **6** or **7**.

Dr Hart has suggested, on the basis of an incomplete list of these alliterative charters, that they were produced by Glastonbury scribes during Dunstan's abbacy.[1] Dunstan was appointed abbot of Glastonbury in 940 by King Edmund and cannot therefore have been responsible for Athelstan's two charters of this type. In support of his suggestion, Dr Hart has emphasized both the possibility that one of the beneficiaries of these charters may have been related to Dunstan and also the fact that two of them were preserved at Glastonbury. These are not compelling arguments and Dr Chaplais has pointed out that the evidence of the formulas tells against any connection between this group of documents and Glastonbury.[2] A much stronger case can be made for Worcester, whose claims are dismissed rather summarily by Dr Hart. Both Professor Whitelock and Dr Chaplais have drawn attention to the remarkable similarities between these charters and a lease granted by Bishop Coenwald of Worcester in 957;[3] and Dr Chaplais has noted other links with Worcester and, in particular, with Coenwald. It is perhaps significant that Coenwald, who was bishop from 929 to 957 or 958, is the only witness common to the thirteen alliterative charters which have full lists of episcopal subscriptions.

Burton Abbey appears to have been a repository for charters belonging to more than one member of the founder's family; and the fact that almost half the known alliterative charters come from Burton may mean that this family tended to have their charters drafted by Bishop Coenwald or someone closely associated with him. Four of these alliterative charters are grants to Wulfric, variously described as *minister*, *proceriali potencia ditatus*, *pedisequus*, and *miles*.[4] The tendency of the alliterative charters to use a great variety of descriptions for individuals may explain these varied descriptions of Wulfric and remove one of the main objections to accepting all four charters as grants to the same man. That these are alliterative charters also increases the likelihood that he was related to Wulfric Spot. The possibility that

---

[1] C. R. Hart, 'Danelaw Charters and the Glastonbury Scriptorium', *Downside Review*, xc (1972), pp. 125–32.

[2] P. Chaplais, 'La chancellerie royale anglaise des origines au règne de Jean sans terre', a paper read at Budapest in 1973, forthcoming.

[3] Sawyer 1290.

[4] Sawyer 472–3, 520, 550.

other kinsmen included Wulfsige the Black and Wulfhelm—who was granted Marchington **(11)** and Aston and Great Barr[1]—is also strengthened by the fact that all these charters are either alliterative or closely connected to the alliterative group.

[1] Sawyer 574.

ABBREVIATIONS

N.L.W.	National Library of Wales
s.	*saeculo*
S.R.O.	Staffordshire Record Office
T.R.E.	*Tempore Regis Eadwardi*

BIBLIOGRAPHICAL ABBREVIATIONS

ASC	*Anglo-Saxon Chronicle*
Birch	W. de Gray Birch, *Cartularium Saxonicum*, 3 vols and index (1885–99)
Bridgeman 1916	C. G. O. Bridgeman, 'Staffordshire Pre-Conquest Charters', *Collections for a History of Staffordshire*, 1916 (William Salt Archaeological Society), pp. 69–137
Bridgeman 1916/1	C. G. O. Bridgeman, 'Wulfric Spot's Will', *Collections for a History of Staffordshire*, 1916 (William Salt Archaeological Society), pp. 1–66
Burton Cartulary	G. Wrottesley, 'The Burton Chartulary', *Collections for a History of Staffordshire*, v, part 1 (William Salt Archaeological Society, 1884), pp. 1–101
Chronicon Abbatum	*Mon. Angl.* iii. 47–50
DB	Domesday Book
DEPN	E. Ekwall, *The Concise Oxford Dictionary of English Place-Names*, 4th edn (Oxford, 1960)
E.P.N.S.	English Place-Name Society
Fl. Wig.	*Florentii Wigorniensis Monastici Chronicon ex Chronicis*, ed. B. Thorpe (1848–9)
Harmer, *Writs*	F. E. Harmer, *Anglo-Saxon Writs* (Manchester, 1952)
Hart	C. R. Hart, *The Early Charters of Northern England and the North Midlands* (Leicester, 1975)
Jeayes 1937	I. H. Jeayes, 'Descriptive Catalogue of the Charters and Muniments belonging to the Marquis of Anglesey', *Collections for a History of Staffordshire*, 1937 (William Salt Archaeological Society)
Kemble	J. M. Kemble, *Codex Diplomaticus Aevi Saxonici*, 6 vols (1839–48)
Luard, *Annales Monastici*	*Annales Monastici*, i, ed. H. R. Luard (Rolls Series, 1864)
Mon. Angl.	W. Dugdale, *Monasticon Anglicanum*, ed. B. Bandinel, J. Caley, and H. Ellis, 6 vols in 8 (1817–30, repr. 1846)

O'Donovan 1972, 1973	Mary Anne O'Donovan, 'An Interim Revision of Episcopal Dates for the Province of Canterbury, 850–950: part I', *Anglo-Saxon England*, i (1972), pp. 23–44; 'part II', ii (1973), pp. 91–113
O.S.F.	W. B. Sanders, *Facsimiles of Anglo-Saxon Manuscripts*, 3 vols (Ordnance Survey, Southampton, 1878–84)
PN Derbys.	K. Cameron, *The Place-Names of Derbyshire* (E.P.N.S., xxvii–ix, 1959)
Robertson, *Charters*	A. J. Robertson, *Anglo-Saxon Charters*, 2nd edn (Cambridge, 1956)
S	For 'Sawyer' in commentaries on the charters
Sawyer	P. H. Sawyer, *Anglo-Saxon Charters: an annotated list and bibliography* (Royal Historical Society, 1968)
Sawyer 1975	P. H. Sawyer, 'The Charters of Burton Abbey and the Unification of England', *Northern History*, x (1975), pp. 28–39
Shaw, *Staffordshire*	S. Shaw, *The History and Antiquities of Staffordshire*, 2 vols (1798–1801)
Stenton 1910	F. M. Stenton, *Types of Manorial Structure in the Northern Danelaw* (Oxford Studies in Social and Legal History, ii, 1910)
Stenton 1971	F. M. Stenton, *Anglo-Saxon England*, 3rd edn (Oxford, 1971)
Stevenson, *Chron. Abingdon*	*Chronicon Monasterii de Abingdon*, ed. J. Stevenson (Rolls Series, 1858)
Stevenson 1911/1	W. H. Stevenson and W. H. Duignan, 'Anglo-Saxon Charters relating to Shropshire', *Transactions of the Shropshire Archaeological and Natural History Society*, 4th ser., i (1911), pp. 1–22
Surveys	C. G. O. Bridgeman, 'The Burton Abbey Twelfth Century Surveys', *Collections for a History of Staffordshire*, 1916 (William Salt Archaeological Society), pp. 209–300
V.C.H.	*The Victoria History of the Counties of England*
Whitelock, *Wills*	D. Whitelock, *Anglo-Saxon Wills* (Cambridge 1930)
Whitelock 1955	*English Historical Documents*, i, c. 500–1042, ed. D. Whitelock (1955)
Whitelock 1959	D. Whitelock, 'The Dealings of the Kings of England with Northumbria in the Tenth and Eleventh Centuries', *The Anglo-Saxons: Studies ...presented to Bruce Dickins*, ed. P. Clemoes (1959), pp. 70–88
Whitelock 1968	*The Will of Æthelgifu: a tenth-century Anglo-Saxon Manuscript*, translated and examined by Dorothy Whitelock with a note on the document by Neil Ker and analysis ... by Lord Rennell (Roxburghe Club, 1968)

LIST OF CHARTERS

THE manuscripts from which the charters have been printed are briefly noted.

1. Æthelflæd, Lady of the Mercians, grants two hides at *Stantun* to Ealhhelm. A.D. 800 [? for 914]: Peniarth 390, fo. 173

2. King Athelstan grants seven hides *æt Hwituntune* to Eadric, *minister.* A.D. 925: Peniarth 390, fo. 173ʳᵛ

3. King Athelstan confirms sixty hides at Hope and Ashford, Derbyshire, to Uhtred, his *fidelis.* A.D. 926: Peniarth 390, fos 173ᵛ–174

4. King Athelstan grants five hides at *Eatun* to Beorhthelm (*Byrhtelm*), *miles.* A.D. 850 [for 939]: Peniarth 390, fo. 173

5. King Edmund grants forty hides at Alrewas, Bromley, Barton, Tatenhill, Branston, Stretton, Rolleston, Clifton, and Haunton, Staffordshire, to Wulfsige the Black (*Þulfsye prenomine Maur'*). A.D. 942: Peniarth 390, fo. 174

6. King Edmund grants land at Walton on Trent, Coton in the Elms, Cauldwell, Drakelow, Derbyshire, Newbold, Staffordshire, and Linton, Derbyshire, to Wulfsige the Black (*Þulfsie prenomine Maur'*). A.D. 942: Peniarth 390, fo. 174

7. King Edmund grants land at Croxall, Catton, Walton on Trent, Drakelow, Stapenhill, Derbyshire, and at *Sulueston'* [? Silverstone, Northamptonshire], to Wulfsige the Black (*Þulfsie*). A.D. 942: Peniarth 390, fo. 174

8. King Eadred grants four hides *in Suthtone*, with licence to buy a fifth, to Ulfketel, *miles.* A.D. 949: Peniarth 390, fo. 174ʳᵛ

9. King Eadred grants land at Bakewell, Derbyshire, to Uhtred, *miles* and *dux.* A.D. 949: Peniarth 390, fos 174ᵛ–175

10. King Eadred grants ten hides at *Eatun* to Athelstan (*Æðestan*), *minister.* A.D. 949: Peniarth 390, fo. 175

11. King Eadred grants land at Marchington, Staffordshire, to Wulfhelm, *miles.* A.D. 951: Peniarth 390, fo. 175ʳᵛ

12. King Eadred grants eight hides *æt Northtune* to Ælfeah, *minister.* A.D. 951: Peniarth 390, fo. 175ᵛ

13. King Eadred grants land at Chesterfield, Derbyshire, to Uhtred Child, *pedisequus.* A.D. 955: Peniarth 390, fos 175ᵛ–176

14. King Eadwig grants eight hides at Braunston, Northamptonshire, to Eadwig, *minister.* A.D. 956: Peniarth 390, fo. 176

15. King Eadwig grants three hides *æt Mortune* to Mæglsothen, his man. A.D. 956: Peniarth 390, fo. 176ʳᵛ

16. King Eadwig grants five hides *æt Niwantune* to Æthelgeard. A.D. 956: Peniarth 390, fo. 176^v

17. King Eadwig grants land at Darlaston, near Stone, Staffordshire, to Æthelnoth, *minister*. A.D. 956: William Salt 84/1/41

18. King Eadred grants five hides at Austrey, Warwickshire, to Wulfric, *minister*. A.D. 958: Peniarth 390, fo. 177

19. King Edgar grants ten hides at Hilmarton and Littlecott, Wiltshire, to Wulfmær, *minister*. A.D. 962: Peniarth 390, fo. 177

20. King Edgar grants three hides *æt Duddestone* [? Duddeston, near Birmingham] and three *æt Ernlege* [? Upper Arley, Worcestershire], to Wulfgeat, *minister*. A.D. 963: Peniarth 390, fo. 177^{rv}

21. King Edgar grants ten hides at Parwich, Derbyshire, to Ælfhelm, *minister*. A.D. 966: Peniarth 390, fo. 177^v

22. King Edgar grants thirteen hides at Breedon, *Wifelesthorpe, Ætheres dune* [? Atterton], and Diseworth, Leicestershire, to Æthelwold, bishop, for the church at Breedon. A.D. 967 [for 972]: Peniarth 390, fos 177^v–178

23. King Edgar grants one hide at *Stantun* [? Stanton by Newhall, Derbyshire], to Wulfric, bishop. A.D. 968: William Salt 84/2/41

24. King Æthelred grants three hides at Brighthampton, two at Aston Bampton, and one at Lew, Oxfordshire, to Ælfwine, *minister* and *scriptor*. A.D. 984: Peniarth 390, fo. 178^{rv}

25. King Æthelred grants twelve hides *æt Æsce* to Æthelsige, *minister*. A.D. 987: Peniarth 390, fos 178^v–179

26. King Æthelred grants land at *Bedintun* [Pillaton, Staffordshire], to Wulfric, *minister*. A.D. 996: William Salt 84/3/41

27. King Æthelred grants three hides at Abbots Bromley, Staffordshire, to Wulfric, *minister*. A.D. 996: William Salt 84/4/41

28. King Æthelred confirms the endowment of Burton Abbey and grants privileges. A.D. 1004: Burton Muniment 1

29. The Will of Wulfric. A.D. 1002 × 1004: Burton Muniment 1

30. King Æthelred grants land at an unspecified place to an unnamed *minister*. A.D. 1007: Peniarth 390, fos 181^v–182

31. King Æthelred exchanges two and a half hides at Rolleston, Staffordshire, for the vills of Aldsworth and Arlington, Gloucestershire, with Abbot Wulfgeat and the Abbey at Burton. A.D. 1008: Loans 30, fo. 10^{rv}

32. King Æthelred grants eight hides at Weston upon Trent, one hide in Morley, one in Smalley and Kidsley, one in Crich, and one in Ingleby, Derbyshire, to Morcar, *minister*. A.D. 1009: William Salt 84/5/41

33. King Æthelred grants two hides at Hallam, Derbyshire, to *Elemod* [? Æthelmod], *minister*. A.D. 1011: Peniarth 390, fos 182^v–183

34. King Æthelred grants five hides *æt Ufre* [? Mickleover, Derbyshire], to Morcar, *minister*. A.D. 1011: Peniarth 390, fo. 183^{rv}

35. King Æthelred grants one and a half hides at Wetmoor, Staffordshire, to Abbot Wulfgeat and the Abbey at Burton. A.D. 1012: Loans 30, fos 10ᵛ–11

36. King Æthelred grants five hides *æt Burtune* to Theodulf, his man. A.D. 1012: Peniarth 390, fos 183ᵛ–184

37. King Æthelred grants two hides *æt Ecgintune* [? Eckington, Derbyshire] to Morcar, *minister*. A.D. 1012: Peniarth 390, fo. 184

38. King Edward grants two hides at *Berghe* to Tofig, *comes*. A.D. 1048: Peniarth 390, fo. 184ᵛ

CONCORDANCE OF THIS EDITION
WITH SAWYER'S LIST AND THE EDITIONS
OF BIRCH, HART, AND KEMBLE

	Sawyer	Birch	Hart[1]	Kemble
1	224	583		
2	395	642		
3	397	658		
4	392	746		
5	479	771		
6	484	772		
7	1606	773		
8	549	876		
9	548	884		
10	545	885		
11	557	890		
12	554	891		
13	569	911		
14	623	978		
15	628	951		
16	599	944		
17	602	954	17	
18	576	1021		
19	707	1081		
20	720	1100		
21	739	1175		
22	749	1283		
23	768	1211	23	
24	853		24	
25	863		25	
26	879		26	
27	878		27	
28	906			710
29	1536			1298
30	917		29	
31	920		30	
32	922		31	
33	923		32	
34	924		33	
35	930		34	
36	929		35	
37	928		36	
38	1017		37	

[1] In Hart's edition the charters are given the numbers they apparently had in the Burton archives. These numbers are used for this concordance; the page references are given below under each charter.

NOTE ON THE METHOD OF EDITING

23, 27, 32 are printed from the single-sheet versions which have some claim to be considered originals and are assigned the siglum A. The other single-sheet versions, given the siglum D **(14, 17, 26, 28, 29),** are either pretended originals or copies and are the basis of the texts printed here except for **14,** which is printed from a cartulary version that is an independent, and better, copy. In **28** some readings from the thirteenth-century cartularies are preferred to those in MS. D, a careless copy. Where single-sheet versions are damaged readings are supplied, if possible, from other manuscripts and the number of missing letters is indicated by dots within square brackets. Peniarth 390 is given the siglum B and in **17** all the orthographic variants are given. Otherwise only the main variants are given from that manuscript and from British Library MS. Loans 30 (here C).

The punctuation, accents, and orthography of the manuscripts have been followed. The letters u and v, i and j have not been normalized; æ, ae, and ę are distinguished, as are uu, w, and þ. Word-division and capital letters have been normalized. Standard abbreviations have been expanded silently, but where there is some doubt the expanded part is printed in italics. The abbreviation *xps* is here expanded as *cristus*.

Interlineations are indicated by the signs ` ´.

The dates of manuscripts and endorsements are indicated in the conventional form, e.g. 's. xii' for the twelfth century, 's. xii¹' for the first half of the century, 's. xii²' for the second half, 's. xii^med' for the middle, while 's. xi/xii' stands for the late eleventh or early twelfth century and 's. xi–xii' for the eleventh and twelfth centuries.

In the measurements of single sheets height is given first.

ADDITIONAL NOTE

The textual notes draw attention to a number of solecisms, some of which were accepted as common form in pre-Conquest charters. At a late stage in the preparation of this volume the following additional examples were noted:

3 line 3 *arbitris* for *arbitri*

4 line 14 and **12** line 14 *violari* for *violare*

11 line 2 *quod precellentior* for either *quod praecellentius* or *quae praecellentior*

19 line 9 *inpenderem* for *inpenderam* or *inpendo*

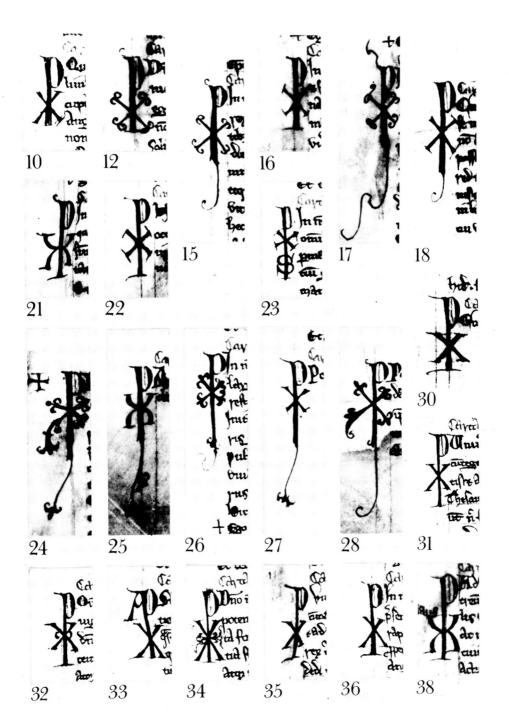

PLATE I. Chrismons reproduced in Peniarth 390, slightly reduced. In that manuscript the following charters have simple initial crosses: **1–9, 11, 13, 14, 19, 20, 37**.

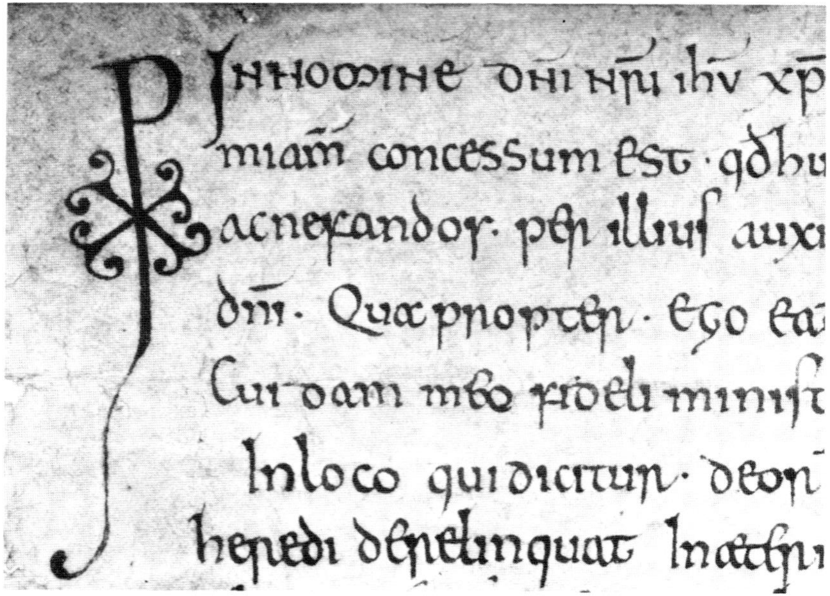

a

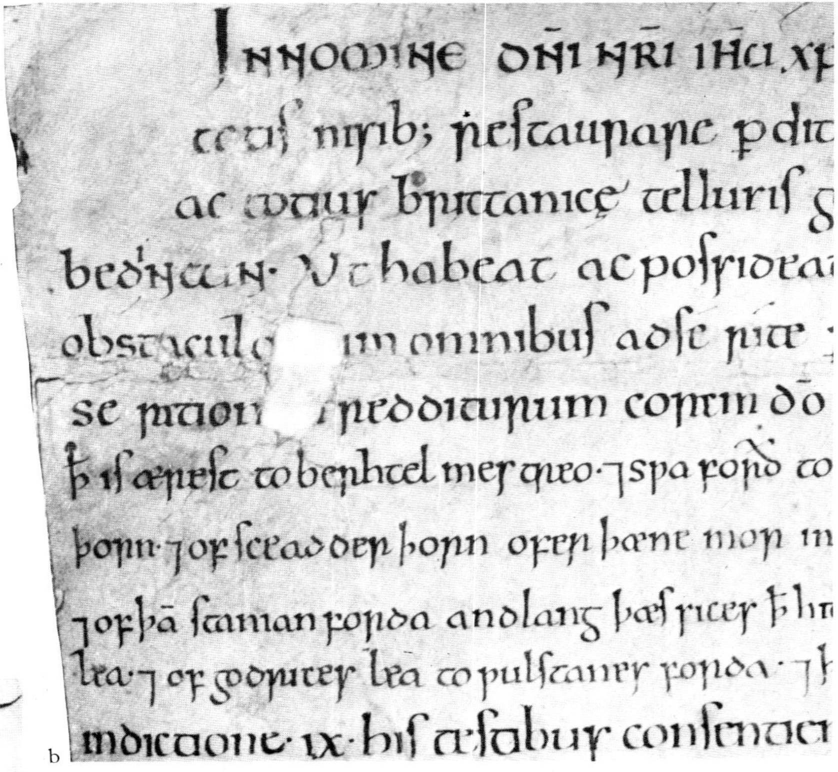

b

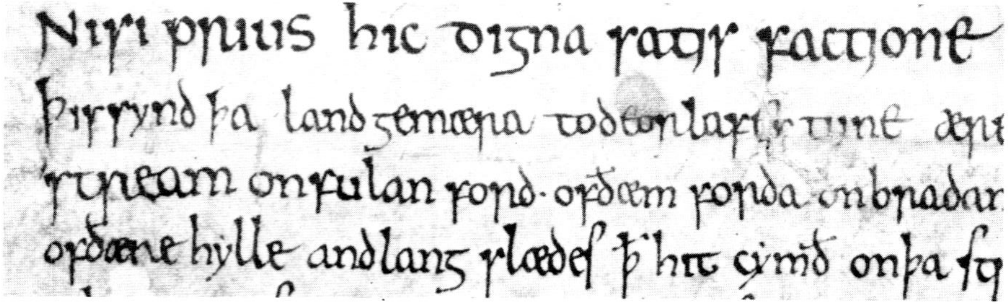

c

PLATE II

Facsimiles of portions of

a. Stafford, William Salt Library, 84/1/41 [**17** MS. A]

b. Stafford, William Salt Library, 84/3/41 [**26** MS. A]

c. Stafford, William Salt Library, 84/1/41 [**17** MS. A]

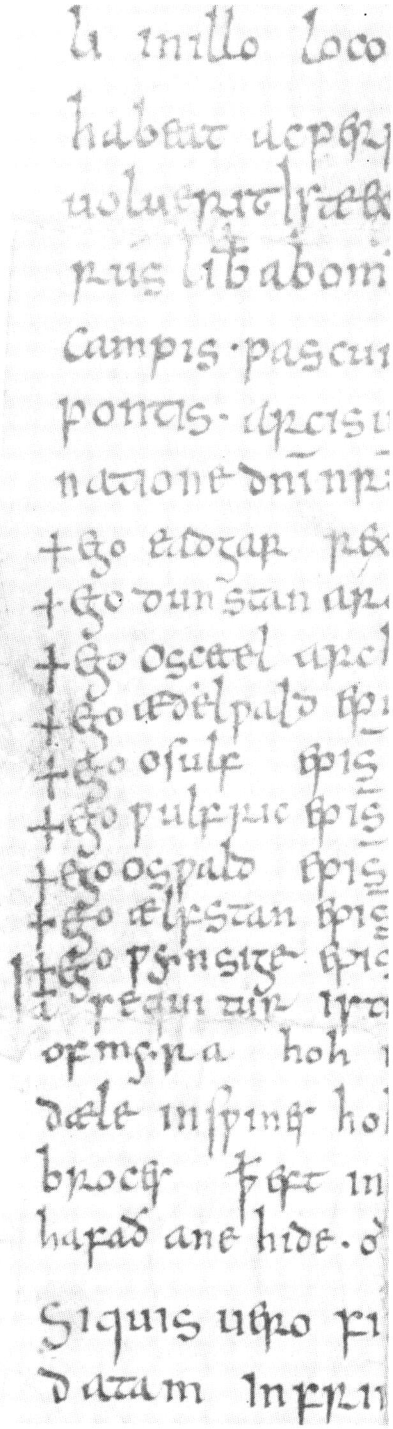

a

b

PLATE III
  Facsimiles of portions of
  a. Stafford, William Salt Library, 84/2/41 [**23** MS. A]
  b. Stafford, William Salt Library, 84/4/41 [**27** MS. A]

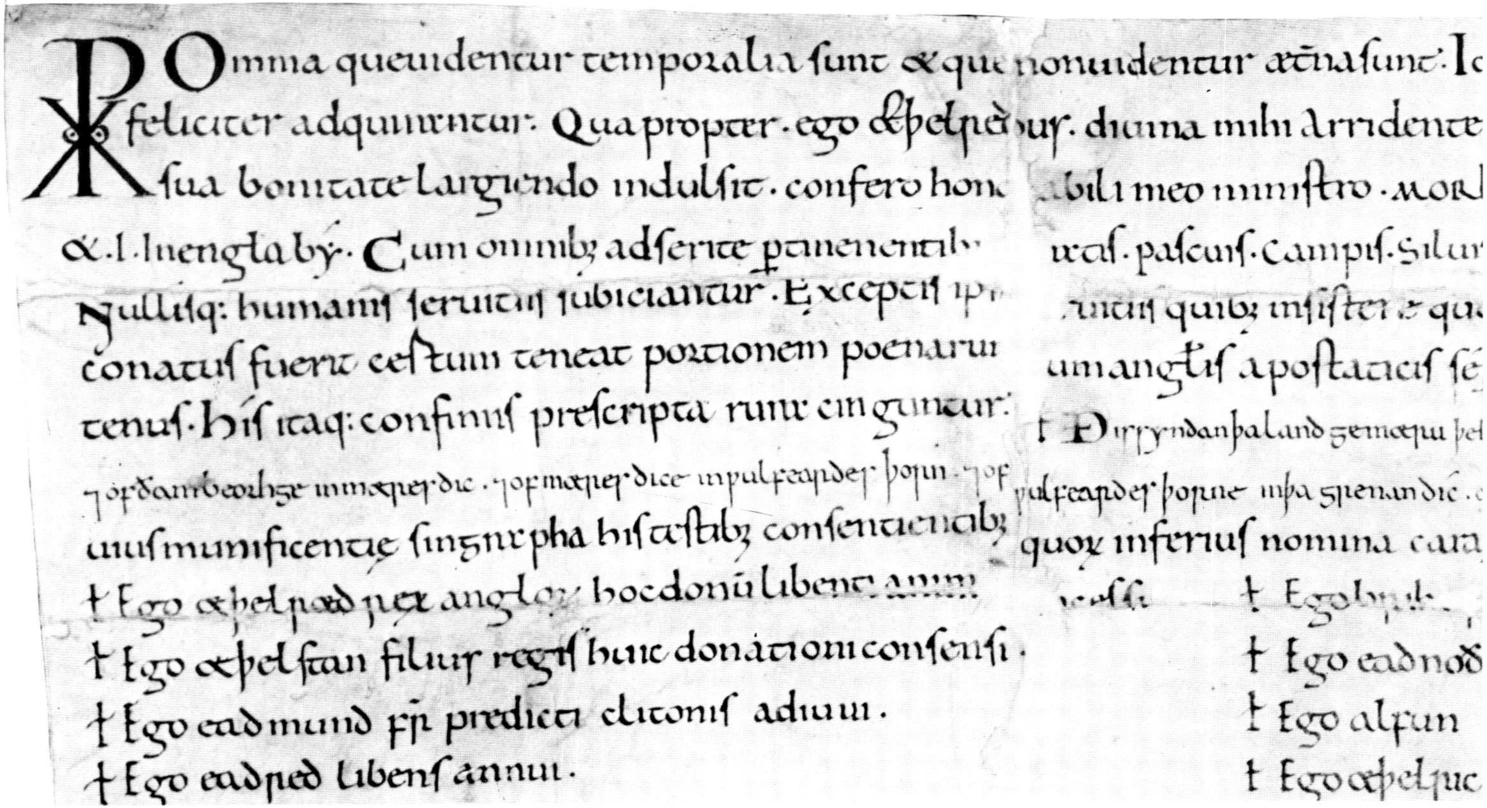

ᴘ Omnia que uidentur temporalia sunt æque non uidentur ætna sunt. Ic
℞ feliciter adquiruntur. Qua propter. ego æþelpꝛð ꝛuꝼ. diuina mihi arridente
℞ sua bonitate largiendo indulsit. confero hoñ ...bili meo ministro. moꝛ...
& .l. Inengla by· Cum omnibᵹ adserite ptinentib· ...ꝛas. pascuis. campis. siluꝛ...
Nullisq· humanis seruitiu subiciantur. Excepteis ip... ...ꝛutiu quibᵹ insister & qui...
conatus fuerit certum teneat portionem poenaru... ...um anglis apostaticis se...
tenus· His itaq· confinis prescripta runt cingutur· † Dirꝼyndanbaland gemære þel
⁊ oꝼðam beohge inmæþer die· ⁊ oꝼmæþer dice inpulꝼcapdeꝛ þoꝛn· ⁊ oꝼ pulꝼcapdeꝛ þoꝛne inþa spenan die·
uius munificentie singnr pha his testibᵹ consentientibᵹ quoꝛ inferius nomina caꝛa...
† Ego æþelpꝛð ꝛex angloꝛ hoc donu libenter annui ...essi † Ego byꝛ...
† Ego æþelstan filius regis hanc donationi consensi· † Ego eadnoð
† Ego eadmund fꝛ predicti clitonis adiui· † Ego alꝼun
† Ego eadꝛed libens annui· † Ego æþelpic

PLATE IV. Facsimile of a portion of Stafford, William Salt Library, 84/5/41 [**32** MS. A]

THE CHARTERS

1

Æthelflæd, Lady of the Mercians, grants two hides (manentes) *at* Stantun *to Ealhhelm.* A.D. 800 [*? for* 914]

B. Aberystwyth, N.L.W., Peniarth 390, fo. 173 (p. 345): copy, s. xiii^{med}
Ed.: Birch 583
Listed: Hart 100, Sawyer 224

Incipiunt carte antique^a

+Superna aspirante gratia ego Æþelfled domina Merciorum dabo meo fideli amico Alchelme aliquam partem terram^b id est . ij . manentium in loco qui dicitur Stantun pro eius humili placabilique obeditione . id est . lx . porcos et . ccc . solidos in argento cum testimonio et consensu meorum amicorum conscribens donabo . ut possidendo felici fruatur euentu dies suos . et quibuscumque post se dare uoluerit perpetualiter liberam in eternam trado hereditatem . Ista terra est circumcincta et determinata terminis et cetera . Si quis uero hanc meam donacionem frangere uoluerit ⸵ Deus reddet ille^c mercedem ante tribunal iudicii . Hii sunt uero testes et confirmatores huius condicionis quorum nomina infra notantur . Anno dominice incarnacionis . dccc . luna indictione . uero . iij^a .

+Ego Ælfled hanc meam donacionem signaculo sancte crucis confirmo .
+Ego Eadferdus episcopus consensi et conscribsi .
+Ego Þerferdus episcopus consensi et subscripsi . et ceteri duces et ministri videlicet . xj^{cim}.
Omnes isti consenserunt ac scripserunt . et in testimonium huius donacionis affuerunt
Deus illum conseruet qui istud conseruet . Deus illum disperdat qui istud dissoluat .

---

^a Incipiunt carte antique *rubric to the whole collection*   ^b *An error for* terre
^c *An error for* illi

This charter, although abbreviated and miscopied, seems to be authentic. Its formulas are paralleled in ninth-century Mercian charters and in particular the *sanctio* may be compared with that in the surviving original grant by Æthelred and Æthelflæd, *trina magestas conservet conservantes . condemnet ledentes* (S 221, see also S 215), and the subscriptions with those in another misdated charter of Æthelflæd (S 225). The date A.D. 800, is obviously wrong and the simplest correction, proposed by Birch in his edition, would be 900 to agree with the indiction, but a grant by Æthelflæd alone seems unlikely at such an early date. She was *domina Merciorum* by right of her husband, Æthelred, who died in 911, apparently after an illness that incapacitated him for some years (Stenton 1971, p. 324 n.). F. T. Wainwright suggested, on the basis of a late Irish source, that Æthelflæd was already acting alone by 902 (*Scandinavian England*, ed. H. P. R. Finberg (1975), pp. 308–9). There is, however, an authentic charter dated 901 in which she made a grant jointly with her husband and they were joint beneficiaries of an authentic lease by Bishop Wærferth of Worcester in 904 (S 221, 1280), which suggests that she is unlikely to have made a grant on her own authority in 900. The curious *luna* between . dccc . and *indictione* in the dating clause is probably a misreading of the original date and it is tempting to suggest that this read . dccccxiiii ., that one *c* was dropped and the four minims were misread as *un*, but the confusion of *x* with *l* is less plausible. The third indiction would be consistent with this emendation, for it began in September 914. It would also be consistent with the two identifiable witnesses, Æthelflæd herself, who died in 918, and Wærferth, bishop of Worcester from at least 872, whose death is recorded by Florence of Worcester in 915 in an annal which may properly belong to 914 (O'Donovan 1973, pp. 112–13). The other witness, Bishop Eadferth, was probably from a Mercian see and his position above Wærferth may mean that he was bishop of Lichfield. That see may have been held by Wilmund or Wilferth in 903 and the next bishop whose name is known was Ælfwine, who first occurs in a charter which should probably be dated 9 September 915 (O'Donovan 1973, pp. 94–5). If the *Stantun* of this charter is correctly identified as Stanton by Newhall in Derbyshire, two miles southeast of Burton, an additional reason for suggesting that this grant should be dated some time after 900 is that the Mercians did not control that part of the Trent valley in 900. Tamworth and Stafford were fortified by Æthelflæd in 913 and she conquered Derby in 917 (Stenton 1971, pp. 326–8). The grant to Ealhhelm may indeed have been part of the process of reconquest and like **3** and, possibly, **5**, **6**, and **7**, this charter may show one of the ways in which English rulers extended their authority at the expense of the Scandinavians.

The grantee *Alchelm*, for Ealhhelm or Ælhhelm, is identified by C. R. Hart (*Anglo-Saxon England*, ii (1973), p. 116) with the ealdorman who occurs in 896 (S 1441. Hart asserts that his sphere of influence 'was limited to the Mercian lands bordering on the northern Danelaw'). This is unlikely; he can probably be identified with the man who witnessed as *minister* from 930 (S 403, 416) and as *dux* from 940 to 951 (S 470, 558), and with the grandfather of Ælfwine who fought at Maldon (*The Battle of Maldon*, ed. E. V. Gordon, revised D. C. Scragg (1976), lines 209–19).

The two *manentes* at *Stantun* were probably the estate whose bounds are described in **23**. That charter is a grant of 1 hide but a note after the bounds explains *ðis send ðara tpegra hida gemæro ðe þulfric biscop hafað ane hide . oðer hafað Ælfnað*. This estate has been identified as Stanton by Newhall, Derbyshire, although no boundary points can be located. The political situation at the beginning of the tenth century makes this Stanton more likely than the others in Derbyshire and the identification is supported by the fact that Burton Abbey held 1 carucate there early in the twelfth century as part of the estate of Stapenhill which the abbey acquired before the Norman Conquest (*Surveys*, p. 240; for the connection with Stapenhill see ibid., p. 295 and Jeayes 1937, nos 4 and, with a wrong identification, 18; for Stapenhill see **7** and p. xlvi). It is therefore likely that this charter was kept by the abbey as one of its title-deeds.

2

King Athelstan grants seven hides (manentes) æt Hwituntune *to Eadric*, minister. A.D. 925

B. Aberystwyth, N.L.W., Peniarth 390, fo. 173^{rv} (pp. 345–6): copy, s. xiii^{med}
Ed.: Birch 642
Listed: Hart 80, Sawyer 395

Carta Æþelstani regis facta cuida,^{a} Edric de Hpitanton' anno domini . dcccc° . xxv .^{b}

+Regnante Theo inperpetuum architectorio·' opere precium constat ut presentium rerum blandimenta et pellax mundi prosperitas nullo monumento^c ducatur^d . Quisque eterne beatitudinis ^{e}gratuita Dei gratia huius vite felicitate conpiscat^e legittimo iure se recipere satagit . quo egregius predicator et sapiens trichelaus^f . quamdiu inquit sumus in corpore peregrinamur a domino . Quapropter ego Æthelstan diuina indulgente clemencia rex Anglorum tociusque climatis ferme cataclismatum gurgitibus Cristiane patrigene preuisor . sollicita fidelium meorum sagacitate cognitam uentilate obedientie causam inuestigarem^g . quatinus meo fideli ministro Eadrice septem manentes in illo loco æt Hpituntune in perpetuam hereditatem condonarem quod et feci tradens enim illi tradidi^h . vt habeat . possideat^i in perpetuam hereditatem . cum siluis pascuis pratis et campis atque omnibus ad se rite pertinentibus . et postquam viam universitatis adiens relinquat cuicumque heredi uoluerit sicut supra diximus in eternam hereditatem . Hac ergo causa imperauimus istum hereditarium librum ita nouiter scribere^k ·' quia illum antiquum hereditarium librum non habebamus . set si quis post hoc illum antiquum librum uel aliud quodlibet contra hanc nostram diffinicionem in propatulo adduxerit ·' ab omni cristianitate irritum fiat . et ad nichilum ualeat . Sit ista predicta terra ab omni mundiali censu libera exceptis istis tribus . expedicione . arcis pontisue construcatione . Si quis hoc nostrum decretum custodire et augere uoluerit ·' augeat omnipotens gubernator omnia presentis sibi et future vite bona . Si quis uero quod non optamus contra hoc nostrum decretum machinari uel infringere uoluerit ·' sciat se racionem grauiter redditurum in die iudicii ante tribunal domini nisi prius hic digna emendauerit penitencia ante mortem . Hec cedula^l caraxatis literulis primo anno regni prefati regis preordinata fuit . Anno ab incarnacione domini nostri Iesu Cristi . dcccc° . xxv° . indictione . xiij^a .

+Ego Æthelstan rex hanc donacionem meam triumphali tropheo sancte + crucis propriis articulis confirmaui atque roboraui . +Ego Ælfpine gracia dei episcopus . +Ego Þinsige episcopus . +Ego Wilfrid episcopus . consensi et subscripsi . +Ego Edgar episcopus consensi et subscripsi . +Ego Cynaht abbas . consensi et subscripsi . et ceteri . duces . presbiteri . et monachi et ministri usque ad . l . vij .

 An error for cuidam   ^b Carta . . . xxv . *rubric*   ^c *For* momento   ^d *Perhaps for* ducantur   ^e · · · · ^e *Read* gaudia Dei gratia concupiscat, huius vite felicitate   ^f *Dr Lapidge comments: No such word appears to be attested elsewhere. It is possibly a grecism, and on that assumption one might make the suggestion that* trichelaus *is a corruption of* trochelates (τροχηλάτης) *which means 'charioteer' and hence 'contestant' (words such as this and* athleta *are frequently applied to Paul on the basis of his words at 1 Cor. 9 : 24)*   ^g *Dr Lapidge has pointed out that the verb in this clause should be indicative, not imperfect subjunctive, since the subordinate clause beginning with* quatinus *is subjunctive. He suggests that* investigarem *may be a mistake for* investigaram, *the syncopated form of the pluperfect or, better still,* investigavi   ^h ? *Delete. The scribe may have copied a gloss into his text, since* tradidi *and* feci tradens *are equivalents*   ⁱ *A conjunction is needed here. Read* habeat possideatque (*cf.* **10**) *or* habeat ac possideat (*cf.* **17**)   ^k Scribi *must be understood here; the error is possibly due to the author of the charter*   ^l *For* scedula

This Mercian charter of Athelstan appears to be authentic; the language and formulas are typical, the indiction agrees with the incarnation date and the witness-list (which includes the relatively rare Abbot Cynath, whose career has been discussed by J. Armitage Robinson (*The Times of St Dunstan* (Oxford, 1923), pp. 35–40) is consistent.

The beneficiary, Eadric *minister,* may be the ealdorman who witnesses 943 to 950 and Robinson argued, on the basis of four charters that he suggested were replacements for documents lost on the same occasion, that Eadric was the son of Ealdorman Æthelfrith (ibid., pp. 45–9). Two of these charters were granted by King Edward in 903 to Ealdorman Æthelfrith as replacements for charters lost by fire (S 367, 371).[1] The other two were grants to Eadric *minister,* one being the present charter and the other a grant by Æthelflæd, of which the correct date appears to be 9 September 915 (S 225: on the date see O'Donovan 1973, p. 113), renewing the charter for Farnborough (Berkshire or Warwickshire) which had been lost in the year of the solar eclipse, namely 878, which year has been mistakenly assigned to the charter itself. It is, however, most unlikely that all these charters were lost at the same time or that they all belonged to the same family when they were lost. The crucial text is the Farnborough charter which makes it clear that Eadric had bought this estate from Wullaf whose great-grandfather Bynna had been granted it by King Offa, and that Eadric needed a replacement because the original had been lost in the fire of 878. The implication is that in 878 Farnborough and its charter did not belong to Eadric but to Wullaf or some other member of his family. There is no suggestion that Eadric bought Farnborough before the fire; had he done so, he could hardly be the ealdorman who ceases to sign in 950, and it would also mean that he waited forty-seven years to obtain a replacement. As there is nothing to suggest that the estates for which Æthelfrith obtained replacement charters had earlier been held by Wullaf, the originals are unlikely to have been lost in the fire of 878. It is also worth pointing out that Robinson's argument implies that Æthelfrith waited twenty-five years to replace his charters. The present text does not say that the original was lost by fire, only that it was not available but might sometime be recovered. As Sir Frank Stenton emphasized

[1] Professor Whitelock has pointed out that S 371, MS. 2, i.e. Oxford, Bodleian, James 23, pp. 33–4, printed by M. Gibbs, *Early Charters of the Cathedral Church of St Paul, London* (Camden Third Series, lviii, 1939), p. 4 as James 8, cannot be extracted from the Glastonbury charter copied in the other manuscripts listed under that entry because James was using a St Pauls manuscript. This is, therefore, from another replacement charter for Æthelfrith, probably issued on the same occasion.

The Latin Charters of the Anglo-Saxon Period (Oxford, 1955), p. 52), charters were lost in many ways, especially in the disturbances accompanying the Viking invasions.

The estate *æt Hwituntune* has been identified as Whittington (Staffordshire), between Lichfield and Tamworth, apparently because of its proximity to Burton; but as other charters in the archive certainly refer to estates in distant parts of the country, that argument is weak. If the choice should be limited to Mercia, as the witness-list suggests, there are at least seven other possibilities, one of which, in Worcestershire, was apparently held by the church of Worcester throughout the whole period (S 180, 1361). Four of the remainder are in DB but none has the same assessment as the Whittington of this charter (DB, i. 167b, 253b, 272a, 301b). Neither Wulfric nor Burton Abbey apparently claimed to hold land in any place called Whittington. The most likely identification is Whittington (Derbyshire), near Chesterfield, which lay close to the frontier between Mercia and Northumbria. Wulfric held extensive estates in the area but Whittington itself was in DB, with Chesterfield, a berewick of the royal estate of Newbold, of which the total assessment was 6 carucates 1 bovate. Sir Frank Stenton used this estate to illustrate manorial instability in the eleventh century, for by 1093 Newbold had become a berewick of Chesterfield (*V.C.H. Derbyshire*, i. 312 and n. 1; cf. Stenton 1910, pp. 52, 68). Chesterfield is also the subject of another Burton charter, **13**, and the presence of both charters in the Burton archive would be explained if they were family deeds. One possibility is that Whittington and Chesterfield were held by Wulfric's brother, Ælfhelm, and passed into direct royal control after his death.

3

King Athelstan confirms sixty hides (manentes) *at Hope and Ashford, Derbyshire, to Uhtred, his* fidelis. A.D. 926

B. Aberystwyth, N.L.W., Peniarth 390, fos 173^v–174 (pp. 346–7): copy, s. xiii ^{med}

Ed.: Birch 658

Listed: Hart 101, Sawyer 397

Carta Æþelstani regis de Hope et Æscford facta Uþtredo^a . dcccc° . xxvi .^{b}

+In nomine domini nostri Iesu Cristi . Cuncta que humanis obtutibus caducarum molimina rerum liquide uidentur decidunt . que uero abdita inuisaque sunt ⁏ eterni arbitris moderamine perpetualiter constant . Haut dubium est hiis qui illa adipisci largiflua Dei largitate ^{c}gracia atque^c mercari posse^d merentibus^e diuina scripturarum documenta pollicentur . Quapropter ego Æthelstanus Angulsaxonum rex^f non modica infulatus^g sublimatus dignitate superno instigatus desiderio fideli meo Uhtredo terram que nuncupatur at Hope et æt Æscforda . lx . manentium quam propria condignaque pecunia id est . xx . libras inter aurum et argento^h a paganis emerat iubente Eadpeardo rege necnon et dux^i Æþelredo cum ceteris comitibus atque ministris in iuris hereditarii

libertatem concedens donabo . habendam possidendamque quamdiu
vixerit . et post obitum suum quibuscumque sibi placitis heredibus dare
uoluerit . Sit autem hec prefata terræ donacio ab omni seculari honore^k
libera preter expedicionem et arcis pontisve constructionem pro com-
petenti pecunia quam ego accepi ab eo . id est . ccc . manc[us]as^l de
puro auro . Si quis uero hanc largicionis munificenciam arrepto pro-
cacitatis stimulo infringere uel mutare aut minuere temptauerit ? sciat
se in illa magna examinis die cum poli cardinis^m terreque fundamenta
simul et inferorum ima pauitando contremiscent latibula . qua vnius-
cuiusque patebit opus et conscientia siue bonum siue malum quod
gessit^n . si non prius satisfactionem^o emendauerit . Secuntur diuise et
mete huius terre . Anno ab incarnacione . domini . nostri . Iesu Cristi .
dcccc . xxvj . indictione . xiiij^a .

+Ego Æthelstanus rex fundamine sancte crucis subarraui . +Ego
Þulfhelm archiepiscopus subscripsi . +Ego Þensige episcopus subscripsi . + . Ego Þeodred episcopus subscripsi . +Ego Beorneht episcopus subscripsi . +Ego Sigelm episcopus subscripsi . +Ego Eadulf
episcopus subscripsi . +Ego Eadgar episcopus subscripsi . +Ego Ealla
episcopus subscripsi . +Ego Cyneferð episcopus subscripsi . et ceteri .
duces . ministri et disciferi . T'.^{p}

^{a} *For* Uhtredo	^{b} Carta . . . xxvi . *rubric*	^{c} · · · ^{c} *For* atque gracia	^{d} ?
Read possunt	^{e} ? *Read* merentibus quod		^{f} rex Angulsaxonum *with*
transposition marks	^{g} ? *Add* et *after* infulatus		^{h} *For* argentum (*cf. S* 396)
^{i} *For* duce	^{k} *For* honere		^{l} *Over erasure,* ? *altered from* marcas
^{m} *Spelling for* cardines		^{n} *Something has been omitted:* ? *add* rationem red-
diturum	^{o} *For* satisfactione digna		^{p} *Birch expands as* Testes

There is nothing suspicious about this charter. The witness-list is consistent
with the date, the formulas are characteristic, and the background of the grant
as described in the charter would itself encourage confidence; this judgement
is further reinforced by the existence in an Abingdon cartulary of an almost
identical charter in which Athelstan granted Chalgrove in Bedfordshire to a
thegn called Ealdred (S 396). The very close similarities between the two texts
suggest that they were both drafted by the same person and that both grants
were made at the same time. As Sir Frank Stenton pointed out in 1910, these
charters show that King Edward in association with Æthelred was encouraging
thegns to buy land from the pagan conquerors of eastern and northern England
(Stenton 1910, pp. 71–5). This purchase must have been made between Edward's accession in 899 and Æthelred's death in 911, with the likelihood of
rather narrower limits because of Æthelred's withdrawal from public affairs
in or before 910 (see p. 2).
    Chalgrove was later given to Abingdon Abbey (Stevenson, *Chron. Abingdon*,
i. 428–9), but there is no evidence that Burton Abbey had any claim to either
Hope or Ashford, nor are they mentioned in Wulfric's will. According to DB
they were held by the king on the eve of the Conquest and were grouped
together with Bakewell to form a triple estate with twenty-seven named berewicks and with a geld assessment of 50 carucates (DB, i. 272b–73). The later
association of these three places suggests that the territory acquired by Uhtred
at the beginning of the century included Bakewell, where a *burh* was constructed
in 920, and this possibility is strengthened by 9, dated 949, granting Uhtred

dux, probably the same man, an unspecified amount of land at Bakewell. This could have been an extension of his estate and the origin of Bakewell's association with Hope and Ashford, but as **9** was said to be for the endowment of a *coenubium* at Bakewell, it is more likely that it was obtained by Uhtred so that he could endow a religious community with part of his estate (Sawyer 1975, pp. 31–4). The difference between the assessment given in this charter and that for the three estates in DB may be due to a mistake in copying, or to some change between 926 and 1086, but the size of the present grant supports the suggestion that Bakewell, which is only two miles from Ashford, formed part of the original estate (cf. Sawyer 1975).

The Uhtred of these two charters was probably the man who witnessed many charters as *dux* from 930 to 949 (S 405, 544). W. H. Stevenson pointed out that apart from the eighth-century *regulus* of the Hwicce most of the bearers of this name were members of the great Northumbrian family from Bamburgh and he suggested that the Uhtred who held Hope and Ashford was the son of Eadwulf of Bamburgh who died in 912 (*The Crawford Collection of Early Charters and Documents*, ed. A. S. Napier and W. H. Stevenson (Oxford, 1895), pp. 74–5). The Uhtred *child* of **13** may have been a member of the same family. The presence of these charters in the Burton archive suggests that these estates were not in the king's hands when the abbey was founded. They were probably deposited at the abbey by a member of Wulfric's family, probably Ælfhelm, in which case they would have been confiscated by the king in 1006 when Ælfhelm was murdered.

4

King Athelstan grants five hides (cassati) *at* Eatun *to Beorhthelm* (Byrhtelm), *miles.* A.D. 850 [*for* 939]

B. Aberystwyth, N.L.W., Peniarth 390, fo. 173 (p. 345): copy, s. xiii[med]

Ed.: Birch 746

Listed: Hart 81, Sawyer 392

Carta Æþelstan Regis .[a]

+Eterne hereditatis territoria et perpetue prosperitatis priuilegia magnis meritorum machinamentis iam concedente Cristo Iesu mercanda sunt . quapropter videlicet Edelstan rex Angulsexna and Norþhymbra imperator . paganorum gubernator Brittanorumque propugnator larga manu confert lucra largissim vti queat firmissime regnorum regimine sublimari . Quamobrem iam nunc locupletat hunc militem Byrhtelm tribuendo ei terram . v . videlicet cassatos in loco quem ruricole Eatun vocitant . pro eius fideli obsequio . et pro eius placabili pecunia . vt possideat eam cum omnibus ad se rite pertinentibus pratis . pascuis . campis . siluis . et post eius discessum cuicumque voluerit heredi derelinquendam . Sit autem predicta tellus libera exceptis istis tribus . expedicione . pontis arcisue constructione . Si qui denique[b] non optantibus nobis nostram hanc cartam cupiditatis liuore depressi violari satagerint agminibus tetre caliginis lapsi vocem audiant examinacionis die arbitris sibi dicentis . discedite a me maledicti in ignem eternum vbi cum demonibus ferreis sartaginibus crudeli torqueantur in pena si non ante mortem digna hoc emendauerint penitentia . Istis terminibus predicta terra circumgirata esse videtur . et cetera . Acta est hec prefata donacio anno ab incarnacione domini nostri Iesu Cristi . dccc . l . indictione . xiij .*c*

+Ego Æðelstan rex Anglorum prefatam donacionem cum sigillo sancte crucis confirmaui .

+Ego þulfhelm Dorobernensis ecclesie archiepiscopus eiusdem regis donacionem cum tropheo agie crucis consignaui .

+Ego Þeodred Lundon*iensis* ecclesie episcopus consignaui

+Ego Ælfheah Þintaniensis ecclesie episcopus triumphalem tropheum agie crucis impressi .

+Ego Cenepald Þigarnensis ecclesie episcopus donum consensi . +Ego Oda episcopus confirmaui . +Ego Ælfric episcopus consignaui . +Ego Þulfhelm episcopus consensi . +Ego Buruhric episcopus confirmaui . +Ego Æþelgar episcopus roboraui . Et Duces . vij . et ministri . xviij .

a Carta . . . Regis . *rubric*   *b* Si qui denique *corrected from* Si quidem tue
c dccc . l . indictione . xiij . *underlined with* nota *in the margin*

This charter belongs to the group of alliterative texts discussed above, pp. xlvii–ix, although it is only partly in the characteristic style of that group. The non-rhythmical formulas were in contemporary use; a very similar *sanctio* occurs in a Winchester charter dated 940 (S 465), and the witness-list, which may be described as of the 'Winchester' type with particular prominence given to Ælfheah's subscription, is very similar to that in an original also dated 940 (S 464; cf. S 497, 510, 528, 535, 532). The combination of two such very different styles or traditions in this charter may be counted in favour of its authenticity; a forger would have been more likely to adapt a model in one style rather than attempt the difficult task of merging two different kinds of text. The date, A.D. 850, is obviously wrong. The witnesses are, however, consistent with the last year of Athelstan's reign and include Wulfhelm of Wells whose pontificate began in 937 or 938 (O'Donovan 1973, p. 107). The indiction, 13, is correct both for 850 and for the year beginning September 939 and would, if accepted, give a remarkably close date for a charter of Athelstan, who died on 27 October 939. Hart, pp. 90–1, argues that this is a forgery. His main reason is the inconsistency of the tenth-century features of the text with the date 850. It is, however, more reasonable to assume that the date was wrongly copied than that a forger was attempting to produce a ninth-century charter. Hart also claims that the king's title could not have been used before 946, and that it first occurs in S 520. In that charter of Eadred this title is also used for his predecessor, Edmund. It was certainly as appropriate a title for Athelstan, especially after his victory at *Brunanburh*, as for his brothers.

The beneficiary, Beorhthelm, cannot be identified with confidence. In the tenth century there were several churchmen with that name but it is rarely recorded as a lay name; apart from the present text it occurs in only two mid-tenth-century charters and one of these is very suspect (S 351). The other is an original of Athelstan, dated 934, with a long witness-list including several northerners (S 425). It is possible that the present charter was a grant to the same man and that he is rarely mentioned because he was a Mercian or Northumbrian who attended court infrequently. *Eatun* has been identified as one of the Staffordshire Eatons but there is no reason to assume that it lay near Burton. Neither the abbey nor Wulfric apparently had any claim to such a place and it could have been any one of the many Eatons in the Midlands or even further afield. **10** is a grant of 10 hides at *Eatun* but in the absence of bounds it is not possible to determine whether **4** and **10** refer to the same place.

5

King Edmund grants forty hides at Alrewas, Bromley, Barton, Tatenhill, Branston, Stretton, Rolleston, Clifton, and Haunton, Staffordshire, to Wulfsige the Black (Þulfsye prenomine Maur').

A.D. 942

B. Aberystwyth, N.L.W., Peniarth 390, fo. 174 (p. 347): copy, s. xiii[med]

Ed.: Birch 771

Listed: Hart 82, Sawyer 479

Carta Sancti Edmundi regis de Alrepasse et Broml' et Barton facta anno domini . dcccc° . xlij° .[a]

+Perpetua hereditas que in sancte trinitatis dei theologia ultra omnia humane mentis machinamenta manet essentialiter ultroneis meritorum . magnopere est mercimoniis comparanda . Quapropter ueraciter paterna priscorum sequens uestigia regum . Eadmund beato dei patrocinio rex et rector Angulsæxna inter innumeras quibus beauit vtriusque certaminis cateruas dapsilitates eternis prouocatur prouerbiis . hilarem datorem et cetera . alacriter Þulsye prenomine Maur' mirifice locupletat et honorat concedens ei has terras eiusque heredibus perpetualiter perfruendas . id est ad Alrepasse . et Bromleg' . et Barton et Tatenhyll' . et Brontiston . ant Stretton . et Roðulfeston . et Clyfton . et Hagnatun . nou is þisses landes feourti hyde . Has denique tellures Eadmund rex anno dominice incarnationis . dcccc° . xlij° . et tercio annorum curriculo ex quo regalia eterni regis gratuita benignitate regebat charismata contulit cum testimonio optimatum quorum nomina inferius adnotantur . Þulfsye salua[b] manu ? non causa philargirie set studio deuotissime fidelitatis habendas .

+Ego Edmund rex huius donacionis dominium in locis campestribus uel siluaticis . seu piscosis laticibus libenter signaculo sancte . +crucis conscribo fruentibus .

+Þulstan archiepiscopus . +Þulfgar episcopus . +Cenpald episcopus . +Þulfhelm episcopus . +Cynsige episcopus . +Æþelmund dux . et ceteri duces . v[que] . in omnes cum ceteris eiusdem milicie sodalibus hec certe territoria triumphali tropheo conscripserunt .

Acta est videlicet hoc regale prerogatiuum in loco celeberrimo qui Wincelcumb nuncupatur . Pax et perhennis prosperitas hiis qui fas diuini priuilegii et ius humani eulogii iugiter seruare decrerint^c . et eis econtra qui negauerint districta dei regula resistat . Reddite ergo que sunt cesaris cesari .' et que sunt dei deo ;-

    ^{a} Carta . . . xlij° . *rubric* ^{b} *For* larga ^{c} *Error for* decreuerint

For comments see **7**.

6

King Edmund grants land at Walton on Trent, Coton in the Elms, Cauldwell, Drakelow, Derbyshire, Newbold, Staffordshire, and Linton, Derbyshire, to Wulfsige the Black (Þulfsie prenomine Maur'). A.D. 942

B. Aberystwyth, N.L.W., Peniarth 390, fo. 174 (p. 347): copy, s. xiii^{med}
Ed.: Birch 772
Listed: Hart 83, Sawyer 484

Carta Sancti Edmundi regis de Waleton' et Caldepell' et cetera . Anno domini . dcccc° . xlij° . ^{a}

+Perpetua hereditas que in sancte trinitatis et cetera ut supra . hilarem datorem et cetera . alacriter Þulsie pre^b Maur' mirifice effert et honorat .' concedens ei has terras nominetenus subnotatas ea ratione interposita vt ipse suaque posteritas regie dignitati fidissima stabilitate obsecundet . Eya^c denominatio terratenus . æt Waletune . 7 suðenne monna Cotuhalfne . 7 æt Caldepællen . 7 æt Dracan hlapen . 7 at Nepan Bolde . 7 at Lintone . Has terras Edmund rex anno dominice incarnationis . dcccc° . xlij° . et tercio annorum curriculo ex quo regalia eterni regis gratuita benignitate regebat carismata dedit cum testimonio optimatum quorum nomina inferius adnotantur . Þulfsie salua^d manu non causa philargirie set studio deuotissime fidelitatis habendas

+Ego Edmund rex huius donacionis et cetera ut supra . +Oda archiepiscopus . +Þu'l'stan archiepiscopus . et ceteri episcopi et duces sicut superius in proxima precedenti .'

+In omnes cum ceteris . ut supra . Reddite que sunt cesaris et cetera . Amen dicat omne os hebraice et latine fiat ;-

    ^{a} Carta . . . xlij° . *rubric* ^{b} *For* prenomine ^{c} *The meaning of this word, which also occurs in the subscriptions to* **8**, *is unknown. Here it could possibly represent* ecce ^{d} *For* larga

For comments see **7**.

7

King Edmund grants land at Croxall, Catton, Walton on Trent, Drakelow, Stapenhill, Derbyshire, and at Sulueston' [? *Silverstone, Northamptonshire*] *to Wulfsige the Black* (Þulfsie).

A.D. 942

B. Aberystwyth, N.L.W., Peniarth 390, fo. 174 (p. 347): copy, s. xiii[med]

Ed.: Birch 773

Listed: Hart 102, Sawyer 1606

Carta eiusdem de Croxale et cetera . dcccc° . xlij° .[a]

+Perpetua hereditate et cetera ut supra . idem rex Edmundus . eidem Þulfsie dedit . Crokeshall' . et Canton' . et Waleton' . et Drakel' . et Stapenh' . et Sulueston' . et cetera ut supra .

[a] Carta . . . xlij° . rubric

5, 6, and 7 belong to the group of alliterative charters discussed above, pp. xlvii–ix. 6 and 7 were apparently identical, apart from the places named, and two of these, Drakelow and Walton, occur in both texts. It is therefore probable that one of these charters is spurious, but it is not possible to determine which. One motive for such a forgery would have been to provide Burton Abbey with a title-deed to one or more of its estates but, as all three charters include places that the abbey acquired after its original endowment, no argument about authenticity can be based on that feature. The differences between 5 and the pair 6 and 7 were apparently limited to the donation clause, the verb in the dating clause (*contulit* 5, *dedit* 6), the omission from 5 of both the final clause *Amen dicat omne os hebraice et latine fiat* and Archbishop Oda's subscription, and the omission from 6 and 7 of the English note about the assessment. Much depends on whether the complete text of 6 and 7 included the clause about the grant being made at Winchcombe. If all three grants purported to have been made in the same place, in almost the same words, and granted land in the same area to the same person, there would be a strong suspicion that two of the three were forged, but if the final *ut supra* of 6 was not intended to represent a clause about Winchcombe it is likely that there were two authentic charters, issued on different occasions. The difference between the witness-lists may well be due to a copying error though it is just possible that Oda was only present on one occasion.

The third regnal year of Edmund began in October 941 and therefore agrees with the incarnation date, 942, which is consistent with the witness-list. The most interesting witness is Archbishop Wulfstan, for he does not subscribe charters between 934 and 942 and, according to a later report in the northern recension of the Chronicle, he was opposed to King Edmund in the dispute about the district of the Five Boroughs (*ASC* 943 D; Whitelock 1959, pp. 71–3). The first original charter of Edmund that he subscribes is dated 944, but he also occurs in a charter of 942 from a Shaftesbury cartulary (S 485, 497).

The beneficiary of all three charters is described as Wulfsige *prenomine Maur'*. Bridgeman speculated that this might derive from Welsh *mawr* meaning 'great', but he alternatively suggested Latin *maurus* meaning 'black' (Bridgeman 1916 ,

p. 83). Support for the second suggestion comes from **27** where Wulfsige *ðĕ blaca* is named, with Æscberht, as a former holder of Bromley, one of the estates granted in **5**. A thegn called Wulfsige occurs in several of Athelstan's charters and by the end of his reign was regularly fourth among the *ministri* (S 477–9; in S 446 he is third *minister*), a position he kept in two of Edmund's charters in 940 (S 464, 470). Three charters of these two kings, dated 934, 935, and 940, have a second Wulfsige *minister* towards the end of the lists (S 425, 430, 464) and one, dated 931, is witnessed by three thegns of that name (S 416). After 940 the name is infrequent and in the next twenty-five years a Wulfsige *minister* only witnessed seven trustworthy charters (S 508, 514, 528, 674, 679, 681, 712). Four of these, dated 958–63, concerned estates in the Midlands and the North, but the absence of a Wulfsige from charters concerning that area between 942 and 958 probably means that these later signatures do not belong to the beneficiary of the present charters. Whether he may be identified with the leading thegn of 940 is uncertain, but if so his disappearance could have been a consequence of the Northumbrian invasion of the Five Boroughs in 940 (Sawyer 1975, pp. 36–7). The reasons for thinking that Wulfsige the Black may have been a kinsman of Wulfric Spot are discussed in the Introduction, p. xl.

No assessment is given in **6** and **7**, possibly because of the abbreviation of those texts, and in **5** it is stated in an unusual form *nou is þisses landes feourti hyde*. The total assessment of the places named in **5** was, according to DB, 23 hides and 3 carucates. With the possible exception of *Sulueston*, which has been identified as Silverstone in Northamptonshire (*DEPN*, s.n.), all the places named in these charters lay on or close to the Trent and within about nine miles of Burton. Three of the places named in **5** were later owned by Wulfric Spot and two of these, Stretton and Bromley (cf. **27**), head the list of his endowment of Burton Abbey (**29**), while the third, Rolleston, later passed, temporarily, into the abbey's possession (**31**). The abbey later acquired several other places named in **5**, **6**, and **7**: Branston (**5**), Cauldwell and Coton (**6**), and Stapenhill (**7**) (see p. xlvi). The assessments and pre-Conquest owners of Wulfsige's estates, as described in DB, were as follows:

	Modern Name	Owner T.R.E.	Assessment	Reference in DB, i
5	Alrewas	Earl Ælfgar	3 hides	246
	Kings Bromley	Earl Harold	3 hides	246
	Abbots Bromley	Burton Abbey	$\frac{1}{2}$ hide	247b
	Barton	Earl Ælfgar	3 hides	246b
	Tatenhill	not in DB, probably part of Barton		
	Branston	Godgifu	$1\frac{1}{2}$ hides	247b
	Stretton	Burton Abbey	$1\frac{1}{2}$ hides	247b
	Rolleston	Earl Morcar	$2\frac{1}{2}$ hides	248b
	Clifton	Earl Ælfgar	8 hides	246b
		Earl Ælfgar	3 carucates	272b
	Haunton	not in DB, probably part of Clifton		
6	Walton	Earl Ælfgar	6 carucates	272b
	Coton	Earl Ælfgar	2 carucates	273
	Cauldwell	Ælfric	2 carucates	273
	Drakelow	Alric	4 carucates	278
	Newbold	not in DB, possibly in Barton		
	Linton	Leofric	2 carucates	274
		?	1 carucate	233b
7	Croxall	Siward	3 carucates	274
	Catton	Siward	3 carucates	274

Walton	see **6**		
Drakelow	see **6**		
Stapenhill	Burton Abbey	4 carucates 2 bovates	273
	Godric	6 bovates	278
Silverstone	Siward	½ hide	227
	Leofric	1 hide	223b
	Asgar	½ hide	227b

8

King Eadred grants four hides (cassata) *in* Suþtone, *with licence to buy a fifth, to Ulfketel, miles.* A.D. 949

B. Aberystwyth, N.L.W., Peniarth 390, fo. 174^{rv} (pp. 347–8): copy, s. xiii^{med}

Ed.: Birch 876

Listed: Hart 103, Sawyer 549

Carta Eadredi regis de Suttone anno domini . dccccº . xlix .^{a}

+Cunctis catholice conuersantibus certum est quod omnis sapiencia a domino constat esse concessa sagacibus . Quapropter studendum est toto mentis iam conamine illius opitulante prerogatiua qui euuangelico paradigmate protulit dicens ꞏ' discite a me quia mitis sum et humilis corde . discere . intelligere . et perseuerare . quia perseuerantibus ꞏ' finetinus^b salus promissa est perpetua . Illuc^c dumtaxat Ealdredus rex Ængulsæxna ond Norðhymbra imperator . paganorum gubernator . Brittonumque propugnator ꞏ' cordetenus anhelando . largiflue cristicolis . melliflue solicolis lucra confert alacriter . Hoc pro certo eiusdem regis satrapa ore veridico potest inumare^d de perenni vsurpacione huius telluris quod sibi suisque heredibus liberaliter preter vrbis pontisque constructione seu expedicionis obsequio magnis rebus ac modicis certa terminacione condonauit Ulfcetele quatuor ruris cassata in Suþtone . quintum quoque comparauit regali licentia ab aliis . Ast sequitur terminatio .

Contulit nempe miles ipse Ulfcetel magno regi beniuolentia^e mentis intencione quinquaginta cocti auri charismata^f quodque precium profert ut eo liberius hec libertas perfruentibus autem^g in euum augeatur . Si qui uero diabolica fraude decepti hoc regale eulogium denichilent ꞏ' ad nichilum redigantur . nisi digne coram Deo reconcilient emendando amen.

+Adest namque dominice incarnacionis annus arithmetica ratione nongentesimus et quadragesimus nonus . in quo denique anno Eadred regali gubernaculo galeatus cum consensu optimatum hanc cartulam consignauit . +Oda quoque ærcabissop . +atque Þulfstan archapresul . +Theodredus episcopus con*signavi*. +Æðelfled consiliarius con*signavi*. + . Ælfred . presul con*signavi* . + . Ældric antistes . con*signaui* .

+Þulfsige pontifex con*signavi* . +Æþelgar . ond Koenpald pontifices . con*signaverunt* . +Þulfhelm biscup con*signavi* . +Cyncige episcopus . con*signavi* . + . Ældred et Æþelpald scripserunt pontificali auctoritate concordantes[h] . + . Eya[i] . et ceteri duces . abbates . ministri . et milites . xxv .

Tali videlicet stabilitate nobilium notum sit hunc codicellum legentibus quod rex prefatus tercio annorum laterculo quo regalia sublimauit diademata paschali sollempnitate in villa famosissima que uulgari uocabulo Sumurtun nuncupatur deo concedente triumphali signaculo hoc prerogatiuum perpetualiter perfruentibus roborauit . —

[a] Carta . . . xlix . *rubric*   [b] *A spelling for* finetenus   [c] *Altered from* Iluc
[d] *Error for* intimare   [e] *Error for* beniuolenti   [f] *Dr Lapidge suggests that* charismata *is a mistake for something like* chremata, *from Greek* χρήματα, 'money'
[g] *Error for* omne *or* evum   [h] *Apparently altered from* concedentes *or vice versa*
[i] *See* 6, *note c*

The witness-list of this alliterative charter is consistent with its date and includes three bishops whose pontificates began or ended at this time: Ældric for Ælfric, of Hereford or Ramsbury, Cynsige of Lichfield, and Æthelwald, possibly of Dorchester (O'Donovan 1972, pp. 38, 42–3; 1973, pp. 95, 99). The close similarity between this list and those in two other alliterative charters of the same date (S. 544, 550) suggests that the Æðelfled who here follows Theodred is an error for Ælfheah.

The beneficiary has an uncommon name. A charter of 949 is witnessed by Ulfketel *miles* (S 547) and two authentic charters of 958 and 959 concerning estates in Nottinghamshire and Yorkshire were witnessed by a *minister* of that name who may have been the beneficiary (S 679, 681). The Sutton of this charter may have been one of the three bequeathed by Wulfric to Burton Abbey but no identification can be suggested with any confidence, although (as explained above, p. xxx) there are grounds for thinking that it may have been Sutton Maddock, Salop.

9

King Eadred grants land at Bakewell, Derbyshire, to Uhtred, miles *and* dux. A.D. 949

B. Aberystwyth, N.L.W., Peniarth 390, fos 174[v]–175 (pp. 348–9): copy, s. xiii[med]

Ed.: Birch 884

Listed: Hart 104, Sawyer 548

Carta Edredi regis de Baþecpall' anno domini . dcccc[us] . xl . nonus .[a]

+Perpetue prosperitatis priuilegium quod constat celesti culmine collocatum . sancte trinitatis dei tripudium rite promerentibus tribuit vsurpando . que adhuc quoque deitatis essentia terrene hereditatis territoria cunctis prestat prout uult ; Hoc preualet . Eadred rex rite Anglorum gloriosissimus . rectorque Noþhanhimbra[b] . et paganorum imperator

Brittonumque propugnator . proculdubio iam propalare ; quem rex regum omnipotens regali gubernaculo totius Albionis sublimauit ; quique confert alacriter larga lucra crucicolis ut deinceps accipiat caritatis[c] karismata ; ruricolis necnon infert perhenniter largitates ; Cuius donum dignanter . imo corde collaudat , miles iste Vhtred et dux modeste cum tellure ad Badecanpelle hilaratus . preter vrbem atque pontem agonemque[d] heredibus usurpata tali terminacio[e] circumcincta . Adest namque annus nongentesimus quadragenus atque nonus . dominice incarnacionis . quartus quoque quo Eadredus regimina rex regebat . et cum archiepiscopis ceterisque consulibus hanc tellurem consignauit . + . Oda Þustan et ceteri episcopi . duces abbates ministri . et milites ut supra cum triumphali signaculo sigillabant celotenus titulantes Ā ω . sequuntur diuise .

+Hoc dumtaxat coenubium Badecanpelle Vhtredo heroica auctoritate ditato suisque heredibus magnis rebus ac modicis a*evum* in euum Ealdredus rex largissimus illuc pertinentibus rite crepundiis charaxauit stabiliter Iam obsecrat imperando et imperat obsecrando cunctos deinceps successores . ut nullus diabolica fraude deceptus audeat uel priscis codicibus . seu saltim ullatenus hoc regale priuilegium adnihilare . sin alias ad nihilum nutu Dei redigantur . nisi dige[f] coram deo et angelis reconcilient ; pax nobiscum .

[a] Carta . . . nonus . *rubric*   [b] *For* Norþanhimbra   [c] *Altered by the scribe from* carisatis   [d] *The meaning of* agonem *is obscure. Dr Lapidge suggests comparison with S 520* (preter arcem atque pontem agonisque obsequium), *where* obsequium agonis *presumably means 'support in or for battle'*   [e] *Error for* terminacione   [f] *Error for* digne

For comments see **3** and pp. xlvii–viii.

10

King Eadred grants ten hides (mansi) *at* Eatun *to* Athelstan (Æðestan), minister. A.D. 949

B. Aberystwyth, N.L.W., Peniarth 390, fo. 175 (p. 349): copy, s. xiii[med]
Ed.: Birch 885
Listed: Hart 84, Sawyer 545

Carta Edredi regis de Eatun . anno domini . dccccᵒ . xlixᵒ .[a]

✠ Quicquid inter seculares in omnibus agendum est terris ⫶ muniri apertis debetur litteris . ut quod obliuiscitur ⫶ mentis memoria presens semper custodiatur littera . ne forte etiam perdatur inuidia cupiditatis quod est iuste adquisitum dono rectitudinis . Vnde ego Eadredus nutu gratie Dei Anglorum rex omnibus meis notum uolo et[b] esse fidelibus quod ego cuidam meo fideli ministro onomate Æðestan proprio amabili obsequio . seu etiam pro sexaginta mancusis de probato et purissimo auro ⫶ do et concedo . x . mansos telluris in loco quem circum manentes

appellant uulgariter Eatun . vt habeat et possideat vita comite . Post sue
etiam terminum vite cuicumque heredi uoluerit derelinquat hereditatem.
Sit autem predictum rus liberum ab omni mundano seruicio . tribus
exceptis . viatici pontis restauracione . arcis regalis constructione .
populari etiam expedicione . Si quis uero quod absit cupiditatis flamma
accensus hoc nostrum infringere temptauerit donum ? sit dampnatus
cum omnibus filiis perdicionis Belial in tartareis tormentis nisi resipi-
scens digna factione*c* emendauerit . Hiis autem terminum finibus predicta terra circumcirca girata esse videtur . Ærst of þære suð mærdic . et
cetera .

Et ut hec cartula inuiolabile robur firmitatis optineat ? +Ego Eadredus
rex primus regali manu confirmo . +Signum Eadgifu genitricis eiusdem
regis .

+Ego Oda Dorobernensis ecclesie archiepiscopus corroboro . +Ego
Þulfstanus Eboracae ciuitatis archiepiscopus adfirmo . +Ego þeodred
Lundoniensis episcopus contestor . +Ego Ælfeh Þintoniensis episcopus
consigno . +Ego Ælfsige episcopus consencio . +Ego Ælfric episcopus
delibero . +Ego Æþelgar episcopus desidero . +Ego Ælfric episcopus cupio .

+Acta est hec cartula anno incarnacionis dominice . dccccº . xlix .
indictione . vij . regn*ante* rege Eadredo . anno . ijº .

---

a Carta . . . xlixº . *rubric*   *b* ? *An error for* id   *c* *An error for* satisfactione

This charter has too many unusual features to be accepted without question
as an authentic grant by Eadred. The indiction, 7, would be right for the year
beginning in September 948 and therefore agrees with the incarnation date,
949, but Eadred's second year ended in May 948. A simple emendation would be
to correct the regnal year to 3, but the use of a regnal year in a non-alliterative
charter of Eadred is itself unusual. The witness-list is consistent with the date
and may be compared with the list in an original of the same year (S 552) but
at least one name appears to have been copied incorrectly. No Bishop Ælfsige
is known at that time and W. G. Searle suggested it should read Wulfsige, of
Sherborne (*Anglo-Saxon Bishops, Kings and Nobles* (Cambridge, 1899), p. 82).
This subscription is in Wulfsige's usual position in lists at that time. There are
two bishops called Ælfric in the list and although that is possible (the sees of
Hereford and Ramsbury were held by men of that name until 949) the second
could be a mistake for Ælfred of Selsey. The variety of verbs used in the subscriptions is much greater than in contemporary charters of undoubted authenticity. Hart, pp. 92–3, points out that many of the formulas have close parallels
in eleventh-century charters and writs.

There are very few subscriptions of a *minister* called Æthestan or Æthelstan
at the time of this charter (S 464, 701) but the occurrence of this name in two
Danelaw charters dated 958 (S 674, 679) may mean that the beneficiary was
a local thegn. There is no means of identifying *Eatun* or of determining whether
it is the same place as in **4**.

11

King Eadred grants land at Marchington, Staffordshire, to Wulfhelm, miles. A.D. 951

B. Aberystwyth, N.L.W., Peniarth 390, fo. 175^{rv} (pp. 349–50): copy, s. xiii^{med}
Ed.: Birch 890
Listed: Hart 85, Sawyer 557

Carta Edredi regis de Marchanton sub Nedwod' . dcccc . li° .[a]

+Prophetica primitus predicacio . et apostolica deinceps disceptacio . et quod precellentior est euuangelica Iesu Cristi promulgatio cuncti[b] indicat dogmata dicens . date et dabitur uobis . Ideoque Eadredus rex Anglorum quos uult honorifice larga manu locupletat . Hoc potest veraciter miles iste Þulfhelmus cum ceteris intimare . quem perhenni huius ruris æt Mærcham usurpacione . preter vrbis . pontisque constructione . et expedicionis obsequio beatizat . concedens ei eiusque heredibus hanc tellurem magnis rebus ac modicis rite pertinentibus perfruendam . . .-
+Eadred rex Albionis alma iam manu hanc munificentiam anno dominice incarnationis dcccc^{mo} . et lj° . sexto quoque quo sceptra regebat regalia annorum laterculo cum consensu senatorum quorum hic calculantur vocabula triumphali videlicet vexillo stabiliter roborauit .
+Oda archiepiscopo[c] cum ceteris suffraganeis . +Theodredo . Ælfrico ꝉ Þulfsigio ꝉ Ælfredo ꝉ Cynsigio ꝉ Koenpaldo ꝉ Æðelgario ꝉ Þulfhelmo ꝉ Oscetelo ꝉ sagaciter consignauit .
+Duces et oerles sex conscribebant . ministri et prefecti . quinque sigillabant .
+Eaðhelm ꝉ abbas atque Dunstan cum signo+sancte crucis hec karismata karaxabant.
Iam imperat rex prefatus obsecrando et obsecrat imperando per clauem euuangelicam quam Petro ipse Iesus Cristus auctore apostolico contulit ligandi atque soluendi potestate tradita quatinus in posterum nullus diabolica fraude deceptus preualeat huius largitatis libertatem delere . set pocius qui studeat adimplere eulogium largitoris ꝉ larga lucra coram Cristo integra karitate cum choris angelicis Iesuali gymnasium[d] sine fine inueniat amen .
Ærest of deues[e] broke an gillundes dic . of ðere dic ꝉ on hine hylle . of hine hille ꝉ on pire broc . of pirebroke ꝉ on pirepasse . of pirpasse ꝉ on ðæne hpitan mor . of þan pitan mor ꝉ on ðæn michalen ac . of ðære mycelen æc ꝉ on stenges healh . of stenges heale ꝉ on potteres lege . of potteres leage ꝉ on cundesleage . of cundeslege ꝉ on cundes fenne . of cundes fenne ꝉ on lind broc . of lind broce . on holan broce ꝉ of holan broke ꝉ an dufan . and long dufan ꝉ eft innan denes broc .

---

[a] Carta . . . li° . *rubric*   [b] *Error for* cunctis   [c] *Error for* archiepiscopus
[d] *? An error for* gymnasii. *If not, read* in Iesuali gymnasio   [e] *For* denes

C

This authentic alliterative charter is very similar to one of the same year concerning land in Huntingdonshire but the differences between the witness-lists make it unlikely that they were issued on the same occasion (S 556). The beneficiary Wulfhelm is probably the Mercian thegn who was later granted land at Aston and Barr in Staffordshire in a charter that is connected, by its final paragraph, with the group of rhythmical texts to which the present charter belongs (S 574; for the identification see also R. Forsberg, *Namn och Bygd*, lviii (1970), pp. 27–39). The same man apparently witnessed several Midland and Northern charters in 958 and 959 (S 579, 677, 679, 681) and may be the thegn who was a regular witness from 960 to 963. The *minister* who witnessed charters of Athelstan and, until 943 or 944, of Edmund, was probably a different man (S 496, 491).

Burton Abbey never had any claim to this estate and it is therefore surprising that the scribe of Peniarth 390 should have copied the bounds. The identifiable boundary points are:

i. *denes broc* which is clearly associated with Densy Lodge, south of Sudbury Station (SK 161 301). In the Needwood enclosures (S.R.O., Q/RDc 58c) several plots east of this Lodge are called Densey Meadow and there is a thirteenth-century reference to meadows in Draycott *que vocatur Denseye* (*The Cartulary of Tutbury Priory*, ed. A. Saltman, *Collections for a History of Staffordshire*, 4th ser., iv (William Salt Archaeological Society, 1962), no. 123).

ii. *pire broc* is Pur Brook which now rises at SK 103 275 and flows south.

iii. *cundesleage* is now Scounslow Green at SK 094 296. In the Tithe Award for Marchington Woodland (S.R.O., D 1528/2/23/4) it is called Scoundslow Green and on the first edition of the Ordnance Survey it is Scounsley Green. The Burton archives include a licence, *temp.* Edward I, to build a granary on *Le Gorstiknol* (cf. Gorsty Hill at SK 100 290) near the way leading to *Cundesleye* (Jeayes 1937, no. 259).

iv. *an dufan*. The River Dove still forms the county and parish boundary. The modern Marchington boundary runs along a well defined valley, in which Woodford now stands (SK 117 316), to join the Dove and this is probably the *holan broc*.

These bounds show that the land *æt Mærcham* is correctly identified as Marchington; they tend to follow the modern bounds of Marchington parish. This estate was later bequeathed by Wulfric to his nephew, Wulfheah. If, as seems likely, Wulfric was related to Wulfhelm, he probably inherited it. T.R.E. it was held by another Wulfric and assessed at 2 hides with a virgate at Agardsley (DB, i. 248b). No assessment is stated in the charter but, to judge by the very similar Huntingdonshire charter, it was given in English at the end of the bounds, and may well have been omitted by the copyist.

12

King Eadred grants eight hides (cassati) *æt Norðtune to Ælfheah, minister.* A.D. 951

A. lost, owned in 1622 by Lord Coke

B. Aberystwyth, N.L.W., Peniarth 390, fo. 175ᵛ (p. 350): copy, s. xiii^med

Ed.: a. W. Burton, *The Description of Leicestershire* (1622), pp. 209–10, from A
    b. Birch 891 from B

Listed: Sawyer 554

Printed from B with variants from Burton's version of A

Carta Eadredi regis Anglorum de Norðtune . dcccc° . lj° . indictione . ix .[a]

✠ Domino dominorum dominante in secula seculorum regna regnorum huius presentis seculi transeunt sicut ignominia[b] et omnis gloria . et locus[c] huius mundi peribit et non sunt eterna . set superna eterna sunt . Vnde ego Eadred[d] rex Anglorum gubernator et rector cuidam mihi fidelissimo ministro quem vocitant nonnulli noto vocamine Ælfeah . viij[e] . cassatos perpetualiter concedo in illo loco ubi iamdudum solicole illius regionis nomen indiderunt . æt Norðtune[f] . vt habeat ac possideat quamdiu viuat et postquam vniuersitatis viam adierit cuicumque voluerit heredi derelinquat . in eternam hereditatem . Sit autem predictum rus liberum ab omni mundiali seruicio cum omnibus[g] que ad ipsum locum pertinere dinoscuntur[h] . tam in magnis quam in modicis[i] rebus . campis . pascuis . pratis . siluis . sine expedicione et pontis arcisve instructione . Si qui denique mihi non optanti[k] hanc libertatis cartam liuore depressi violari satagerint ⫽ agminibus tetre[l] caliginis lapsi vocem audiant examinacionis die arbitris sibi dicentis . discedite a me maledicti in ignem eternum vbi cum demonibus ferreis sartaginibus crudeli torqueantur in pena . si non ante mortem digna hoc emendauerint penitentia . Istis terminis ambitur predicta tellus . et cetera[m] .

Hec carta karaxata est anno ab incarnatione . domini nostri Iesu Cristi ⫽ dcccc . lj° . indictione . ix .

+Ego Eadred[n] rex Anglorum prefatam donacionem indeclinabiliter concessi .   +

+Ego Eadgifu[o] eiusdem regis mater cum sigillo sancte crucis[p] confirmaui .

+Ego Oda Dorobernensis ecclesie archiepiscopus eiusdem regis donationem subscripsi et confirmaui .[q]

+Ego Ælfheah Pintaniensis[r] ecclesie episcopus triumphalem tropheum agie crucis impressi .[s]

+Ego Cynpald episcopus consignaui .

+Ego Osulf episcopus adquieui .

+Ego Æþelgar episcopus corroboraui .

+Ego Pulfsige episcopus non renui

+Ego Oscytel episcopus conclusi[t]

+Edmund dux

+Æþelstan dux

+Ealhhelm dux

+Æþelmund dux

+Æþelsige . dux[u]

+Pulfric minister .

+Æþelgeard minister .

+Ælfred minister .

+Ælfheah minister .

+Pulfric minister .[w]

+Ælfsige . minister[x]
+Ælfgar minister
+Birhtferþ minister
+Ordheah minister
+Ealdred minister
+Ælfric . minister .[y]

[a] Carta . . . indictione . ix . *rubric in* B   [b] *Sic Burton;* ignominica B   *An error for* iocus (*cf. S 730, 872*)   [d] Eldred *Burton*   [e] Ælfelh vni *Burton*   [f] Et Northtune *Burton*   [g] seruicio cum omnibus *omitted Burton*   [h] -ter *Burton*   [i] modis *Burton*   [k] obstanti *Burton*   [l] atre *Burton*   [m] et cetera B; This sant thalangemara to Northtune, &c. *Burton*   [n] Eldred *Burton*   [o] Eadgifa *Burton*   [p] + *omitted Burton*   [q] +Ego Odo Dorouernensis Ececlesiæ Archiepiscopus eius Domini regis donationem subscripsi . *Burton*   [r] Ælfeah Wintoniensis *Burton*   [s] *The first four subscriptions are on separate lines in* B; *in Burton the remaining subscriptions are as follows, in two columns*

+Ego Cenfal Episcopus consignaui .   +Ego Æthelrise Dux .
+Ego Osulf Episcopus adquieui .   +Ego Wulfricus .   mis .
+Ego Æthelsan Episcopus corroboraui .   +Ego Ethelred .   mis .
+Ego Wulfrig Episcopus non renui .   +Ego Eldred .   mis .
+Ego Oscitel Episcopus conclusi .   +Ego Elfelh .   mis .
+Ego Edmundus Dux .   +Ego Elfrig .   mis .
+Ego Athelstanus Dux .   +Ego Elfgar .   mis .
+Ego Æthelmus Dux .   +Ego Birfirth .   mis .
+Ego Athelmundus .   +Ego Ordeah .   mis .

[t] *First column of subscriptions ends here*   [u] *Second column of subscriptions ends here*   [w] *Third column of subscriptions ends here*   [x] *This subscription is inserted above the fourth column, on the same line as the subscription of Ælfheah, bishop of Winchester*   [y] *The fourth column of subscriptions ends here*

Some of the errors in Burton's 1622 version (*Eldred* for Eadred, *Ælfelh* for Ælfeah) suggest that he was using a pre-Conquest manuscript with a form of the letter *a* that could be mistaken for *l*, cf. *Eadpig* in **14** MS. D which the scribe of MS. B misread as *Eldpig*. The cartulary version was probably taken from the same text, but without the same mistakes. Burton's version of the witness-list is very carelessly copied, with such mistakes as *Ethelred* for Æthelgeard and *Eldred* for Ælfred. He also appears to have left out names that he thought had already been listed; the second Wulfric is omitted and so too are the last witnesses, Ealdred and Ælfric, presumably because he had already listed *Eldred* and *Elfrig* as mistaken readings for Ælfred and Ælfsige.

The witness-list, which includes the earliest subscription of Oswulf, bishop of Ramsbury (O'Donovan 1973, p. 99), is consistent with the date of the charter, 951, which also agrees with the indiction. The formulas are typical; the proem occurs in S 730 and the *sanctio* is common, see **4**. The very early use of *chi rho* as the chrismon should be noted.

The beneficiary Ælfheah may have been the later ealdorman who had very extensive estates but as his will makes no mention of a Norton (S 1485) a more likely identification is with the *minister* who begins to subscribe in 955 and who was granted land in Huntingdonshire in 958 (S 674). Burton prints this charter under his description of Norton juxta Twycross in Leicestershire and although he gives no reason for the identification it may be correct. Norton juxta Twycross was held in DB by Godgifu, and assessed at 6 carucates, and she also held 3 carucates in the adjacent Appleby (DB, i. 231b) where Burton Abbey held 4 hides, one of which had been alienated to Godgifu (DB, i. 273a). Appleby had been held by Wulfric and formed part of his endowment of Burton Abbey.

He also bequeathed a Norton to his nephew Ufegeat but that was presumably confiscated when Ufegeat was blinded in 1006. The fact that Norton and Appleby are adjacent and were partly held by the same person in DB may be no more than coincidence, but it is interesting to note that Wulfric also held land nearby at Austrey (cf. **18**, **29**, and p. xxvii). He appears to have had a substantial interest in this area and the present charter could have been his title-deed to that Norton.

13

King Eadred grants land at Chesterfield, Derbyshire, to Uhtred Child, pedisequus. A.D. 955

B. Aberystwyth, N.L.W., Peniarth 390, fos 175^v–176 (pp. 350–1): copy, s. xiii^{med}

Ed.: Birch 911

Listed: Hart 105, Sawyer 569

Carta Eadredi regis de Cestrefeldo facta Uhtredo Child . dcccc . lv .^{a}

+In principio creauit Deus celum celestibus celorum agminibus ethraliter conflagrando . et terram terrestribus trutinauit tripudialiter tribuendo ita dicens . Celum mihi thronus est . et tellus scabellum pedibus . id est cetus angelicus et culmen apostolicum . Iam illuc anhelans Eadred rex Angulsæxna et Norþhimbra imperator paganorum gubernator . Brettonumque propugnator toto cordis ac mentis conamine Iesum Cristum totius lucri largitorem laudat et glorificat . Ideoque anno dominice incarnationis nongentesimo et quinquagesimo quinto . nonus quoque annus adest ex quo regalia erexit^b regimina . quos uult letificat honorifice euuangelica sequendo paradigmata . gratis accepistis ? gratis date . Hoc dumtaxat pedissequus^c Vhtred Child alacriter in huius telluris ad Cesterfelda perhenni liberalitate subterius terminandum magnis rebus ac modicis preter vrbis pontisque constructione et expedicionis obsequio cum suis collaudat heredibus . Ecce testes hoc volumen munientes .

+Eadred rex tocius Britannie hec karismata triumphali vexillo sancte crucis consignauit . +Oda archabisco*p* . +Berhtsige episcopus . +Elfsige pontifex . +Ospulf didasculus . +Þulfsige antistes . +Berhtelm presul . +Ælfpald biscop . +Cynsige episcopus . +Oscetel pontifex . +Koenpald monachus . +Þulfhelm presul . +Aldred antistes . +Eadgeofu euax . +Eadpig cliton . +Eadgar æþeling . et ceteri duces . principes . milites et ministri . xxvj . consensum prebuerunt .

En imperat prefatus rex obsecrando et obsecrat imperando per clauem euuangelicam quam Cristus Iesus Petro principi apostolico potestate tradita ligandi ac solvendi contulerat ut nullus deinceps diabolica fraude deceptus audeat hoc eulogium violare . Ve ve inueniant violantes . Euge euge tu adaugens hic et in euum amen . fas diuinum . jus humanum .

^a Carta . . . lv . *rubric*   ^b *Error for* rexit   ^c *Erasure above* -us

The witnesses of this authentic alliterative charter are consistent with its date. The most unusual is Ealdred, bishop of Chester le Street, who otherwise witnesses three charters dealing with land in the Midlands and the North (S 675, 679, 681). Uhtred *Child* may have been a kinsman of the Uhtred of **3** and **9** and he was probably the *dux* who subscribed four Midland charters in 956 and 958 (S 659, 674, 677, 679). Chesterfield is not mentioned in Wulfric's will and Burton Abbey held no land there. For the possibility that Chesterfield was held by Ælfhelm see the comment on **2**.

14

King Eadwig grants eight hides (mansae) *at Braunston, Northamptonshire, to Eadwig, minister.* A.D. 956

B. Aberystwyth, N.L.W., Peniarth 390, fo. 176 (p. 351): s. xiii^{med}

D. Burton upon Trent Museum, Burton Muniment 2: single sheet, parchment, s. xi¹, 240 × 580 mm., damaged by folding

    Endorsements: (1) by the scribe of the charter: +*þis is seo land bóc to Brantestune þe Eadˋpigˊ cing gebocade Eadpige his þegne ón ece yrfe* (2) in a hand of s. xiii: *Dcccc . lv . indictione . xiiij* . (3) in a hand of s. xiii: *Brontestonˋ* (4) in a medieval hand: *XIIII*

Ed.: a. *O.S.F.*, iii Anglesey 1 (facsimile, transcript, and translation) from D

    b. Birch 978

Listed: Hart 4, Sawyer 623

Printed from B with bounds, subscriptions, and main variants from D

+^aRegnante imperpetuum^b domino nostro Iesu Cristo Manifestum est cunctis quod omnia celestia et terrestria prouidentia Dei gubernantur^c . que sollicitudo mortalis vite in carorum amicorumque amissione^d conqueritur ac defletur . Ideo certis adstipulationibus mellita oracula^e diuine clamationis nos frequentatiuis hortationibus^f suadet^g . ut cum hiis^h fugitiuis et sine dubio transitoriisⁱ possessiunculis iugiter mansura regna Dei suffragio adipiscenda sunt . Idcirco ego Eadpig rex Anglorum ceterarumque^k gentium in circuitu persistentium cuidam^l fideli meo ministro^m vocitato nomineⁿ Eadpig^o aliquam partem terre in loco qui dicitur Brantestun . viij^p . mansas terre . ut habeat et possideat^q vite sue^r et post se cuicumque uoluerit heredi derelinquat in eternam hereditatem . Sit autem predicta terra libera cum omnibus que^s rite pertinentibus ad ipsam^t campis pascuis pratis . excepto^u istis tribus expeditione . pontis arcisve^w instructione . Si quis uero quod non^x optamus contra nostrum hoc decretum machinari^y uel infringere uoluerit ⫶ sciat se racionem grauiter redditurum in die iudicii ante tribunal domini . nisi prius hic digna^z emendauerit^{aa} ante mortem .

þis^{bb} syndon þa landgemæro to Brantes tune óf þes stod faldes east hyrnan ón þone pýt . of þam pytte on þone suðran beorh of þam beorge

ón þone þorn styb of þa*m* stybbe to þes cumb[es] heafde of þam cumbe
on geriht in on limenan adún 7lang streames oð hit cymð on þiliabys ón
þone lytlan ðorn óf þa*m* ðorne ón middan þone mere of þa*m* mere on
riht to þa*m* lytlan bro[ce] up 7land cumbes to þam sceardan beorge of
þa*m* sceardan beorge to þa*m* rugan hlæpe óf þa*m* rugan hlæpe ón stan
beo`r´h óf stan beorge eft ón þone stod fald .

Acta*cc* est autem hec*dd* donatio anno . dcccc . lvj . incarnationis*ee*
dominice . indictione . xiiij .   +

Ego Eadpig rex Anglorum hóc confirmaui titulo sancte crucis*ff*
Ego Eadgar indoles corroboraui
Ego*gg* Oda archipresul impressi .

Ego Ælfsige	episcopus	consensi.
Ego Oswlf*hh*	episcopus	annui .
Ego Byrhtelm	episcopus	dictaui
Ego Daniel	episcopus	subscripsi .*ii*
+Æðelstan*kk*	dux	
+Æþelsig	dux	
+Eadmund	dux	
+Ælfhere	dux	
+Æþelpold	dux	
+Æþelmund	dux*ll*	
+Ælfgar	m*inister*	
+Byrhtferð	m*inister*	
+Ælf[ ]	m*inister*	
+Æðelmær	m*inister*	
+Ælfred	m*inister*	
+Þulfric	m*inister*<i>mm</i>	

Description of D: Three horizontal and three vertical folds. Ruled with a stylus,
one bounding line to left, prickings survive in left margin. Written area 210 ×
540 mm. Written in Anglo-Saxon minuscule by an inexpert scribe. The short
form of *s* is not used initially, *a* and *e* are normally horned and in some ligatures
e has a tall loop. The names of the beneficiary and the place are in capitals,
initial *R* in the invocation and *M* of the proem are uncial, and capital *G* occurs
in *Eadgar*. The *E* of *Ego* in the subscriptions is in both rounded and straight

forms and they are written in the left margin. The script of the Old English bounds and of the witnesses' names is only distinguished by the use of ð, þ, p, and 7. Some words are divided internally, e.g. *cunc tis*, *ter restria*. The chrismon is a plain cross in the left margin, the crosses of the subscriptions are plain and occur only in the second and third columns. The last four subscriptions in the first column are out of line. ∴ is used as the *signe de renvoi*.

D appears to be a very clumsy eleventh-century copy of an authentic charter. There are many mistakes, apart from those corrected by the scribe; the royal title is incomplete, there is no verb of donation, the assessment should be introduced by *videlicet* or something similar, the anathema lacks *penitentia* or equivalent word and the date is odd. It is probable that B was copied from a lost version that shared several of the major deficiencies of D. B certainly has many better readings than D, and these are unlikely to have been corrections by the scribe of B for he does not demonstrate such competence elsewhere. The witness-list is acceptable, the indiction is correct and the beneficiary could be the man who occurs infrequently between 961 and 970 (S 697, 715, 781). The reference in the bounds to the River Leam and to Willoughby shows that the estate was Braunston, Northamptonshire, the western boundary of which is still the River Leam. It has been suggested that the boundary elsewhere generally follows the modern parish boundary (J. E. B. Gover, A. Mawer, and F. M. Stenton, *The Place-Names of Northamptonshire* (E.P.N.S. x, 1933), pp. 14–15; M. W. Beresford, *History on the Ground* (1957), pp. 41–4). This seems likely but it should be emphasized that the argument is entirely topographical and is not supported by other identifiable names. Neither Wulfric nor Burton Abbey had any interest in Braunston which was T.R.E. held by two men, Thorir and Sæwine, with a total assessment of 3 hides 3 virgates (DB, i. 220, 226). It is possible that this charter was mistaken for a title-deed of Branston in Staffordshire, which did belong to Burton Abbey.

Hart, pp. 56–7, expresses some reservations about the authenticity of this charter. His reasons include the alterations to the witness-list and endorsement, but as MS. D is clearly a copy, and a very bad one, that argument has no force. He also emphasizes the close similarity of this charter to one dated fourteen years earlier (S 482) but that, as he recognizes, is not a decisive argument against authenticity.

15

King Eadwig grants three hides (mansae) æt Mortune *to* Mæglsothen, *his man.* A.D. 956

B. Aberystwyth, N.L.W., Peniarth 390, fo. 176[rv] (pp. 351–2): copy, s. xiii[med]
Ed.: Birch 951
Listed: Hart 106, Sawyer 628

Carta Eadpig regis de Mortune . dcccc . lvj .[a]

✠ In nomine domini nostri Iesu Cristi . Anno uero dominice incarnacionis . dcccc . lvj° . indictione . xiiij . ego Eadpig rex Anglorum ceterarumque gentium in circuitu persistentium gubernator et rector . audiui a sapientibus et prudentibus hanc mellitam dulcedinem sermocinacionis diuine . quod bona voluntas in die examinacionis pro bono opere re-

putabitur . Idcirco dedi cuidam meo homini vocitato nomine Mæglsoþen
tres mansas ei libenter largiendo donaui . in illo loco ubi ruricole antiquo
usu nomen indiderunt . æt Mortune . eatenus ut hoc diebus suis possideat . tramitibusque vite sue . et post se cuicumque uoluerit heredi
derelinquat in eternam hereditatem . Sit hec predicta terra cum omnibus
ad se rite pertinentibus libera . campis . pascuis . pratis . siluis . excepto
istis tribus . expedicione . pontis arcisve coedificacione . Si quis uero
minuerit hanc donationem ¿ sciat se reum omni hora vite sue . et tene-
brosum in tartarum succedere .
   Istis terminis hec tellus ambita videtur . et cetera .

+Ego Eadpig rex Anglorum indeclinabiliter concessi . +Ego Eadgar
eiusdem regis frater consensi .

                                   +
+Ego Oda archiepiscopus cum signo sancte crucis roboraui .

                                   +
Ego Ælfsing presul sigillum agye crucis inpressi . +Ego Cenpald
episcopus consignaui . +Ego Oscytel episcopus confirmaui . +Ego
Osulf episcopus adquieui . et ceteri duces et ministri . ix .

   ᵃ Carta . . . lvj . *rubric*

This charter appears to be authentic. The dating criteria are consistent and the
formulas are characteristic of the period. The closest parallel is an original of
Eadred dated 948 (S 535; other charters by the same scribe have some similarities,
e.g. S 526); similar formulas are used in charters of Eadwig (S 582, 613), and
the anathema occurs in several charters of that period (S 600, 601, 620, 642, 645).
The witness-list is identical to that in **16**. The beneficiary does not occur in
other charters; for the name, compare the Maelsuðan who was a moneyer at
Chester in Edgar's reign (*Sylloge of Coins of the British Isles*, ii, nos 678, 739;
v, nos 93, 94, 107). *Mortun* cannot be firmly identified but it is possibly the
Morton in Derbyshire which Wulfric bequeathed to Burton Abbey (see above,
p. xxxii). If so this charter is a title-deed of one of Wulfric's estates that Burton
had a claim to.

16

King Eadwig grants five hides (mansae) æt Niwantune *to
Æthelgeard, his* karus. A.D. 956

B. Aberystwyth, N.L.W., Peniarth 390, fo. 176ᵛ (p. 352): copy, s. xiiiᵐᵉᵈ
Ed.: Birch 944
Listed: Sawyer 599

Carta Eadpig regis de Nipantune . dcccc . lvj . indictione . xiiij .ᵃ

✠ In nomine cosmi saluatoris et humani generis redemptoris Iesu
Cristi domini nostri qui solus cum patre et spiritu sancto regnum tenet
inmortale ¿ ego Eadpig disposicione gentis Angligene et diuersarum
nationum industrius rex vni meorum karorum quem cordetinusᵇ diligo

nomine Æðelgeard . v . mansas dedi illi ubi uulgariter dicitur æt Nipantune . Quamdiu hic corpus animatum habere videbitur nostri doni priuilegium sibi vendicet . et postero denique suo quemcumque elegerit perhenniter imperciat[c] . cum campis pascuis pratis siluis . Sit uero hec terra ab omni seculari negocio libera . excepta expedicione et pontis ac arcis constructione . Si quis uero hominum hanc meam donacionem cum stulticie temeritate iactitando infringere certauerit . sit ipse grauibus per colla depressus catenis inter flammiuomas tetrorum demonum catenas[d] . nisi prius hic ad satisfactionem venire maluerit . Istis terminis circumgirata asseritur ante scilicet supradicta terra . et cetera . Acta est hec prefata donatio anno ab incarnatione domini nostri Iesu Cristi . dcccc . lvj . indictione . xiiij .

+Ego Eadpig rex Anglorum indeclinabiliter concessi . +Ego Eadgar eiusdem regis frater consensi .

+

+Ego Oda archiepiscopus cum signo sancte crucis roboraui . et ceteri ut supra episcopi . duces et ministri .

[a] Carta . . . xiiij . *rubric* [b] *A spelling for* cordetenus [c] *A spelling for* imperceat [d] *An error for* cateruas

This charter appears to be authentic. The witness-list is the same as in **15**, also dated 956, and the indiction is right. The anathema occurs in several contemporary charters including an original of 949 (S 552) and an undated charter of Eadwig for Abingdon (S 663) which has other similarities, notably the clause introducing the bounds (which is also in an original of 956 (S 624)). An Æthelgeard *minister* was a frequent witness between 942 and 958 (from S 481 to 650) and was granted several estates in Hampshire and Berkshire in that period (S 463, 488, 523, 641, 1663; see Whitelock, *Wills*, p. 117). *Niwantun* cannot be identified with confidence but it is likely to have been the Newton in which Wulfric had 'a little estate' which he bequeathed to Burton Abbey (see above, p. xxix). This has been identified as Newton Solney in Derbyshire which was held T.R.E. by Earl Ælfgar and, with its berewick Bretby, was then assessed at 7 carucates (DB, i. 272b).

17

King Eadwig grants land at Darlaston, near Stone, Staffordshire, to Æthelnoth, minister. A.D. 956

B. Aberystwyth, N.L.W., Peniarth 390, fo. 176[v] (p. 352): ? copy of D, s. xiii[med]
D. Stafford, William Salt Library, 84/1/41: single sheet, parchment, s. xi², 230 × 360 mm.
    Endorsements: (1) by the scribe of the charter: +*Deorlafestunæs boc* :— *an hid æ[t] þan hame . oðer æt stapulforda* . (2) in a hand of s. xiii: *Anno ab incarnacione domini . dcccc . lvi . regnauit Ædwig* . (3) in a hand of s. xiii (?): *. dcccc . lvj* . (4) in a medieval hand: *XVII*
Ed.: a. Birch 954, from B
    b. Hart, pp. 172–9, from D

Listed: Sawyer 602
Printed from D with all variants from B except punctuation

✠ In*a* nomine domini nostri Iesv*b* Cristi . Omnibus quibus cristianitatis censuram a Dei arcipotentis poli per suam largifluam misericordiam concessum est . quod huius instantis labentisque uitæ*c* prosperitas totis nisibus restaurare perditos ac nefandos . per illius auxilium possumus ceu psalmigraphus ita fando dixit . initium sapientiæ*d* timor domini*e* . Quapropter . ego Eadƿig . rex Anglorum ac totius*f* Bryttanicæ*g* telluris gubernator et rector . cuidam meo fideli ministro quem nonnulli uocitant noto uocamine*h* . Æðelnoðe aliquam partem terrę*d* in loco qui dicitur . Deorlauestun . vt habeat ac possideat quandi*i* uiuat*k* . et post sé cuicumque uoluerit heredi derelinquat in æternam*l* hereditatem . Sit autem predictum*m* rús liberum ab omni mundiali obstaculo cum omnibus ad sé ríte pertinentibus . campis . pascuis . pratis . siluis . sine expeditione*n* . et pontis . arcisue*o* instructione . Si quis *autem**p* infringere temptauerit quod absit . sciat sé rationem redditurum coram Deo et angelis eius . nisi prius hic digna satisfactione emendare maluerit . Istis terminis ambitur prędicta*q* tellus . þis synd þa landgemæra to Deorlafestune ærest*r* hit fehð on trentan þær fulan bróc scýt*s* on trentan . þonne andlang broces ongean stream on fulanford . of ðæm forda*t* on bradan*u* ford . of bradan forda ƿest andlang stræte on hƿæte croft of ðæm crofte on grenan hylle of ðære hylle andlang slædes ꝥ hit cymð on þa*w* stræt*x* to þæm*y* ðrym landgemæran*z* . þonne andlang*aa* peges on ðære dic ende . of ðære díc on gerihtna*bb* to sceortan stane . of ðæm stane on ðone pylle*cc* . of þǽm pylle on fǽrdene . of ðære dene þæt eft on trentan .

    Hæc carta scripta est . anno dominicę*d* incarnationis . dcccclvi . indictione . xiiii .*dd*

+Ego Eadƿig rex Anglorum indeclinabiliter concessi .
+Ego Eadgar eiusdem regis frater*ee* celeriter consensi .
                   +
+Ego Oda archiepiscopus cum signo sancte crucis roboraui .
                   +
+Ego Ælfsinus pręsul sigillum agię crucis impressi .
+Ego Byrhthelm episcopus consignaui .
+Ego Cenpald episcopus adquieui
+Ego Oscytel episcopus subscripsi .*ff*
+Ego Osulf episcopus .
+Ego Byhthelm episcopus .
+Ego Aþulf episcopus*gg*
+Æðelstan   dux .
+Ælfhere   dux .
+Æðelsige   dux .
+Aþelpold   dux .
+Byrhtnoþ   dux .

+Ælfheah	mi*nister* .	
+Ælfsige	mi*nister* .	[hh]
+Ælfric	mi*nister* .	
+Ælfred	mi*nister* .	
+Ælfsige	mi*nister* .	
+Ælfnoþ	mi*nister* .	
+Ælfpig	mi*nister* .	
+Eadric	mi*nister* .	
+Byrnric	mi*nister* .	[ii]

[a] Carta Eadpig regis de Derlaueston . dcccc . lvj . indictione . xiiij . *rubric in* B
[b] Iesu B   [c] vite B   [d] -e B   [e] *Dr Lapidge comments: The formula* a Dei arcipotentis poli, *which occurs in several charters in this form, must originally have read either* a Deo arcipotentis poli *or* a Dei arcipotentis polo. *This opening sentence is very deficient in other respects*   [f] tocius B   [g] Brittanice . B   [h] vocamine B
[i] D; B *correctly reads* quamdiu   [k] viuat B   [l] eternam B   [m] predi*c*tum B
[n] expedicione B   [o] arcisve B   [p] D *uses the insular abbreviation for* autem; hoc B   [q] predi*c*ta B   [r] Derlauestone . Erst B   [s] scyet B   [t] forde B
[u] braden B   [w] þæ B   [x] stræte B   [y] þam B   [z] landgemæren B
[aa] andlan B   [bb] gerithna B   [cc] þylle B   [dd] . dcccc . lvj . indictione . xiiij . B   [ee] B *ends here* . et cetera . ut . supra . *with* ? *in the margin*   [ff] *First column of subscriptions ends here*   [gg] *This and the preceding two subscriptions form a second column, parallel with the last three in the first column, inserted under the longer subscription of* Ælfsinus   [hh] *Third column of subscriptions ends here*   [ii] *Fourth column of subscriptions ends here*

Description of D: Three horizontal and two vertical folds. Ruled with a stylus, prickings survive in left margin. Written area 210×315 mm. Written in Anglo-Saxon minuscule with little distinction between Latin and Old English. The long, short, and round forms of *s* are used throughout, and the last, which does not occur in the bounds, is unusually high. The *cc* form of *a* occurs and *e* has a prominent horn. Long *i* is used after *t*, medial tall *i* occurs once, in *eiusdem*, and *æ* occurs once with Caroline *a* in the bounds. The invocation is in uncials, uncial *G* is used in *Ego Eadpig* in the text and in the short second column of subscriptions. Capital *L* occurs in the place-name in both Latin text and endorsement. The insular abbreviation for *autem* is used. The elaborate chrismon, which is very similar to that in Eadwig's charter to Oda (S 646) and in a Winchester document (S 649), is in the margin and extends to the seventh ruled line. The crosses of the subscriptions have prominent serifs, and the first column of them, together with the *H* of *Hæc carta*, are in the left margin, in line with the vertical of the chrismon. B is probably a copy of D. There are only two variant readings that could be taken as evidence to the contrary: at note *i* B has *quamdiu* in place of the *quandi* of D, but that is plausibly a correction, and at note *p* B reads *si quis hoc infringere* where D has *si quis autem infringere*, a difference that is most reasonably explained on the assumption that the scribe of B misunderstood the insular abbreviation for *autem* in D. *Infringere* nevertheless needs an object and the *hoc* of B is probably correct. It is therefore possible that B and D are independently derived from a copy that read *si quis autem hoc infringere*. **26** is based on the same text but unfortunately MS. D is damaged at both these critical points, B reading *quamdiu* for the *quand*[. .] of D, and *si quis autem et cetera* where D has a hole large enough for an abbreviated *hoc* after *autem*. The chrismon of **17** D is carefully reproduced in B, and a similar form is given in **26** B where the single sheet, D, has a blank.

   The witness-list is consistent with the date and the proem occurs in an Abingdon charter granting land to a Wulfric in 951 (S 558). If the present charter had

only been preserved in a cartulary copy it could reasonably have been accepted
as authentic, despite the unusual absence of an assessment. The production
of such a careful 'facsimile' in the late eleventh century, with a chrismon of
a type used a century earlier and an endorsement is, however, most suspicious,
whatever the source of B. Even if B was not derived from D there is no reason to
believe that it came from an authentic original. Had an original of this charter
survived until the thirteenth century there would have been no need to produce
D, even less to do so in such an elaborate manner. Hart's discussion of this
charter, pp. 174–9, is based on the mistaken view that the script of D is mid-
tenth-century.

Burton Abbey had undisputed title to Darlaston, part of the original endowment which it retained until the Dissolution (see above, p. xxxi; in DB, i. 247b
it was assessed at 3 virgates), and this charter may have been produced to give
greater authority to the bounds which appear to be older. It was clearly based
on some authentic text which may also have served as the model for **26**. The
beneficiary, if he existed, would probably have been a local thegn who does not
occur elsewhere. He is unlikely to have been the Æthelnoth *minister* who was
a frequent witness in 947 and 948 and the beneficiary of charters dated 941 and
946 granting land in Somerset(S 476, 509). No witness of that name then appears
until the reign of Æthelred, although, according to an Abingdon charter dated
956, an Æthelnoth *minister* was granted land in Berkshire (S 603).

The bounds are in grammatically correct Old English and are unlikely to
have been compiled at the time the charter was produced. Separate bounds,
unconnected with a charter, were sometimes kept and it is possible that the
boundary clause of the present charter derives from such a set of bounds for
Wulfric's estate at Darlaston. Only two boundary points can be firmly identified,
the River Trent and Filly Brook(*ful broc*) which flows into the Trent at SJ 897
337. The *dic ende* is unlikely to have been associated with the great earthwork
of Bury Bank SJ 882 359 because there are too many boundary points between
that and the Trent; it may have been the end of the ditch that formerly ran
along the line of the new road in the vicinity of Blakelow, SJ 869 354. No Roman
roads are known in this area, but the street of these bounds may have been along
the line of the interrupted track that leads south-east from Swynnerton SJ 853
354. The Trent and Filly Brook were the boundaries of Darlaston township
in the Tithe Award and it is possible that the early boundary followed the same
general line for the whole of its length (S.R.O., SMS 417). According to the
endorsement this estate was assessed at 1 hide with another *æt Stapulforda* which
Hart, pp. 176–7, suggests was Stableford, five miles north-west of Darlaston.

18

King Eadred grants five hides(mansae) *at Austrey, Warwickshire,
to Wulfric, minister.* A.D. 958

B. Aberystwyth, N.L.W., Peniarth 390, fo. 177 (p. 353): copy, s. xiii[med]
Ed.: Birch 1021
Listed: Hart 54, Sawyer 576

Carta Eadredi regis Merciorum de Alduluestrep . dcccc . lviij . indictione . prima .[a]

✠ Cum fas licitumque deifico jure omni regio[b] habena vtenti esse liquet

hoc pro libito elidere posse malignos*c* . verum etiam arbitrio venerari
potius benignos ·' cur nostre curulas*d* sceptris perstringere non audeat
penna indissolubilia monimenta a nobis Deo auctore conserta . a quo et
dandi et possidendi facultatem oportunitatis id temporis exceptam Deo
gratias haurimus ·' Quocirca ego Eadred rex Merciorum diuina pro-
curante gratia ritu parentele*e* et pie et strenue exposcente . Albionis
monarchiam solus exercens cuidam mihi deuoto ministro Þulfrico
nomine . v . mansas in loco qui dicitur æt Alduluestreoþ in hereditatem
perpetualiter possidendam . et tradendam cui voluerit heredi . Soluimus
etiam idem rus omni iugo regali preter expedicione . pontis arcisve
reedificacione . Si quis uero hoc minuere temptauerit ·' sentiat dei
offensam ·' nisi satis emendet . Istis terminis et cetera . Acta est hec
donatio ·' anno dominice incarnationis . dcccc . lviij . indictione . prima .

+

+Ego Eadred rex Anglorum hanc meam donacionem sancte crucis signo
corroboravi .

+Ego Eadpig et Eadgar indoles hec confirmauimus . +Ego Oda archiepiscopus confirmavi . + . Ego Ælfæh episcopus . + Ego Cenpald
episcopus . + Ego Leoupine episcopus confirm*avi* . et ceteri duces . et
ministri . xv .

a Carta . . . prima . *rubric*　　　*b* *An error for* regia　　　*c* Eadred rex Merciorum
in margin in hand of uncertain date　　　*d* *An error for* curulis　　　*e* *An error for*
parentali

A spurious charter, possibly produced as a title-deed for Burton Abbey's estate
at Austrey. It purports to be a grant by Eadred but is dated 958 with the correct
indiction for that year. The description of Eadred as *rex Merciorum* suggests
that he has been substituted for Edgar, who was king of Mercia in 958.[1] The
witness-list, which includes Bishop Ælfheah, who died in 951, appears to have
been taken from a charter of 946–51, but charters of Eadred were normally
witnessed by Eadgifu, who is not listed here, and Eadwig and Edgar, who are,
do not appear in authentic texts until the end of Eadred's reign (Whitelock 1968,
p. 43). Austrey was bequeathed by Wulfric to Morcar's wife. In DB Burton
Abbey held 2½ hides there as a gift of Earl Leofric. Other tenants in chief were
Henry de Ferrers, who held 2½ hides, and Nigel de Albini, who held 5 hides and
3 virgates (see above, p. xxvii).

19

King Edgar grants ten hides (mansae) *at Hilmarton and Littlecott,
Wiltshire, to Wulfmær, minister.* A.D. 962

B. Aberystwyth, N.L.W., Peniarth 390, fo. 177 (p. 353): copy, s. xiii^med
Ed.: Birch 1081
Listed: Sawyer 707

[1] Cf. S 677. Professor Whitelock has, in a private communication, drawn my
attention to two charters in which Eadred's name has apparently been substituted for
Eadwig's; S 579, which is subscribed by Oscytel as archbishop of York, a title that
he does not use until after Eadred's death, and S 1662, in which Edgar's subscription,
ejusdem regis frater, is in the form normal in charters of Eadwig.

Carta Eadgari regis Anglorum de Helmerdigtun . dcccc . lxij .^a

+Regnante Theo imperpetuum architectorio qui sua ineffabili rite potencia omnia disponit atque gubernat . vicesque temporum . hominumque mirabiliter decernens . terminumque incertum prout uult equanimiter inponens . et de secretis celorum . glorie humaneque nature misteriis docet . vt cum hiis fugitiuis et eui cursibus transitoriis possesiunculis iugiter mansura Deo largiente fragilique nature consolacionis subleuamine adipiscenda sunt . Quapropter ego Eadgar rex Anglorum cuidam meo fideli ministro uocitato nomine Þulfmær in eternam hereditatem hilariter inpenderem . x . mansas in duobus locis ubi ruricoli antiquo vsu nomen imposuerunt . Helmerdingtun et æt Lytlacoton . vt ille bene perfruatur . ac perpetualiter possideat quamdiu uiuat . et post se cuicumque uoluerit heredi derelinquat . ceu supradiximus in eternam hereditatem . Sit autem predicta terra cum omnibus ad se rite pertinentibus libera . campis . pratis . pascuis . siluis . excepto istis tribus . expedicione . pontis arcisve constructione . Si quis uero quod non optamus contra nostrum hoc decretum machinari uel infringere aliquid uoluerit ? sciat se racionem grauiter redditurum in die iudicii ante tribunal domini . nisi prius hic digna emendauerit penitencia ante mortem . Istis terminibus predicta terra circumgirata esse videtur . et cetera . Anno dominice incarnationis . dcccc . lxij . scripta est hec carta . hiis testibus consentientibus quorum inferius nomina carraxantur .

+Ego Eadgar rex Anglorum corroboraui .
+Ego Dunstan archiepiscopus   confirmaui .
+Ego Oscytel archiepiscopus   consolidaui
+Ego Byrthelm   episcopus   corroboraui .^b
+Ego Osulf   episcopus   adquieui .
+Ego Aþulf   episcopus   non renui .
+Ego Æþelpold^c   abbas
et ceteri duces et ministri ? xviij .

^a Carta . . . lxij . *rubric*   ^b *First column of subscriptions ends here*   ^c +Eg Æþelpold *B*

This appears to be an authentic charter of Edgar. The witnesses are consistent with the date and the formulas are contemporary; the proem also occurs in an authentic charter of 964 from Romsey Abbey (S 727; it also occurs in S 448, 459, and the spurious 1214). A Wulfmær *minister* witnessed many of Athelstan's charters and another occurs, much less frequently, 986–1005 (Robertson, *Charters*, p. 386), but in the intervening period the name is rare. A Wulfmær *minister* subscribes charters in 959 and 972 (S 660, 786) and was granted land in Somerset in 973 (S 793). A Wulfmær *miles* of King Edgar is mentioned in the *Vita Oswaldi* as an ambassador to Otto II (J. Raine, *The Historians of the Church of York and its Archbishops* (Rolls Series, 1879), i. 435). The places named in this charter can be identified with confidence as Hilmarton and Littlecott in Wiltshire. The early forms of these names are very close to those in the charter and the identification is supported by the fact that Littlecott is a hamlet in Hilmarton parish (J. E. B. Gover, A. Mawer, and F. M. Stenton, *The Place-Names of Wiltshire* (E.P.N.S. xvi, 1939), pp. 268–9).

There is no evidence that Wulfric or Burton Abbey had any interest in these places. Wulfric and Wulfmær may have been kinsmen, and the charter may have been deposited at Burton by a member of the founder's family (see above, p. xli).

20

King Edgar grants three hides (cassati) æt Duddestone [? *Duddeston, near Birmingham*] *and three* æt Ernlege [? *Upper Arley, Worcestershire*], *to Wulfgeat, minister.* A.D. 963

B. Aberystwyth, N.L.W., Peniarth 390, fo. 177^{rv} (pp. 353–4): copy, s. xiii^{med}
Ed.: Birch 1100
Listed: Sawyer 720

Carta Eadgari regis de Ærnlege . dcccc . lxiij .^{a}

+Annuente altithroni moderatoris imperio tocius Albionis triuiatim potitus regimine non inmemor ob hoc mihi recidiua fore concessa vt hiis strenue eterna lucrarer ⁊ ego Eadgar rex Anglorum quandam ruris particulam duobus in locis diremptam . tres videlicet cassatos loco^b qui celebri æt Duddestone nuncupatur vocabulo . tres itidem æt Ernlege cuidam ministro mihi oppido fideli qui ab huiusce patrie gnosticis nobili Þulfget appellatur uocabulo pro obsequio eius deuotissimo perpetua largitus sum hereditate . vt ipse vita comite cum omnibus vtensilibus pratis videlicet^c pascuis . siluis voti compos habeat . et post vite sue terminum quibuscumque uoluerit cleronimis^d inmunem derelinquat . Sit autem predictum rus omni terrene seruitutis iugo liberum tribus exceptis rata videlicet expedicione pontis . arcisve restauracione . Si quis autem hanc nostram donationem in aliud quam constituimus transferre voluerit ⁊ privatus consortio sancte dei ecclesie æternis barathri incendiis lugubris iugiter cum Iuda Cristi proditore eiusque complicibus puniatur . si non satisfactione emendauerit congrua quod contra nostrum deliquit decretum . Hiis metis rus hoc giratur . et cetera .

Anno dominice incarnationis . dcccc . lxiij . scripta est hec carta hiis testibus consentientibus quorum inferius nomina notantur .

+Ego Eadgar rex Anglorum concessi
+Ego Dunstan archiepiscopus   corroboraui .
+Ego Oscytel archiepiscopus   confirmaui .
+Ego Osulf   episcopus   consolidaui .
+Ego Byrhthelm   episcopus   adquieui .^{e}
+Ego Eþelpold abbas . et ceteri duces et ministri . nouem .

^{a} Carta ... lxiij . *rubric* ^{b} *Read* in loco ^{c} r *in the margin against the line* videlicet pascuis ... cleronimis ^{d} *An error for* cleronomis ^{e} *The four episcopal subscriptions are set out in two columns*

The witness-list of this apparently authentic charter is consistent with its date,

963, and must have been before Æthelwold was elected bishop of Winchester, presumably some time before his consecration on 29 November in that year. The closest parallel is an original of the same date (S 717). Four other charters by the same scribe have been identified (S 687, 690, 703, 706), some with points of similarity with this text, e.g. two have the same anathema. The most interesting comparison is with S 706, dated 962, which, as far as the surviving text of **20** allows comparison, has an identical dating clause and witness-list, the only difference being in Beorhthelm's subscription with *consensi* in place of the present *adquieui*. This charter, like **20**, has nine *duces et ministri* after Æthelwold and it is therefore possible that they were granted on the same occasion and that the date of **20** is miscopied. Other closely related charters, which do not survive as originals, come from Wells and Abingdon (S 709, 722).

The beneficiary is probably the *minister* who regularly subscribed from 964 to 974 and who was a kinsman of Wulfrun (Whitelock, *Wills*, pp. 164–5). Wulfrun granted land at *Ernleie* to Wolverhampton and the bounds show this to be Upper Arley, Worcestershire, north of Bewdley; an estate held in DB by the church of Wolverhampton and then assessed at 2½ hides in comparison with the 3 of the present charter (S 1380; DB, i. 247b). As Professor Whitelock has pointed out, neither of the places in this charter is mentioned in Wulfgeat's will and, if the testator is the beneficiary of this charter, either his will must have been made before he acquired the estates or he disposed of them before making the will. *Æt Duddestone* has been identified as Duddeston near Birmingham, which is not named in DB. It is about twenty miles east of Upper Arley and the distance between them has been considered a reason for doubting the identification (J. E. B. Gover, A. Mawer, and F. M. Stenton, *The Place-Names of Warwickshire* (E.P.N.S. xiii, 1936), p. 32), but the charter clearly implies that they were separated.

21

King Edgar grants ten hides (mansae) *at Parwich, Derbyshire, to* Ælfhelm, *minister.* A.D. 966

B. Aberystwyth, N.L.W., Peniarth 390, fo. 177ᵛ (p. 354): copy, s. xiiiᵐᵉᵈ
Ed.: Birch 1175
Listed: Hart 107, Sawyer 739

Carta Eadgari regis de Peuerwich dcccc . lxvj .ᵃ

☧ In nomine Dei summi et altissimi Iesu Cristi . Nihil intulimus in hunc mundum . verum nec auferre quid possumus . quare de hiis que velud aporiatum peripsema contempnuntur . atria vite emenda sunt . vbi cum beatis celicolis eternis gaudiis natura nostre humanitatis Cristo triumphante extat feliciter coniungenda ⫶ ac sine metu deifice amenitate contemplacionis iugiter perfruenda . Quapropter ego Eadgarus tocius Albionis dei disposicione regni fastigium optinens cuidam mihi dilecto ministro qui a gnosticis scibili Ælfhelm appellatur onomate quandam telluris particulam . x . videlicet mansas animo libenti concedo in eo loco qui Anglica relacione Peuerpich appellatur . quatinus ille hanc hereditaria libertate voti compos possideat sue vite diebus . et post se

D

cuicumque sibi placuerit heredi derelinquat . Sit autem predictum rus omni terrene seruituti[b] iugo liberum et cetera ut supra . Si quis igitur hanc nostram donacionem euertere studuerit ꝛ sancte Dei ecclesie priuatus et cetera ut supra . Hiis metis rus istud percingitur . Anno dominice incarnationis . dcccc . lxvj . Scripta est hec cartula . hiis testibus consencientibus quorum hic nomina visuntur .

+Ego Eadgar tocius Anglice nationis basileos hanc donacionem libenter confirmaui .

+Ego Dunstan Dorobernensis ecclesie archiepiscopus subsigillaui+

+Ego Oscytel Eboracensis ecclesie archiepiscopus subscripsi .

+Ego Eadperd clito ꝛ	adnotaui .
+Ego Ælfryð eiusdem regis coniux ꝛ	roboraui .
+Ego Æþelpold episcopus	karessi .
+Ego Ælfstan episcopus	confirmaui .
+Ego Osulf episcopus	consignaui .
+Ego Ospold episcopus	consolidaui .
+Ego Alfpold episcopus	supposui .[c]
+Ego Byrhthelm episcopus	pretitulaui .

+Ego Æspig abbas

+Ego Orgar[d] abbas

+Ego Ælfstan abbas

+Ego Ordbyrht abbas

+Ego Æþelgar abbas .[e]

et ceteri duces et ministri ꝛ vndecim .

---

[a] Carta . . . lxvj . rubric   [b] Error for seruitutis   [c] First column of subscriptions ends here   [d] Error for Osgar   [e] Second column of subscriptions ends here

This charter has some suspicious features. The witnesses are consistent with the date but are a remarkably ill-balanced assembly for such a grant, with eight bishops, five abbots, and eleven others. The only authentic charter to include both Edward clito, who was then about four years old, and Ælfthryth is Edgar's refoundation of New Minster, a grant of great importance made in the same year, 966 (S 745). This charter could have been granted on the same occasion but the form of the royal subscription is not found in other charters of Edgar (it would have been more appropriate in the time of Æthelred) and the verbs in the episcopal subscriptions are unusually varied, including some that were not used in other charters of Edgar. The royal title is also unique, its nearest parallel being an authentic charter of Edgar for Abingdon which also quotes the same passage from 1 Tim. 6:7, although in a slightly different form (S 689). The chrismon is very similar to the form used in three authentic charters of 961–2 (S 690, 703, 706). Hart, pp. 107–8, considers that despite the idiosyncrasies of this charter there are no grounds for suspecting its authenticity.

The grant purports to be of 10 hides in Peuerwich which Sir Frank Stenton reasonably suggested was Parwich in Derbyshire (Stenton 1910, p. 73), an estate that was Terra Regis in DB when it was the head of a manor with 3 berewicks and was assessed at 4 hides (DB, i. 272b). An Ælfhelm minister is a fairly frequent witness in the third quarter of the tenth century and two acceptable charters dated 970 and 972 have two Ælfhelms (S 781, 786). An Ælfhelm bequeathed land in and near East Anglia (S 1487) including a Cambridgeshire estate granted to him in 974 (S 794). The area covered by that will suggests that it was another Ælfhelm who was granted land at Witney in 969 (S 771) and he may have been the purported beneficiary of this charter. If the Ælfhelm for whom this charter was made, apparently in Æthelred's reign, was Wulfric's brother, its presence in the Burton archive, and the later royal owner-ship of Parwich, would be explained.

22

King Edgar grants thirteen hides (cassati) *at Breedon,* Wifeles-thorpe, Ætheres dune [? *Atterton*], *and Diseworth, Leicester-shire, to Æthelwold, bishop, for the church at Breedon.* A.D. 967 *[for 972]*

B. Aberystwyth, N.L.W., Peniarth 390, fos 177^v–178 (pp. 354–5): copy, s. xiii^{med}

Ed.: Birch 1283

Listed: Hart 37, Sawyer 749

Carta Eadgari regis de Breodune facta cuidam episcopo dcccc . lxvj .^{a}

+ Nobilita[. . .]^b mundane fastigium semper inhiat cupiditatibus . gaudet honoribus . inflatur occursibus . rapinis pascitur . calumpniis delectatur . rubiginosi auri talenta desiderat . ingeritque ei congeries auri ּ׃ sitim ardua^c possidendi . sicut Prudentius agit^d . Auri namque fames parturit^e maiorum^f ab auro . Vnde fit ut dum gaudet pompis seculi et vanis honoribus oblectari ּ׃ nichil ei de mansuris dignitatibus in memoriam reuocetur nec respicit ad ea que non videntur . dummodo illa que satiari animum putat inoportune possideat . Quapropter ego Eadgarus tocius Brittannie basileos quedam^g ruris particulam . xiij . videlicet cassatos in loco qui celebre^h Æ[t] Breodone nuncupatur voca-bulo cuidam episcopo nomine Æþelpaldo mihi fidelissimo largitus sum hereditate ut vite sue diebus voti compos possideat . et post vite sue terminum sacri ordinis virorum quocumque^i voluerit ^{k}in munere^k derelinquat . Nullus successorum meorum ipsius terre portionem ab ecclesia dei que in Breodone sita est numquam presumptuosus auferat . Et est autem predicta tellus hiis locis compta . iij . videlicet cassati æt Æbredone . et . iij . æt ÞifelesÐorpe^{lm}. æt Æþeredes dune . iiij . scilicet æt Digþespyrþe . Sit autem predictum rus cum certis ac cognitis terri-toriis omni terrene seruitutis iugo liberum tribus exceptis ratum videlicet expeditione pontis arcisve constructione . Si quis autem hoc donum fastu superbie inflatus in aliud quam constituimus transferre uoluerit ּ׃ priuatus a consortio sancte ecclesie eternis baratri incendiis lugubriter deputetur . si non satisfactione emendauerit congrua quod contra decre-tum satagerit nostrum .

Anno ab incarnatione domini . dcccc . lxvij^n . hec donatio facta est . hiis testibus consentientibus quorum inferius nomina carraxantur .

+Ego Eadgarus rex prefatam donacionem signo crucis corroboraui .

+Ego Dunstan Doruernensis ecclesie archipresul consensi et subscripsi .

+Ego Oswald archiepiscopus consensi et subscripsi .

+Ego Æþelpald episcopus corroboraui hanc prefati regis donationem .

+Ego Ælfstan episcopus confirmaui .

+Ego Alfpald episcopus conscripsi.*o*

+Ego Osgar abbas

+Ego Æþelgar abbas

+Ego Cynepered abbas

+Ego Ordberht abbas

+Ego Freoþegar abbas*p*

et ceteri duces et ministri decem .

<ul>
<li>a Carta . . . lxvj . rubric   b Read Nobilitatis   c An error, perhaps for ampla</li>
<li>d Spelling for ait (cf. 25, note e). The quotation is from Hamartigenia 257   e Error</li>
<li>for parto fit   f Error for maior   g Error for quandam   h For celebri</li>
<li>i Error for cuicumque; cf. no. 24   k . . . k Error for immunem; cf. no. 24</li>
<li>l Þifeles Ðorpe   m iij with caret in hand of uncertain date; 3 inserted in</li>
<li>modern hand above the line in the text   n Error for . dcccc . lxxij .   o The</li>
<li>first column of subscriptions ends here   p The second column of subscriptions ends</li>
<li>here</li>
</ul>

This authentic, but misdated, charter is a good example of Æthelwold's prac-
tice of obtaining the sites of former monastic houses, no doubt with a hope of
restoring them.[1] The formulas are typical of the period although the proem is
unparalleled and the anathema does not occur elsewhere in this form (cf.
S 702, 706, 716), but such originality would not be surprising in a charter for
Æthelwold. The witness-list includes Archbishop Oswald and cannot therefore
be right for 967. This date is probably a mistake for 972; the identifiable witnesses are consistent with that date. Hart, pp. 69–70, suggests that the correct
date was 974 because of the occurrence of Freothegar who he claims succeeded
Osweard as abbot of Evesham no earlier than 974 (pp. 335–6). The only evidence for an Abbot Freothegar at Evesham is the Evesham Chronicle in which
his appointment by Ealdorman Ælfhere is clearly associated with the anti-
monastic reaction after Edgar's death. This is not a satisfactory basis on which
to identify the witness in this charter as abbot of Evesham in Edgar's reign.
Sir Frank Stenton (*V.C.H. Leicestershire*, i. 316, 349) suggested that the lands
granted in this charter formed part of the post-Conquest Leicestershire manor
of Tonge, and they may have been the lands *æt Twongan* which Wulfric bequeathed to Æthelric for life, with reversion to Burton Abbey (see above,
pp. xxvii–viii).

[1] This suggestion has been made, in a private communication, by Professor Whitelock, who has drawn attention to Æthelwold's acquisition of Barrow upon Humber
(S 782, D. Whitelock, 'The Authorship of the Account of King Edgar's Establishment
of Monasteries', *Philological Essays . . . in Honour of Herbert Dean Meritt*, ed. James L.
Rosier (The Hague, 1970), pp. 125–36). Æthelwold also acquired another Mercian
estate, *Madanlieg* (S 801), which is shown by the boundary point *in wriman ford* to be
Madeley, near Newcastle, Staffordshire, cf. W. H. Duignan, *Notes on Staffordshire
Place-Names* (1902), and *DEPN*, *s.n.* Wrinehill (in Madeley parish), but there is no
evidence for an earlier religious community there.

23

King Edgar grants one hide (unum mansas) *at* Stantun [? *Stanton by Newhall, Derbyshire*], *to Wulfric, bishop.* A.D. 968

A. Stafford, William Salt Library, 84/2/41 : original, parchment, 300 × 240 mm., damaged by folding
   Endorsements : (1) by the scribe of the charter : Þulfrices boc bisc̄ æt stan tune á on ece erfe . (2) in a hand of s. xiii : dcccc . lxviij . indictione . xjᵃ . (3) in a hand of s. xiii : *Santon'*. (4) in a hand very similar to 3 : *Santoñ* (5) in a medieval hand : *XXIII*. (6) in a hand of s. xviii : *Stantn A boundrye*
B. Aberystwyth, N.L.W., Peniarth 390, fo. 178 (p. 355) : copy of A, s. xiiiᵐᵉᵈ
Ed.: a. Birch 1211 from B
      b. Hart, pp. 179–86, from A
Listed : Sawyer 768
Printed from A with main variants from B

℞ Inᵃ nomine Dei summi Cuncta que in hoc seculo temporaliter uersantur . sine ullo respectu articulo omnibus horis atque momentis properanter ad finem festinant . et tunc sine fine inreuocabilia permanebunt . Quapropter ego Eadgar rex Anglorum ceterarumque gentium in circuitu persistentium gubernator et rector . dedi cuidamᵇ uni meo episcopoᶜ nuncupato uocamine Þulfric unum mansas agelluli in illo loco ubi uulgari nomen inposuerunt Stántun . quatenus habeat ac perpetualiter possideat quamdiu uiuat . et post se cuicumque uoluerit iste exenium derelinquat in æternam hereditatem . Sit autemᵈ predictum rús liberᵉ ab omni mundiali obstaculo cum omnibus ad se rite pertinentibus campis . pascuis . pratis . siluis . excepto communi labore expeditione pontis . arcisuæ coedificatione . Hæc kartula karaxataᶠ . est . anno ab incarnatione domini nostri Iesu Cristi dccccº lxº viiiᶜᵍ . indictione uero xiº .

+Ego Eadgar rex hanc meam donationem sabulo glorioso roboraui
+Ego Dunstan archiepiscopus consignaui
+Ego Oscetel archiepiscopus inpressi
+Ego Æðelpald episcopus consensi
+Ego Osulf episcopus confirmauiʰ
+Ego Þulfric episcopus conclusi
+Ego Ospald episcopus subscripsi
+Ego Ælfstan episcopus roboraui
+Ego Þynsige episcopus inpresiⁱ .
+Ælfere dux
+Æþelstan dux
+Ælfheah dux
+Æðelpine dux
+Berhtnoð dux
+Eanulf discifer

+Ælfpine discifer
+Þulfstan discifer[k]
+Æðelsige   pedisecus
+Þulfric   minister
+Æðelm   minister
+Þulfgár   minister
+Þulfsige   minister
+Ælfhelm   minister
+Þulfmær   minister[l]

I*am* sequitur istius ruris terminatione[m] ærest of alde píc þ spa[.]n myra hoh . of myra hoh in ðæt dæl þ spa on æðeredes . hoh . of æðeredes h[oh] in þ dæl . of ðæm dæle in spines hoh þ spa 7long dæles þ in ðone stanegan fórd . of þæm fórda 7long broces þ eft in þ alde píc. ðis send ðara tpegra hida gemæro ðe Þulfric biscop hafað ane hide . oðer hafað Ælfnað Si quis uero filargyrie spiritu inflatus hanc meam munificentiam pro deo datam infringere ausus fuerit . sit anathema ab omnipotenti deo et a congregatione omnium sanctorum . nisi hic cum satisfactione digne deo et hominibus emendauerit . Pax perpetue prosperitatis augeatur coram Cristo . sanctorum patrocinio patrocinante .

---

[a] Carta Eadgari regis de Stantun dcccc . lxviij . indictione . xj . *rubric in* B   [b] duidam B   [c] m *erased before* episcopo A   [d] hoc B   [e] A; liberum B, *correctly*   [f] cartula karraxata B   [g] v *written over* i A   [h] *The first column of subscriptions ends here in* A;   [i] *The first column of subscriptions ends here in* A; *the second column of subscriptions ends here in* B; B *ends here* et ceteri duces . disciferi . pedissequi . et ministri quindecim .   [k] *The second column of subscriptions ends here in* A   [l] *The third column of subscriptions ends here in* A   [m] *Error for* terminatio

Description of A: Two horizontal and three vertical folds. Ruled with a stylus; evenly spaced ruling for text and anathema, closer spacing with some irregularity in subscriptions and bounds. Two bounding lines to left, no prickings survive. Written area 270 × 255 mm.

The script is an idiosyncratic square Anglo-Saxon minuscule with a number of archaisms. In the Latin *d*, *f*, and *g* are insular; *e* is always horned, *a* and *c* occasionally, *l* usually descends below the ruled line; the bow and tail of *r* are sharply articulated as in the uncial *r* of insular majuscule, while round *r* occurs twice after *o*; *s* is normally round with a clumsy lower bow but short insular *s* does occur, mainly in ligatures, and *y* is straight. Ligatures after *e* are common and include *ec* and *eþ*. Capital *Q* occurs twice; uncial *G* is found once, in the donor's name. The script of the Old English bounds is distinguished only by the use of ð, þ, p, *f*-shaped *y*, the long and short forms of insular *s*, and the absence of round *s*. Abbreviations include the insular symbol for *autem*, *miniĩ* for *minister*, and .*e*. once for *est*. ꝺ- used in the subscriptions for *con-*. The chrismon is unusual and is very similar to that occurring in a late medieval copy of a charter of Burgred of Mercia, dated 862 (S 209; *O.S.F.* ii. Bodleian). It is in an indented space on the first two lines, its vertical is on the inner bounding line, and it appears to have been drawn before the text was written. The crosses of the subscriptions are simple, and in the first column are on the inner bounding line.

This has been judged on palaeographical grounds to be contemporary with the date of the charter and despite the errors—*unum mansas* and the altered date—it is probably an original. The script has some archaic letter forms which, with the chrismon, suggest that it was in part modelled on a ninth-century exemplar. The formulas are appropriate for a charter of Edgar's reign and the witnesses are consistent with the date. The word *discifer* is used in Edgar's reign (S 597, 651 and, wrongly expanded by Birch as *discipulus*, 782). Professor Whitelock has suggested that the beneficiary, Wulfric, was bishop of Hereford (Whitelock 1955, p. 514). He does not occur often but subscribes from 958 to 970 (S 677–777; in S 838 Kemble misread Wulfsige as Wulfric).

The estate has been identified as Stanton by Newhall, Derbyshire (*PN Derbyshire*, pp. 659–60), apparently because Burton Abbey later owned a carucate there as part of its holding in Stapenhill (see above, p. xlvi). None of the boundary points can be positively identified but the modern parish boundary of Stanton and Newhall agrees very well with the boundary in the charter. Beginning with *alde wic* to the west of Stanton House at SK 256 197, *myra hoh* would be the ridge between Stanton and Stapenhill on which the modern boundary turns at SK 270 216. The next spur, *æðeredes hoh*, would be the ridge north of Newhall where the modern boundary crosses the Burton–Ashby road at SK 292 216 and the following *dæl* would be the steep valley to the east where the modern boundary turns at SK 313 213 and *swines hoh* would be back on the ridge, possibly near SK 301 209. The modern boundary then drops to the southwest into the valley west of Swadlincote and later follows a stream, possibly the *broc* of the charter, from SK 278 194 to 258 193. Stoney Dale at SK 285 198 may be no more than a coincidence and have no connection with the stony ford of the charter. These bounds are stated to describe 2 hides of which Wulfric had one. The same estate is probably the subject of **1**. It is possible that Bishop Wulfric was a member of Wulfric Spot's family. Hart, pp. 185–6, suggests that the bounds agree well with those of the modern parishes of Stanton in the Peak and Birchover, Derbyshire, but acknowledges that none of the names of boundary points can be identified. The possibility that **1** refers to the same estate and Burton's later interest in Stanton by Newhall are reasons for preferring the identification proposed here.

24

King Æthelred grants three hides (cassati) *at Brighthampton, two at Aston Bampton, and one at Lew, Oxfordshire, to Ælfwine,* minister *and* scriptor. A.D. 984

B. Aberystwyth, N.L.W., Peniarth 390, fo. 178^{rv} (pp. 355–6): copy, s. xiii^{med}

Ed.: Hart, pp. 187–92

Listed: Sawyer 853

Carta Æþelredi regis totius Albionis de Byrhtelmingtun^a . dcccc . lxxxiiij^b

+✠ Regnante domino nostro Iesu Cristo inperpetuum^c . qui ante mundi constitucionem decem angelorum agmina mirifice collocauit . decimaque^d post per superbiam cum suo Lucifero in barathrum voraginis elapsis^e ʒ nouem in sua stabilitate misericorditer conseruauit . quique decimam^f adimplere cupiens postquam celum terramque conderet ፦ hominem ex limo terre formauit . formatumque prothoplastum serpentinus liuor ad mortem usque perduxit . omneque humanum genus post illum . et quando dei inmensa misericordia hoc perspexit . condoluit . vnicumque filium suum mittens satum de intemerata virgine Maria per crucis mortem omne humanum genus piissime redemit . Qui assidue nos sacro precio mercatos admonet vt iugiter intenta mente meditemus qualiter in hanc erumpnosam vitam deuenimus . vel quali fine iterum hinc redire oporteat . quia ut beatus Iob ait . nudi egressi sumus de vtero matris . nudi iterum in terram matrem omnium ire debemus . Ideo pernecessarium est vnicuique ut ex caducis et deficientibus istius mundi diuiciis eternas indeficientesque diuitias lucretur . Hiis et aliis quampluribus exemplis roboratus ego EÐelred diuina concedente gratia rex et monarchus tocius Albionis aliquam portiunculam ruris . videlicet . sex cassatos in communi tellure diremtis[g] . iij . scilicet ubi gnostici vocitant Byrhtelmingtum . ij . ubi a ruricolis nuncupatur æt Eastun . i . uero situm in loco qui dicitur æt Hlæpe cuidam mihi oppido dilecto fidelique ministro videlicet meo scriptori qui a notis noto Elfpine nuncupatur vocabulo pro eius amabili humilique obsequio quo iugiter instanter deseruit in sempiternum condono . ut vita comite teneat eternamque in hereditatem possideat cum omnibus que ad se rite pertinent . videlicet campis . pratis . pascuis . Cum uero dei prouidente gratia de hoc volubili mundo migrauerit ፦ cuicumque sibi placuerit cleronomi inmunem per omnia derelinquat . Hoc uero meum donum firmum perseueret . et ab omni seculari seruicio firma libertas permaneat . tribus exceptis causis que ab omnibus notissime constant . Si quis hanc . meam donacionem amplificare uoluerit ፦ hic presentem vitam illi augeat dominus et in futuro perpetuam in terra viuentium . quod si aliquis aliter quod absit inflatus diabolica temeritate aliquid in hoc dono minuere uel mutare satagere nisus fuerit ፦ sciat se a sanctorum omnium consortio esse exortem . nisi prius fauente Dei gratia emendauerit . Hec autem scedula carraxata est anno dominice incarnationis . dcccc . lxxxiiij . indictione . xij . Hiis testibus consentientibus subscribentibusque quorum vocabula inferius scripta cernuntur .

+Ego EÐelred rex Anglorum huius donacionis libertatem regni tocius fastigium tenens libenter concessi .

+Ego Dunstan archiepiscopus Doruernensis ecclesie cum signo sancte semperque adorande crucis roboraui .

+Ego Ospaldus Eboracensis ciuitatis archipresul crucis taumate confirmaui .

+Ego Ælfstanus	episcopus	consignaui .
+Ego Æðelgar	episcopus	consolidaui .
+Ego Æscpig	episcopus	adquieui .
+Ego Aðelsige	episcopus	adnotaui .
+Ego Þulfgar	episcopus	corroboraui .[h]
+Ego Sigegar	episcopus	faui .

+Ego Ælfric episcopus inpressi .[i]
+Ego Ælfeah episcopus subscripsi .
+Ego Æðulf episcopus conclusi .[k]
et ceteri duces sex . abbates : iiij[or] . disciferi : iiij[or] . pincerne . iiij[or] . ministri . vndecim .

[a] *Altered from* Byte- [b] Carta . . . lxxxiiij *rubric* [c] *Altered from* imperpetuum [d] *Read* decimoque [e] *Read* elapso [f] *An error for* decimum [g] *Error for* diremtos [h] *First column of subscriptions ends here* [i] in *written over an erasure* [k] *Second column of subscriptions ends here*

There is no reason to doubt the authenticity of this charter. Its formulas are characteristic of the early part of Æthelred's reign, the witnesses are consistent with the date and the form of their subscriptions may be compared with those in an original dated 987 (S 864). The places named appear to have been part of the great royal estate of Bampton from which other grants were made by Eadwig to Bampton minster (*O.S.F.* ii, Exeter 16) and by Edgar to Brihtnoth (S 911, cf. *V.C.H. Oxfordshire*, i. 375 n., 378). Aston is not named in DB but Brighthampton was divided between at least two fiefs and assessed at 7½ hides; Lew belonged to another fief and was assessed at 1½ hides (DB, i. 154b, 156a, 157b, 161a). Ælfwine is not otherwise known but the importance of this charter as evidence for a royal *scriptor* was emphasized by Sir Frank Stenton (1971, p. 353).

25

King Æthelred grants twelve hides (mansae) æt Æsce *to Æthelsige,* minister. A.D. 987

B. Aberystwyth, N.L.W., Peniarth 390, fos 178[v]–179 (pp. 356–7): copy, s. xiii[med]
Ed.: Hart, pp. 193–6
Listed: Sawyer 863

Carta Æþelredi regis tocius angligene gentis de Æsce . dcccc . lxxxvij . Indictione . xv .[a]

☧ Annuente Dei patris ineffabili humane proli clementia qua adnullata primi terrigene piaculo noue restauracionis admirabile quoddam mundo decus eterne consortem maiestatis filium suum misitare[b] dignatus est . qui terrene fragilitati custodite[c] per uirginei pudicitiam flosculi affatu angeli virginis claustra subintrans noue incarnacionis misterium se ostentando dedicauit . ostendens se dictis uerborum factisque miraculorum quibus deifice pollebat dominum . curans omnium imperanti sermone egrotationum pondus . tandem quadrati pro nobis ferens supplicia ligni iugum hereditarie mortis absumens . diu longeque interdicte reserauit limina porte . Pro cuius inenarrabilis glorie recordatione[d] ego Æðelredus gratia Dei sublimatus rex et gubernator tocius angliene[e] gentis . aliarumque gentium in circuitu persistentium cuidam meo fideli ministro vocitato nomine Æðelsige pro sua humilissima deuocione quandam telluris particulam . xij . videlicet mansas largiendo libenter concedens perdonabo . illic ubi colones antiqui ita nuncupando nomen indiderunt æt Æsce . vt habeat ac perhenniter possideat quamdiu viuat in eternam hereditatem . et post se cuicum*que sibi placuerit inmunem derelinquat ceu supradiximus in eternam possessionem . Si quis igitur hanc nostram donacionem in aliud et cetera . Sit autem predictum rus . istis terminibus et cetera . Anno ab incarnatione domini . nostri . Iesu Cristi . dcccc . lxxxvij . indictione . xv . scripta est hec cartula et cetera ut supra .

+Ego Æðelred rex Anglorum huius donacionis libertatem regni tocius fastigium tenens libenter concessi .

+Ego Dunstan archiepiscopus Doruern*ensis* . ecclesie cum*ᶠ* signo sancte crucis confirmaui .

+Ego Ospold archiepiscopus Eborace ciuitatis crucis taumate adnotaui .

+Ego Ælfstan episcopus consensi .

+Ego Ælfeh episcopus adquieui .

+Ego Æðelgar episcopus consolidaui .

+Ego Æscpyᵍ episcopus inpressi .

+Ego Æðelsige episcopus roboraui .

+Ego Sigeric episcopus non renui .

+Ego Ælfpold episcopus conclusi . et ceteri duces . abbates et ministri . viginti et vnus . [1]

ᵃ Carta . . . xv . *rubric*   ᵇ *A spelling for* missitare   ᶜ *A verb such as* condolens *has fallen out here*   ᵈ '*Two*'-*shaped* r *after* o *altered to long* r   ᵉ *A spelling for* angligene, *showing OE palatalization of intervocal* -g- (*for a related example, cf.* **22**, *note d*)   ᶠ c *is written over* s   ᵍ Ærcpy

[1] After Oswald the episcopal subscriptions are arranged in three columns of two. Contemporary charters suggest that these columns were intended to be read in turn, as here. Ælfwold's subscription, printed last here, is written on the same line as Oswald's, above the third column, and it is therefore possible that it should come before Æthelsige. I am indebted to Mr Simon Keynes for drawing my attention to this point.

This charter appears to be authentic. The witness-list is consistent with the date, the indiction is correct, similar formulas are found in other charters of the same date (S 866, 867). Æthelsige *minister* is a frequent witness from 979 to 994 but he does not occur after that, suggesting that he was the Æthelsige who fell out of favour at that time (he subscribes S 883, dated 995, but Professor Whitelock (1955, p. 525) has shown that this date is probably wrong). Wulfric himself acquired land at Dumbleton in 995 by exchange with Hawas who had obtained it after its forfeiture by Æthelsige for theft (S 886) and in a charter of 998 Æthelred restored to Rochester land at Bromley that had been taken from the church at the instigation of Æthelsige who had killed the king's reeve (S 893). Neither Wulfric nor Burton Abbey had any interest in a place called Ash. It has been identified as Ash in Derbyshire but that was assessed in DB at 2 carucates (DB, i. 274b), in contrast to the 12 of this charter. As the Burton archive included charters for places in Oxfordshire and Wiltshire, this place need not have been in the Midlands. One possible identification is Ash in Hampshire, assessed in DB at 8 hides (DB, i. 47a), but in the absence of bounds no identification can be made with any confidence.

26

King Æthelred grants land at Bedintun [*Pillaton, Staffordshire*]
to Wulfric, minister. A.D. 996

B. Aberystwyth, N.L.W., Peniarth 390, fo. 179 (p. 357): copy of D, s. xiii^med
D. Stafford, William Salt Library, 84/3/41: single sheet, parchment, s. xi², 150 × 540 mm., damaged by folding
   Endorsements: (1) by the scribe of the charter: + *Bedintunes boc* (2) in a hand of s. xiii: *Ethelredus regnauit anno ab incarnacione domini . dcccc . xciij . Endentones boc .* (3) in a medieval hand: *XXVI*
Ed.: Hart, pp. 196–200
Listed: Sawyer 879
Printed from D with some damaged letters supplied from B and 17 MS. D

^aIn nomine domini nostri Iesu Cristi . Omnibus quibus cristianitatis censuram `a´ Dei^b . arcipotentis poli per suam^c largifluam misericordiam concessum est . quod huius [ins]tantis^d labentisque uitæ prosperitas nisibus restaurare perditos ac nefandos . per illius auxilium possumus . ceu spalmigraphus^e ita fando dixit . Initium sapientiæ timor domini^f . Quapropter . ego Æðelred . rex Anglorum ac totius Brittanicę telluris gubernator et rector . cuidam meo fideli ministro quem nonnulli uocitant noto uocamine . Þulfric . aliquam^g partem terre . in loco qui dicitur Bed`i´ntun . ut habeat ac possideat . quamdiu^h uiuat . et post sé cuicumque uoluerit heredi derelinquat, in æternam hereditatem . Sit autem predictum^i . rus liberum ab^k omni mundiali obstaculo cum^l omnibus ad sé ríte pertinentibus^m . campis . pascuis . pratis . siluis . sine expeditione . et pontis . arcisue instructione . Si quis autem [. .]^n infringere temptauerit quod absit . sciat se rationem^o redditurum coram Deo et angelis eius . nisi prius hic digna satisfactione emendare maluerit.^p Istis terminis ambitur prædicta tellus^q Her^r sutelat þa landgemæru into Będintun .

Þ is ærest to berhtelmes treo . 7 spa forð to mearðes s[ca]ge . 7 spa forð ofer þa blace`le´ge to sproges forda . of sproges forda . andlang þǽs broces to gáte brycge . 7 of gate brygce into spompes næpe . 7 of spompes hnæpe into sceddern þorn . 7 of sceadder þorn ofer þæne mor into þā sur æppeltreo æt þære nearapan sætan . 7 fram þære nearapan sætan . in þæne holgan bróc æt þulfgares more . 7 spa forð andla`n´ges þæs broces forð þ hit cymð to þam stanian forda . 7 of þā stanian forda andlang þæs sices þ hit cymð to þam smæle æcels . 7 þanone to þam blacan hale . 7 þanone in þone broc . 7 spa forð andlangas þæs broces forð þ hit cymð to hryxies mæne peig . 7 þanone oð þ hit cumð to godrices lea . 7 of godrices lea to pulstanes forda . 7 þanone oð þ hit cymð under þære blacan ecge to þære srtæte . 7 ofer þa stræte . eft in [ber]htelmes treo:-
Hic^s bellus^t caraxatus est anno incarnationis dominice . d . cccc . xc . ui^u . indictione . ix . his^w testibus consentientibus quorum nomina inferius annotantur :·^x

+Ego Æðelred rex Anglorum hoc nostrum donum fir[m]a ratione roborare curaui .

*y*Ego Ælfric Dorouernensis æcclesiæ archiepiscopus . signum sanctę crucis imposui . Ego Ealdulf Ęboracensis æcclesię archiepiscopus . consensi . Ego Ælfheah Þintoniensis*z* episcopus . iussu domini mei annotaui*aa*. Ego Þulfstan Lundoniensis æcclesię episcopus assensum prebui . Ego Ælfheah Licetfeldnensis æcclesię episcopus adquieui . Ego Æscpig Dorcensis æcclesię episcopus . subscripsi . Ego Ordbriht*bb* Australium Saxonum æcclesie episcopus . titulaui . Ego Goduuine episcopus . Ego Ælfðryð mater regis . Ego Æþestan filius regis . Ego Ecgbriht*cc* filius regis . Ego Eadred*dd* filius regis . Ego Ælfsige . abbas . Ego Ælfpeard . abbas . Ego Þulgar . abbas . Ego Byrhtelm*ee* abbas . Ego Leofric abbas . Ego Byrhtnoð abbas . Ego Kenulf abbas*ff* . Ego Æðelpard . dux . Ego Ælfric dux . Ego Leofpine . dux . Ego Leofsige . dux . Ego Æðelm[.]er minister . Ego Ordulf minister . Ego Æðelmær minister . Ego Bryhtpold . minister . Ego Æðelric . minister . Ego Æðelpard . mi[nister] . Ego Leofpine . minister . Ego Goduuine . minister .

a Carta . Æpelredi regis de Bedintun . dcccc . xciij . indictione . ix . facta Þulfrico . *rubric in* B; *blank space for chrismon* D; ✠ B   *b* censurimus Dei B   *c* sitam B   *d* [. .]tantis D; perstantis B; instantis **17** *MS*. D   *e* psalmigraphus B, *correcting* D's *error*   *f* B; [. .]omini D   *g* B; a[. .]quam D   *h* B; quand[. .] D; cf. **17** *MS*. D quandi   *i* B; aute[. .]rædictum D   *k* et cetera ut supra . Si quis autem et cetera . B   *l* **17** *MS*. D; [. .]m D   *m* **17** *MS*. D; pertinentib[.]s D   *n* D *is damaged along a vertical fold, the missing parchment being space for about two letters. For other consequences of the same damage see notes d, f, g, i*   *o* **17** *MS*. D; ration[. .] D   *p* infringere . . . maluerit . *omitted in* B   *q* B; a[. . . . .]r predicta t[. . .]us . D   *r* et cetera *in place of bounds* B   *s* B *resumes here*   *t* libellus B   *u* *Altered from* . d . cccc . xi . D; dccc . xciij . B   *w* Hiis B   *x* consentientibus . . . annotantur : · *omitted in* B   *y* B *supplies a cross before each episcopal subscription*   *z* B *adds* ecclesie   *aa* B; m[. . .]nnot[. . .] D   *bb* Orobriht B   *cc* Ægbriht B   *dd* Ædred B   *ee* Byrchelm B   *ff* B *ends* et ceteri duces et ministri duodecim .

Description of D: Two horizontal and three vertical folds. Ruled with a stylus, single bounding lines in both margins. No prickings survive for horizontal lines, one prick for bottom of left bounding line. Written area 130 × 530 mm.

The handwriting—impure Caroline minuscule for the Latin; Anglo-Saxon minuscule for the Old English—is similar to that of **28**. In the Latin text insular *a*, *d*, and *s*, long, short, and round, are normal but Caroline forms also occur as does the *cc* form of *a*. Round *r* is used after *o*, and insular *f*, *g*, and *r* are used throughout, with one occurrence of Caroline *g* in *mater regis*. *k* occurs in the subscriptions. The Old English bounds were written by the same scribe with a finer pen, and are distinguished by the use of þ, ð, p, the absence of Caroline *a*, *d*, and *s*, the use of horned *e*. ð has a long, slightly sinuous ascender, tagged on the left, similar to the form in **28**. The invocation and place-name are in uncials, the *g* of *digna* in the anathema is a capital while the other letters of that word are uncials, capital *G* is frequent in the subscriptions, and capital *Q* is used three times in the text. The layout is most unusual; the subscriptions are not in columns and there is only one cross, before the king's subscription. A blank space is left for the chrismon by the indentation of the first three lines.

There are many similarities between this spurious charter and **17**. The boundary clause is in good Old English and is unlikely to have been compiled when the charter was produced in the second half of the eleventh century and the bounds describe an estate that was given to Burton Abbey by Wulfric and retained by it until the Dissolution. The motive for producing this text was probably the same as that suggested for **17**, to lend some authority to an authentic set of bounds that had hitherto been unattached to a charter. The text, down to the boundary clause, is identical with **17** and the witness-list is taken from **27**. The date has been altered and seems originally to have been 911 although possibly 1001 was intended. The layout of the charter is unusual. The chrismon, which is not found in the single-sheet version, is supplied in Peniarth 390 from **17** or its source, cf. p. 29. The misreading of *censurimus Dei* for *censuram a Dei* shows that B derives from D in which the *a* inserted above the line *censuram* `a` has been mistaken for the abbreviation *-us*, and the *cc* form of *a* in the ligature *ra* has been read as *ri*. According to DB the abbey held ½ hide at *Beddintona* which the twelfth-century Surveys describe as at *Bedintona et Pilatehala* and which survives as Pillaton near Penkridge (see above, p. xxix).

The bounds, which include many names of great interest, cover an area that has been greatly affected by modern developments, but a remarkable series of estate maps prepared in 1754 makes it possible to locate several points (S.R.O., D 260/M/E/353 a). *blacelege* is probably Blakelees Cross at SJ 967 140 where the modern boundary comes to a very marked point; *swompes hnæpe* may be Snapes, a field at SJ 935 123, still a marshy area; the *mor* may be preserved in Broad Moor which in 1754 is shown north of Moor Hall cottages SJ 936 131; *wulfgares mor* was Wolgaston Moor; *holgan broc* is presumably the brook that flows across this Moor from Quarry Heath and in 1754 there was a stony ford in this stream at SJ 946 137.

27

King Æthelred grants three hides (cassati) *at Abbots Bromley, Staffordshire, to Wulfric,* minister. A.D. 996

A. Stafford, William Salt Library, 84/4/41: original, parchment, 285 × 460 mm., damaged by folding and bad repairs
   Endorsements: (1) in a hand of s. xiii: *Ethelredus Rex . Wlfrico Bromleg'* .
   (2) in a medieval hand: *XXVII*
B. Aberystwyth, N.L.W., Peniarth 390, fo. 179ʳᵛ (pp. 357–8): copy of A, s. xiiiᵐᵉᵈ

Ed.: Hart, pp. 201–7

Listed: Sawyer 878

Printed from A with main variants and some damaged letters from B

✠ Pollente*ᵃ* perpetualiter domini nostri Iesu Cristi regno . Huius instabilitas uitae fortuitis atteritur*ᵇ* casibus . ac uariis uilescendo meroribus . terminum sue commutabilitatis iamiamque praesignat affuturum ⸴ ut ueritatis praesagio prędicta eius*ᶜ* multiforma*ᵈ* malorum iacula electorum corda non ad desperationem seu tedium diuini amoris peruertant*ᵉ* ⸴ uerum etiam ad desideria regni celęstis . et ad piae deuotionis famulatum magis magisque acuant ⸴ iuxta illud dominicum . His autem fieri incipientibus respicite^f et leuate capita uestra ꝫ quoniam appropinquat redemptio uestra . Huiusmodi diuini documenti oraculis pręmonitus ego Aeðelred^g rex Anglorum . cuidam meo fideli ministro a populis Þulfric apellato . quandam ruris trium scilicet cassatorum in loco quem accolę uicini æt Bromleage^h cognominant partem impendo ꝫ ut ipse dum sospitatem uitae habuerit illam sibi in usum necessarium sicut mater ei largita est uoti compos optineat ꝫ et post uitae suae terminum cuicumque sibi placuerit relinquat superstiti . Consistat autem suprascripta tellus ab omni seruitute secura . tribus exceptis . expeditione . arcis . pontisue constructione^i . Qui uero nostrum hoc^k donum euertere laborauerit ꝫ timeat se in profundo auerni inmersum aeternaliter torqueri: nisi quantotius a sua peruersitate discedat . Attamen si quislibet antiquum siue nouum protraxerit libellum . et hanc nostram titulationem superare nisus fuerit . binis mortis^l periculis obiurgetur obnoxius . quia aut rapina . aut furto illum subdole adeptus est . Huiusmodi terminis prędicta tellus circumducitur . Of ðam lytlan hlapan to þan longan snapan on ða stræte forþ æfter strete oð cume to þan readan ácon 7 ðær ðpers ofer ða puda þæt cyme in pire broces heafde 7 æfter pire broc ðæt hit gæþ in bliðe up æfter bliþe oð hit cyme in ceabbe broc æfter broce þæt cume in ðan forde from ðan forde æfter þære strete þeligeð cumb pelle léa oð cume on þa grene pege 7 forð æfter grene pege oð hit cymeþ æft to ðan lytlan laupan . ðus hit hæfde eadelm 7 ælfred 7 æþelpold spa spa hit^m Þulfsige ðé blaca 7 æscbryht^n hit geærdeden heom . Hic libellus caraxatus est anno incarnationis dominice . dcccc^o . xc^o . ui . indictione^o ix . his testibus consentientibus quorum nomina^p inferius annotantur .

+Ego Æþelred rex Anglorum hoc nostrum donum firma ratione roborare curaui .

+Ego Ælfric Dorouernensis^q ęcclesiae archiepiscopus signum^r sanctae crucis imposui .

+Ego Eadulf Eboracensis ecclesię archiepiscopus consensi .

+Ego Ælfæah Þintoniensis ecclesie episcopus iussu domini mei annotaui .

+Ego Uulfstan^s Lundoniensis ecclesie . episcopus assensum prebui .

+Ego Ælfheah Licetfeldensis ecclesie　　episcopus adquieui .

+Ego Æscpig Dorcensis　　ecclesie　　episcopus subscripsi .

+Ego Ordbryht Australium Saxonum ecclesie　　episcopus titulaui .

+Ego Godpine Hrofensis　　ecclesie　　episcopus non restiti .

+Ego Alfpold Cridiensis ecclesie　　episcopus confirmaui .^{t}

+Ego Uulfsige^u Scireburnensis ecclesie episcopus inpressi .^{w}

+Ego Sigar Uuyllensis　　ecclesie　　episcopus nil[. . . . .]sui .^{x}

+Ego Ealdred Cornubiensis ecclesie　　episcopus corroboraui .^{y}

+Ego Sigeferð　　　　episcopus dignum iudicaui .^{z}

+Ego Aðulf Herefordensis ecclesie　　episcopus consolidaui .^{aa}

+Ego Aelförið mater regis .^{bb}

+Ego Æþestan fil[ius re]gis .
+Ego Ecgbyrht fili[us] regis .
+Ego Eadmund filiu[s] regis .
+Ego Eadred filius regis .

+Ego Ælfsige	abbas
+Ego Ælfpeard	abbas .
+Ego Uulfgar	abbas .
+Ego Byrhtelm	abbas .
+Ego Leofric	abbas
+Ego Byrht[	]bbas .
+Ego Keanulf	abbas
+Ego Æþelric	[a]bbas
+Ego Aeþeluueard	[. .]x .
+Ego Ælfric	[d]ux .*cc*
+Ego Leofþine	dux .
+Ego Leofsige	dux .
+Ego Æþelmær	minister .
+Ego Ordulf	minister .
+Ego Æþelmær	minister .
+Ego Byrhtþold	minister .
+Ego Æþelric	minister .
+Ego Æþelpeard	minister .
+Ego Þulfpeard	minister .
+Ego Leofpine	minister .
+Ego Leofpine R	minister .
+[E]go Siperd	minister
+Ego Sired	minister
+Ego Godpine	minister
+	*dd*

a Carta Æþelredi regis facta Þulfrico de Bromleg' . dcccc . xciij . *with last minims altered to* uj . *rubric* B   *b* B; fortui un[. . .]teritur A   *c* B; [. . .]s A   *d* Error for multiformia   *e* B; peruer[.]ant A   *f* B; respi[.]ite A   *g* Eðelred B   *h* æt Bromlege B   *i* B *substitutes* et cetera . *for* expeditione . . . constructione .   *k* hoc nostrum B   *l* B; mort[.]s A   *m* B; spa spa [. . . .] A   *n* Ærcbriht B   *o* B; indict[. .]ne A   *p* B; nomi[. .] A   *q* The ou has been repaired upside down A   *r* B; archi[. . . . . .]num A   *s* Þulfstan B   *t* B; co[.]fi[.]-maui A   *u* Þulfsige B   *w* B; ecclesie [   ] A   *x* Wyllensis ecclesie episcopus . B   *y* B; corr[. . . .]aui A   *z* B; dig[. . . .]udicaui . A   *aa* B; consol[.]daui . A; *the first column of subscriptions ends here* A   *bb* B; AelfÐdryÐ [   ]s . A; B *ends here* et ceteri filii regis ut supra . et ceteri abbates . viij . duces . iiij . et ministri . xij .   *cc* The second column of subscriptions ends here   *dd* The third column of subscriptions ends here

Description of A : Three horizontal and three vertical folds. Ruled with a stylus, single bounding line to left. Written area 265 × 430 mm. The Latin and Old English scripts are clearly distinguished; the Latin is Caroline minuscule, the Old English is Anglo-Saxon minuscule with rounded *y* and, normally, short insular *s*, but round and long forms are also used, the latter once initially. Capitals **are** used for *EGO . EÐELRED* in the text and for some initials, e.g.

H, N. R. The beneficiary's name is in insular script and the place-name in Caroline. In the subscriptions *EGO* and some names, viz. the name of the first *dux*, the title of the first abbot, the first names in the second and third columns and the last two names, are in rustic capitals. The names of witnesses are normally in Anglo-Saxon minuscule and their titles in Caroline, but there is some confusion, e.g. insular *r* in *rex*, and insular *d, r,* and short *s* in *dorouernensis.* In the Latin the *punctus elevatus* is used. The chrismon is a plain, but bold, *chi rho* and the first five lines of text are indented to make room for it. The crosses in the subscriptions are simple, the first column being in the margin. There is space for another column of subscriptions. The absence of a contemporary endorsement is noteworthy.

This charter is probably authentic. It is palaeographically acceptable, the indiction is right for 996, and the witness-list is consistent with that date. It includes Wulfstan who became bishop of London in 996 and Sigar of Wells who died on 28 June 998. Sigeferth is presumably the bishop of Lindsey who otherwise attests from 997 to 1004, making this his first appearance. The fact that he alone is given no see in this charter may reflect some uncertainty on the part of the drafter about its temporary revival. The note after the bounds about Wulfsige the Black's former ownership of part of Bromley is consistent with the grant made to him in 942 (**5**) and taken with the statement in the charter that Wulfric's mother had held the estate (*sicut mater ei largita est*) supports the suggestion that Wulfric and Wulfsige were related (see above p. xl).

Bromley formed part of Wulfric's endowment of Burton Abbey and in DB the abbey held ½ hide there while 3 hides at Bromley were *Terra Regis* and had been held by Earl Harold (DB, i. 246, 247b). These two estates clearly correspond to the two places Abbots and Kings Bromley. They were already separate at the time of this charter for the bounds certainly describe Abbots Bromley. *Pire broc* is Pur Brook, which also occurs in the bounds of **11**, and the boundary point *in pire broces heafde* is unusually precise. The modern boundary of Abbots Bromley parish (Tithe Award Map in Lichfield Diocesan Record Office) follows Pur Brook from its source at SK 105 275 almost to its confluence with the Blithe. As in the charter the southern boundary is formed by that river (*bliþe*). The western boundary is formed by Tad Brook which is probably the *ceabbe broc* of the charter. The northern boundary is not so well marked but the street may be represented by the straight stretch of boundary from SK 081 294 to 092 292. According to the charter this estate was assessed at 3 hides which suggests that the DB assessment of ½ hide had been greatly reduced, or that there was some confusion between the two parts of Bromley.

The reference to the possibility that old or new deeds might be produced and the mention of rapine or theft may mean that Wulfric or his family had lost some of their charters. This may explain why Burton Abbey needed to produce charters for two of the estates given by Wulfric, Darlaston and *Bedintun*, **17, 26.** It is curious that the bounds of the present, authentic, charter are not in as careful Old English as those of **17** and **26.**

28

King Æthelred confirms the endowment of Burton Abbey and grants privileges. A.D. 1004

B. Aberystwyth, N.L.W., Peniarth 390, fos 179ᵛ–180ᵛ (pp. 358–60): s. xiii^med.
    Endorsements 1, 3, 2 on fo. 181ᵛ (p. 362)

C. London, British Library, MS. Loans 30, fos 8–9: copy from same exemplar as B, s. xiii[1]. Endorsements 1, 2 on fos 9ᵛ–10

D. Burton upon Trent Museum, Burton Muniment 1: single sheet, parchment, s. xi[2], 520×385 mm., damage mainly due to folding. For endorsements see pp. xxxiv–viii

E. Cambridge, Corpus Christi College, 111, pp. 278–9: copy of ? s. xvi

F. London, British Library, Cotton Vespasian E iii, fo. 4: incomplete copy, s. xiii

G. London, British Library, Harley 358, fos 40ᵛ–41: copy of D, s. xvi

H. London, British Library, Lansdowne 447, fo. 28ᵛ: incomplete copy of B, s. xvii

I. Oxford, Bodleian, Dodsworth 38, fos 25–26ᵛ: incomplete copy of D, s. xvii

K. Oxford, Bodleian, Dugdale 11, fos 9–10: claims to be from C but Latin text comes from D, although C was apparently used for the list of estates and for endorsement 1, s. xvii

L. Oxford, Bodleian, James 25, pp. 163–4: incomplete copy of C, s. xvii

Ed.: a. *O.S.F.* iii, Anglesey 2 (facsimile, transcript and translation) from D
b. Whitelock, *Wills*, pp. 50–1, endorsement 1, with translation, from D
c. Kemble 710 from *Mon. Angl.*
d. *Mon. Angl.* iii, pp. 39–40 from K
e. Luard, *Annales Monastici*, i. 183 from F

Listed: Hart 40, Sawyer 906

Printed from D with main variants and better readings from B and C.

Damaged parts of D are indicated by square brackets and the missing letters supplied from B and C. Illustrative readings are given from other versions.

Postquam[a] malesuada ueneniferi serpentis suggestio primum generis humani parentem inuida fraude uetiti[b] seduxit edulio pomi . mortis continuo sententia huiusque uitę erumnosa ipsi prot[ho]plasto opponitur peregrinatio[c] . unde et in posteros mortifere cumulus dampnationis ob multiplices iniquitatum exercitationes a Deo excreuit . ut totius [a]dinuentor malitię diabolus ab ipsius quo prediximus radice originis totam ferme sibi hominum[d] progeniem diuina permissione et culpa exigente ad pęnas consociaret gehennales . eius túmidę ab initio satellitumque[e] conspirantium preparatas elationi . donec unicus ęterni patris uerbigena substantiam dolens perisse quę suę ymaginabitur similitudini . mysterio secretiori in ultima sęcli aetate uirginea sésé carne uelaret . ac uerus deus uerusque homo inter homines sine peccati macula in persone conuersaretur unitate . idque supernum consilium inimico in tantum celebatur . ut ipsum gula . uana gloria . auaritia . quibus armis primum[f] prostraret[g] hominem adgredi non diffideret . autumans ipsum qui totius bonitatis fons caputque est laqueo inique posse inretiri preuaricationis . sed sacre testimonio scripturę tertio ab ipsa transuerberatus ueritate vmbras denuo uictus repedat infernales . hac[h] nostre auctori salutis mox famulatus adfuit angelicus . Hisque omnibus ita ut diximus humanitatis exactis . Iesus sancto refertus pneumate . sapientia ę[t]ate . proficiens et gratia medicamenta restaurationis humane tali protinus proposuit institutione . poenitentiam inquiens agite . appropinquabit enim regnum celorum . Haecque et alia

E

suę documenta pietatis multiplicium dignatus [est]^i confirmare signis^k
miraculorum . cęcos inluminando . surdis auditum reddendo . mutis
loquendi officium . mancis manuum utilitatem . claudis gradiendi pos-
sibilitatem . paraliticis menbrorum integritatem . leprosis cor[po]ris
emundationem lunaticis ^{l}demoni'acis'sque sensum^l mentis . mortuis
uitam . uiuis uiam uitę huiusmodi sententi[is rese]rando . C[urrite dum
luc]em habętis . ut ^{m}uos tenebre non comprehendant^m . Verumptamen
hostis insidiis antiqui infidelium corda Iudęorum inter hęc omnia ob-
duruerunt . ut ipsum mediatorem^n dei et hominum post illata probra
ac flagella cruci adfigere animo non metuerent cęcato . qui tamen
corpus animatum tert[ia die incorruptibile] uictor resumpsit et in-
mortale^o . discipulisque palpandum clausis exhibuit^p ianuis . quadra-
ginta inter eos crebrius illis apparendo conuersatus ymeras . illisque
adstantibus et intuentibus die quadragessimo cęli petiit habitacula col-
locans se cum nostre carnis substantia^q in paterni^r dextera throni .
angelis^s hęc uerba apostolis^t pronuntiantibus . sic ueniet quemadmodum
uidistis eum euntem in cęlum . De quo sui aduentus die ita ipse per^u
prophętam . dies inquid ille . dies [i]re . dies calamitatis et miserię . dies
tribulationis et angustię . dies tenebrarum et caliginis. dies nebule^w et
turbinis . dies tube et clangoris . Tanti siquidem f[or]midine diei^x
adtactus . et tam districto^y iudici plac[er]e gestiens . ego . Æþelred rex
Anglorum offero ipse^z domino nostro Iesu Cristo libertatem monasterii
cuiusdam uulgari usu . æt Byrtun . appellatur . ut sit [s]emper cum
omnibus quę sibi subiacent . villulis . prędiis . campis . siluis . pratis .
pascuis . aquarum decursibus piscationum hostiis et cunctis neces-
sitatis humane utensilibus eterna securitate liberrimum ut illud no[bil]is
progeniei minister . Þulfric^{a2} . extruxit . et exstructum^{b2} collegio in-
stituit monachico . dominium loci et in eo habitantium męę regali com-
mittens dominationi . habeatque abbas uocabulo . Þulfgeat^{c2} . qui ad hoc
ordinatus . est . primus . liberam facultatem interius exteriusque sub
mea dicione illud gubernandi postposito cuiuslibet alterius hominis
dominio . Hęc uero libertas huius priuilegii annotatione [ide]o robora-
tur . quatenus in ipso loco eiusdem quo^{d2} prediximus ordinis familia
iugiter regulari more sub abbate tunc sibi prelato iuxta 'regulam'
militans sancti Benedicti^{e2} adgregetur . spesque prescripti ministri qui
hoc Cr[isto] contulit monasterium . per puram in ipso habitantium
conuersationem sanctamque eorum intercessionem . ad cęlestium re-
munerationem erigatur diuitiarum . Verum si quispiam altioris inferio-
risvae persone h[unc] locum deuastare uel quisquam ex eo abstrahere .
seu minuere aut in seruitutem studuerit redigere . tribus tantummodo
exceptis expeditione scilicet . arcis . pontisue constructione^{f2} . sciat se
a cęlesti alienari^{g2} [gloria] et gehennalia subire tormenta . vbi uermis est
non moriens . et ignis indeficiens . dentiumque stridor [int]olerabilis .
^{h2}ni citius a sua resipiscat^{i2} prauitate . E contrario siquis hoc donum
quod Cristo offertur aug[ment]are uoluerit . nouerit cęlestia se

recipere pręmia . vbi Cristus omnia in omnibus . dies sine nocte . lux
inde[f]iciens . claritas sempiterna . vita perpętua . gloria ineffabilis .
requies ęterna[h2] . gaudium sine fine . Haec autem[k2] sunt nomina uilla-
rum . quę pręfatus minister ipsi sancto deuotissime subegit monasterio:-
Ærest Byrtun þe þ mynster onstent . 7 Strættun[l2] . 7 Bromleage . 7
Bedintun . 7 Gageleage[m2] . 7 Þitestun[n2] . 7 Langanford[o2] . 7 Styrcleage[p2] .
7 Niþantun æt þære pic . 7 Hpædedun[q2] . 7 oðer Niþantun[r2] . 7 Þines-
hylle . 7 Suðtun . 7 Tycenheale[s2] . 7 þ æt Scenctune . 7 þ æt Halen . 7
Remesleage . 7 þ æt Sciplea . 7 þ æt Suþtune[t2] . 7 þ æt Actune[u2] tpegra
manna dæg ealspa þa forepord sprecað 7 þ æt Deorlafestune . 7 Lege
mid eallon þan ðe[w2] þær to hereð[x2] . 7 Hilum[y2] . Ácofre mid eallon þam
þe þærto hereð[z2] . 7 Bregdesheale[a3] . 7 Mortun . 7 eal seo socne[b3] þe
þær[c3] to hereð[d3] . 7 Pyllesleage[e3] . 7 Taþapyllan[f3] . 7 Æppelbyg[g3] .
7 þ æt Burhtune . 7 æt Þesttune[h3] . 7 þ æt Þicgestane . 7 þ æt Scearnforda . 7 þ æt 'Ealdes' purðe[i3] . 7 þ æt Ælfredingtune[k3] . 7 þ æt Þaddune .
7 þ æt Snódespic 7 þ æt Þynnefelda . 7 þ æt Oggodestune[l3] forð inn
mid Mortune . 7 þ æt Hereburgebyrig . 7 þ æt Ecclesheale[m3] . 7 þ æt
Suðtune . 7 þ æt Morleage[n3] .
Scripta[o3] siquidem est huius libertas priuilegii anno ab[p3] incarnatione
Cristi [q3] . millesimo . iiii[to] . indictione . ii[a] . horum testimonio sapientum
quo[rum n]omina inferius annotata esse cernuntur .
Ego Æþelred rex Anglorum hoc donum perpętua ditaui libertate .
Ego Æþelftan[r3] filius regis .
Ego Ecgbyrht[s3] filius regis .
Ego Eadmund[t3] filius regis .
Ego Eadred[u3] filius regis .
Ego Eadpig[w3] filius regis .
Ego Eadgar[x3] filius regis .[y3]

Ego Ælfric . archi .	episcopus composui .
Ego Þulfstan[z3] . archi .	episcopus conclusi .
Ego Ælfheah .	episcopus consignaui .[a4]
Ego Ælfhyn[b4] .	episcopus consensi .
Ego Lyuuingc[c4] .	episcopus condixi .
Ego Æþeric[d4] .	episcopus confirmaui .
Ego Ælfhelm .	episcopus corroboraui .
Ego Ordbyrht[e4].	episcopus assensi .
Ego Godpine .	episcopus adquieui .
Ego Ælfgar .	episcopus adunaui .
Ego Godpine	episcopus affirmaui .
Ego Sigeferð[f4] .	episcopus auxiliatus sum .[g4]
Ego Ælfpardus[h4] .	abbas .
Ego Ælfsinus[i4] .	abbas .
Ego Þulfgarus	abbas .
Ego Keanulfus[k4] .	abbas .
Ego Ælfsinus .	abbas .

Ego Germanus .	abbas .
Ego Godemannus .	abbas .
Ego Þulfricus .	abbas .
Ego Leofricus[l4] .	abbas .
Ego Bryhtpoldus[m4] .	abbas .
Ego Eadred[n4] .	abbas .
Ego Ælmær .	abbas .[o4]
Ego Ælfric .	dux .
Ego Ælfhelm[p4] .	dux .
Ego Leopine[q4] .	dux .
Ego Æþelmær	[ministe]r .
Ego Ordulf .	m[inister]
Ego Þulfgeat[r4] .	minist[er]
Ego Þulfheah[s4] .	minister .
Ego Þulfstan[t4] .	minister .
Ego Styrr[u4] .	minister .
Ego Morkare .	minister .
Ego Fræna[w4] .	minister .
Ego Æþeric[x4] .	minister .[y4]
Ego Æþelmær[z4] .	minister
Ego Ælfgar .	minister
Ego Aþelpold[a5] .	minister .
Ego Ulfcytel[b5] .	minister
Ego Eadric .	m[ini]st[er]
Ego Godric .	m[inister][c5]
Ego Godpine .	minister
Ego Æþelpeard[d5] .	minister
Ego Ælfgar .	minister
Ego Leofpine[e5] .	minister
Ego Byrhtere[f5] .	minister
Ego Leofpine[g5] .	minister
Ego Ælmær[h5] .	minister[i5]

[a] Carta Wlfrici Spoti Monasterii Burthoniensis fundatoris . *rubric* C; *chrismon in* B; P *omitted and space left for chrismon in* D   [b] B, C, H; fraude uenti D, G, I, K   [c] B, D, H, K; peregrinando C   [d] C, D; humanam B   [e] B, D; satellitumque sibi C   [f] C, D; B *omits* primum   [g] B, D, K; prostrauerat C   [h] C, D; ac B   [i] B; C *omits* est   [k] C, D; signius B   [l · · · l] demoniisque obsensum *altered by another hand to* demon'iacis'que sensum D; demoniisque obsessum C; demoniisque sensum B; demoniacisque obsensum I   [m · · · m] B, C; non tenebre uos conpraehendant D, I, K   [n] B, C; medicatorem D, I, K   [o] B, D; immortale K; mortale C   [p] B, D; C *omits* exhibuit   [q] C, D; substantiam B   [r] B, C; paterna D   [s] L *begins here*   [t] C, D; angelis B   [u] B; *omitted* D   [w] B, C; nubule D   [x] C, D, L; die B   [y] B, C, L; districtio D   [z] ipso C, D; ipsi B   [a2] C; Wlfric B, D   [b2] B, D; instructum C, L   [c2] C; Wlfgeat B, D   [d2] ? *an error for* quem (*or* quoad)   [e2] C; iuxta sancti militans Benedicti B, D, K   [f2] L *ends here*   [g2] B, C; aligenari D (*for this spelling, cf. no.* **25**, *note e*)   [h2 · · · h2] ni citius . . . requies eterna . *omitted* B   [i2] D, K; resipiscat a sua C   [k2] B, D; autem *omitted* C   [l2] C, D; Strætton B   [m2] C, D; Gagesleage B   [n2] C, K; Þites[.]un D;

Ƿitestan B [o2] D; Langeford B; Laganford C, K [p2] C, D; Styrclege B [q2] D; Ƿædedun B, C, K [r2] C, D; Nyƿantun B [s2] D; Ticenheale B, C [t2] D; Suðtune B, C [u2] B, C; A[ ]tune D [w2] B, C; þ[.] D [x2] D; hyrð B, C [y2] C, D; Hylum B [z2] D; þa*m* ðe ðer into hyrð B; þa ðe ðar into hyð C [a3] D; Brægdesheale B, C [b3] D; socna B, C [c3] D; ðer B; ðær C [d3] C, D; herð B [e3] D; Pillesleage B, C [f3] D; Taðeƿyllan B; Taðaƿyllan C [g3] D; Æppelby C; Appelbi B [h3] C, D; Ƿestone B [i3] D; Ealdƿyrðe B; Ealdesƿyrðe C [k3] D; Ælfredincgtune B, C [l3] D; Oggedestune C, K [m3] D; Eccleshale B, C [n3] D; Morlege B, C [o3] B, C; Sripta D [p3] B, C; ab *omitted* D [q3] B, D; domini nostri Iesu Cristi C, K [r3] D; Æþelstan B, C, F [s3] D; Ecgbrith B; Ecgbryht C [t3] D; Ædmund B, C, F [u3] D; Ædred B, C [w3] D; Ædƿig B, C [x3] B, D; Ædgar C [y3] *The first seven subscriptions are written on one line in* D *and are not arranged in columns* B *and* C [z3] D; Ƿulstan B; Ƿlfstan C [a4] Cant' Ebor' Lych' *in the margin of* B *against the first three episcopal subscriptions* [b4] D; Ælfhun B, C; Ælfhim F [c4] D; Lyuuing B, C [d4] D; Æþelric B, C [e4] D; Ordbryht B, C [f4] C, D, F; Sigeferd B [g4] *The first column of subscriptions ends here* D; *in* C *this subscription is followed by a blank line and the remaining subscriptions are arranged in two columns* [h4] D; Ælƿeardus B, C [i4] C, D; Ælfƿinus *with* ƿ *over an erasure* B [k4] C, D; Koeanulfus B [l4] C, D; Lefricus B [m4] D; Byrthƿoldus B; Byrhƿoldus C [n4] C, D; Edred B [o4] *The second column of subscriptions ends here* D; *in* C *this subscription is followed by a blank line* [p4] C, D; Ælfelm B [q4] D; Lefƿine B; Leofƿine C; *this subscription is followed by a blank line in* C [r4] B, D; þulfgeat C [s4] B, C; *altered to* Ƿulfheah *from* Ƿulfheoh D [t4] B, C; Ƿulstan C [u4] D; Styrs B, C [w4] C, D; Freona B [x4] D; Æþelric B, C [y4] *The third column of subscriptions ends here* D [z4] D; Æþelmer B, C [a5] D; Æþelƿold B; Æþelþold C [b5] C, D; Ulfcetel B [c5] *This subscription omitted* B, C, K [d5] C, D; Æþelƿerd B [e5] D; Lefƿine B, C [f5] D; Byrthere B; Byrthere *altered from* Brithere C [g5] D; Lefƿine B, C [h5] D; Ælmer B, C, K [i5] *The fourth column of subscriptions ends here* D

Description of D: Damage mainly due to folding. Three vertical and five horizontal folds. Ruled with a stylus on the dorse, no prickings. The left margin is cut down to the edge of the written area, which measures 510×385 mm. **29** follows on the same sheet. Both texts and endorsement 1 were written by one scribe whose hand is very similar to that of the scribe of **26**. The Latin text is in Caroline minuscule but with occasional insular features: insular *r* occurs once and *e* is often horned. A round *r* is used after *o*, *y* is rounded and capital *Q* occurs initially and in the abbreviation *Q;* for *-que*. The ligatures include *ra*, with the *cc* form of *a*, and a distinctive *rt*. The list of estates, the names of witnesses, and the will (**29**) are in Anglo-Saxon minuscule in which rounded *s* occurs especially in the subscriptions, and *ð* has a long, slightly sinuous ascender, tagged on the left, similar to the form in **26** MS. D. The names of the king, Wulfric, and Abbot Wulfgeat are in coloured rustic capitals. Rustic capitals are also used for the invocation and valediction of the will and for the *Sic Fiat* of endorsement 1. Initials are alternately in red and blue.

For the endorsements, see pp. xxxiv–viii.

29

The Will of Wulfric. A.D. 1002×1004

B. Aberystwyth, N.L.W., Peniarth 390, fos 180v–181v (pp. 360–2): copied from the same exemplar as C, s. xiii^med

C. London, British Library, MS. Loans 30, fo. 9^{rv}: copied from the same exemplar as B, s. xiii[1]

D. Burton upon Trent Museum, Burton Muniment 1, s. xi[2]. For description and endorsements see above pp. xxxiv–viii, 53

K. Oxford, Bodleian, Dugdale 11, fos 10–11: copy of C, s. xvii

L. Oxford, Bodleian, James 25, p. 164: incomplete copy of C. s. xvii

M. Oxford, Bodleian, Rawlinson B 350, fos 70, 71: copy of C. s. xvii

N. London, British Library, Stowe 780, fos 1–2: translation, s. xvi, ? from O

O. Nottingham, University Library, MiDc 7, fo. 35^{v}: translation in modern English, s. xvi

Ed.:   a. *O.S.F.* iii. Anglesey 2 (facsimile, transcript, and translation) from D

     b. Whitelock, *Wills*, pp. 46–51 (no. 17), with translation, from D and Thorpe

     c. Kemble 1298

     d. B. Thorpe, *Diplomatarium Anglicum Ævi Saxonici* (1865), pp. 543–9 from C

Listed: Hart 39, Sawyer 1536

Printed from D with main variants from B and C and readings from B and C where D is damaged. Illustrative readings are given from other versions.

In^a Nomine Domini^b . Her sputelað Þulfric his hleofan^c hlaforde his cpyde 7 eallon his freondon^d . þ is þ ic geann minon hlaforde tpa hund mancessa goldes . 7 tpa seolforhilted speord . 7 feoper hors . tpa gesadelode . 7 tpa ungesadelode . 7 þa pæpna þe þærto gebyriað . 7 ic geann ælcu*m* bisceope^e . v . mancessa goldes . 7 þa*m* tpa*m* arcebisceopan . heora ægþran tyn mancusas^f goldes . 7 ic geann into ælcu*m*^{g} munucregole . i . pund . 7 ælcon abbode . 7 ælcon abbatissan . v . mancusas^h goldes . 7 ic geann Ælfrice ^{i}arcebisceope þæs^i landes æt Dumeltan^k forð mid þon oðran for minon saple . pið þan þe he freond . 7 fultu*m* ðe betere sy into þære stope þe ic geporht^l hæbbe . 7 ic gean Ælfhelme^m . 7 Þulfage^n þære landa betpux Ribbel . 7 Mærse^o . 7 on^b Þirhalu*m*^{q} . þe heo hig dælan him betpeonan . spa hig efnost magon . butan heora ægðer his agen habban^r pille^s . on þ gerad þonne 'sceadd' genge sy . þ heora ægðer sylle . iii . þusend sceadda . into þæra stopa æt Byrtune^t . 7 ic geann^u Ælfhelme Rólfestun^w . 7 Heórlfestun^x . 7 ic geann Þulfage^y þæs landes æt Beorelfestune . 7 æt Mærchamtune^z 7 ic geann Ælfhelme þæs landes æt Cunugesburh^{a2} . pið þon þe he do þ þa mvnucas . habban ælce geare þriddan^{b2} dæl þæs fisces . 7 he ða tpá dæl . 7 ic geann Þulfage þæs landes æt Alepaldestune . 7 ic geann Ufegeate þæs landes æt Norðtune^{c2} . on þ gerad þ he freond . 7 fultu*m* þe betere sy into þære stope . 7 ic geann minre earman dehter^{d2} þæs landes æt Elleforda^{e2} . 7 þæs æt Aclea^{f2} . mid eallon þa*m* þe þær nu to herð . þa hpile hire ðe hire dæg^{g2} bið . 7 ofter hire dæg gá þ land into þære stope æt Byrtune^{h2} . 7 heo hit náge mid nanon þinge to forpyrcenne . ac hæbbe heo ðone bryce þa hpile þe heo hit geearnigean cann . 7 gá hit syððan into þæra stope æt Byrtone^{i2} . forðon þe hit þæs mines godfæder gyfu . 7 ic pille 'þ Ælfhelm' si hire múnd . 7 þæs landes . 7 þ æt Tampurþin^{k2} hire to nanon^{l2} ^{m2}þeopdome . ne nanon^{m2} geborenan men . butan þ

heo þone ealdordom hæbbe . 7 ic geann Ƿulfgare[n2] minan cnihte þæs
landes æt Baltryðeleage[o2] . ealspa his fæder hit him begeat . 7 ic
becƿeðe Morcare ꝥ land æt Ƿaleshó . 7 ꝥ æt Ƿeogendeþorpe[p2] . 7 ꝥ
æt Hƿitepylle[q2] . 7 ꝥ æt Clune . 7 ꝥ æt Barleburh . 7 ꝥ æt Ducemannestune[r2] . 7 ꝥ æt Moresburh . 7 ꝥ æt Eccingtune . 7 ꝥ æt Bectune .
7 ꝥ æt Doneceastre[s2] . 7 æt Morlingtune[t2] . 7 ic geann his pife
Aldulfestreo[u2] . ealspa hit nu stont mid mete . 7 mid mannon . 7 ic
geann Ælfhelme[w2] minan mæge . þæs landes æt[x2] Paltertune . 7 þæs ðe
Scegð me becpæð . 7 ic geann Æþelrice ꝥ land æt Ƿibbetofte . 7 ꝥ æt
Tƿongan . his dæg . 7 ofer his dæg . ga ꝥ land for mine saple . 7 for
[y2]minre meder[y2] . 7 for his into[z2] Byrtune[a3] . And þys synd þa land þe ic
geann into Byrtune[b3] . ꝥ is ærest Byrtun[c3] þe ꝥ mynster on stent . 7
Strættun[d3] . 7 Bromleage . 7 Bedintun . 7 Gageleage . 7 Ƿitestun[e3] .
7 Laganford[f3] . 7 Styrcleage . 7 Nipantun æt[g3] þære[h3] pic . 7 Ƿædedun[i3] .
7 ꝥ lyttle land þe ic ah on oðer Nipantune . 7 Ƿineshylle . 7 Suttun . 7
Ticenheale . 7 ꝥ[k3] æt Scenctune . 7 ꝥ[k3] æt Ƿicgestane . 7 ꝥ æt Halen .
7 Hrémesleage[l3] . 7 ꝥ æt Sciplea . 7 ꝥ æt Suðtune . 7 ꝥ æt Actune tpegra
manna dæg ealspa þa foreƿord sprecað . 7 Deorlafestun . 7 ꝥ þærto
hereð . ꝥ is Rudegeard[m3] . 7 min lyttle land on Cotepaltune[n3] . 7 Lege
mid eallon þam þe þærto hereð . Ácofre mid þam[o3] þe þærto hereð .
ꝥ is[p3] Hilum . 7 Celfdun[q3] . 7 Cætesþyrne[r3] . 7 ꝥ heregeatland æt
Suðtune[s3] . 7 Morlege . 7 Bregdeshale[t3] . Mortun . 7 eall seo socna þe
ðærto hereð . 7 ꝥ land þyderinn æt Pillesleage[u3] . 7 Oggodestun . 7 Ƿinne-
feld[w3] . 7 Snodespic into Mortune . 7 ꝥ æt Taðapyllan[x3] . 7 ꝥ land æt
Æppelby[y3] . þe ic gebohte mid minum féó . 7 ꝥ[z3] æt Ƿestune . 7
Burhtun . 7 seo hid æt Scearnforda . into Ƿiggestane . 7 ꝥ æt Hereburgebyrig . 7 Ealdespurðe[a4] . 7 Ælfredingtune . 7 Eccleshale . 7 æt
Ƿaddune . 7 an hida æt Sceon . And ic geann þam hirede in Tampurðin .
ꝥ land æt Langandune . ealspa hi hit ær me to leton[b4] . 7 habban hi
þone bryce healfne . 7 healfne[c4] þa munucas[d4] into Byrtun[e4] . ge on
mete . ge on mannon . 'ge on yrfe' ge on eallon[f4] þingon . 7 se bisceop fó
to his lande æt Bubba'n'dune[g4] . 7 fon ða munucas[h4] into *Byrtune* . to
þam þe on þam lande is . [i4]ge on méte[i4] ge on mannon . ge on eallon
þingon[k4] . 7 ꝥ land þam bisceope æt þære sýle . 7 ic pylle ꝥ se cyning beo
hlaford . þæs[l4] mynstres[m4] ðe ic getimbrede . 7 þære landára þe ic
ðyderinn becpeden hæbbe gode to lofe . 7 to purðmynta minan hlaforde[n4] . 7 for minre[o4] saþl[p4] . 7 Ælfric arceb . 7 Ælfhelm[q4] min broðor .
ꝥ hig beon mund . 7 freond . 7 forespreocan[r4] . into ðære stope pið
ælcne geborenne mann . heom to nanre agenre æhta . butan into sanctus[s4]
Benedictus regole . 7 ic geann minre goddehter[t4] Morkares[u4] . 7 Ald-
gyðe[w4] . ꝥ land æt Strættune . 7 ðone[x4] búle þe pæs hire ealdermoder .
7 into þam mynstre[y4] æt Byrtune . an hund pildra horsa . 7 sextena tame
hencgestas[z4] . 7 þærto eall ꝥ ic hæbbe on libbendan[a5] . 7 on licgendan .
butan 'þan' ðe ic becpeden hæbbe 7 god ælmihtig[b5] hine apende of
eallum godes dreame . 7 of ealra cristenra[c5] gemánan . se ðe þis[d5] apende .

butan hit min án cynehlaford sy . 7 ic hópyge[e5] to him spa gódan . 7 spa
míldheortan . þ he[f5] hit nylle sylf dón . ne eac nanum oþrum menn
geþafian . Valete in Cristo . Amen[g5] .

[a] Testamentum Þulfrici . *rubric* B　　　　[b] In . . . Domini *capitals in* D　　　　[c] D;
leofan B, C, K, M　　[d] B; freodon C; freon[. .]n D　　[e] C; biscop B; bisce[. .]e
D　　[f] B, C; mancses D　　[g] B, C; ælc[. .] D　　[h] B, C; manxes D
[i . . . . i] C; arcebiscop þæs B; arcebis[. . . . .]æs D　　[k] C, D; Dumeltun B
[l] C; geproht B; geporh D　　[m] C, D; Ælfelme B　　[n] C, D; þulfgage B
[o] C, D; Merse B　　[p] B, C; [. .] D　　[q] C, D; Þirhalon B　　[r] D; habben
B, C　　[s] B, C; [. . . .] D　　[t] C, D; Byrtone B　　[u] B, C; gea[. .] D
[w] C, D; Roluestun B　　[x] D; Heorelfestun B, C, K　　[y] C, D; Þulfhage
B　　[z] D; Marchamtone B, Merchamtune C, M　　[a2] C, D; Cunugesburg B
[b2] B, C; þridd[. .] D　　[c2] C, D; Noĉtune B　　[d2] C, D; dohtter B　　[e2] C, D,
M; Helleforda B; Ælleforde K　　[f2] B, C, K; Ácclea D　　[g2] B, C; d[. .] D
[h2] C, D; Byrtone B　　[i2] B, C; By[. . . . .] D　　[k2] Tompurðin . B, C
[l2] B, C; na[.]on D　　[m2 . . . m2] þeopdome . ne nanon *omitted* B　　[n2] B, C;
Þulfgar[.] D　　[o2] C, D; Baltriðelege B　　[p2] C, D; Þeoogende-
þorpe B　　[q2] B, D; Hpiteþille C, K, M　　[r2] B, C; Ducema[　]nestune D
[s2] C; Duneceastre B; Donecestre C, K, M　　[t2] D; Morlincgtune B; Morlig-
tune C, K, M　　[u2] C, D; Alduluestreo B　　[w2] C; Ælfelme B; Ælfelm[.] D
[x2] on B, D　　[y2 . . . y2] D; his modor B, C, M; his moders O　　[z2] C; int[.] D; in
to B　　[a3] B; Byrtone . C; [. . . . .] D　　[b3] D; Byrtone B, C　　[c3] C, D;
Byrtune B　　[d3] B, D; Stræton C　　[e3] B, C; Þitestan D　　[f3] C, D;
Langeford B　　[g3] C, D; 7 B　　[h3] D; ðære B, C　　[i3] C, D; Þededun B
[k3] þ *omitted* B, C　　[l3] D; Remesleage B, C　　[m3] B, D; Rudegard C
[n3] C, D; Cotepaletune B　　[o3] D; þon B; þon *over erasure* B　　[p3] B, C;
[. .] D　　[q3] D; Cealdun B; Celfdum C　　[r3] C, D; Cætesþurne C　　[s3] D;
Suttune B, C　　[t3] C, D; Brægdeshale B　　[u3] D; Pilleslege B; Pyllesleage C
[w3] B, C; Þynnefe[. .] D　　[x3] C, D; Taðaþillan B　　[y3] C; Æppebbyg D;
Appelby B　　[z3] þ *omitted* B, C　　[a4] B, C; Ealdespy[. . .] D　　[b4] B, C;
[.]eton D　　[c4] B, C; healf[. .] D　　[d4] B, D; munecas C　　[e4] B; B*yrtun*
C, D　　[f4] D; ælcon B, C　　[g4] D; Bubandune B, C　　[h4] C, D; munacas
B　　[i4] D; ge on mete *omitted* B, C　　[k4] B, C; þing[. .] D　　[l4] B, D; þær
C　　[m4] C; mynste > mynstres C; minstres B　　[n4] B, C; hlafor[. .] D
[o4] C, D; mynre B　　[p4] D; saplan B, C　　[q4] C, D; Ælfelm B　　[r4] B, C;
forespre[. .]an D　　[s4] C; santus B; sa[. . . . .] D　　[t4] C, D; goddohter B
[u4] B, D; Morcares C　　[w4] B, D; Ealdgyðe C　　[x4] B, D; ðon[.] D　　[y4] C;
-tr- *damaged* D; mynster B　　[z4] C, D; hengestas B　　[a5] B, D; libbandan C
[b5] L *begins here*　　[c5] B, D; cristenre *altered from* cristenra C　　[d5] þis *in*
capitals D　　[e5] B, D; hopege C, L　　[f5] B, C; [.]e D　　[g5] Valete . . .
Ame[.] *in capitals* D; Cristo *in capitals* C; Amen *omitted* B, C, N, O, K, M

For translation and comments see pp. xv–xxxiv

30

King Æthelred grants land at an unspecified place to an unnamed
minister. A.D. 1007

B. Aberystwyth, N.L.W., Peniarth 390, fos 181[v]–182 (pp. 362–3): copy,
　s. xiii[med]

Ed.: Hart, pp. 208-11

Listed: Sawyer 917

Carta Æðelredi regis de terra . annis et cetera . dcccc . xc . bisque quinis necne septenis .[a]

✠ Cum enim nos liquide in extrema decrepitacione huius senescentis mundi viteque momentanee tamquam ultime prosapie abortiuos filios procreatos nouerimus ׃ opus omnimodis habemus ut tanto in hoc laborioso spatiolo simus cautiores ׃ quanto patulo scimus illecebrosas nunc antiqui hostis plus priscorum tempore patrum augmentatas fore temptacionum suadelas . quibus animo acriter quatimur iunctis ima[b] simul in ortuis[c] calamitatum informationibus quas in corpusculo dematis nostri cordisque iugi scrutinio graui maceracione sustinemus . utpote uelut pauidi sub vigiliarum excubiis mancipii bellis attriti clade multati extreme prestolantes clangorem buccine quo genus omne hominum quod fuit . quod est . et quod erit futurum ad vnius aggregabitur uerissimi arbitris sub attonito pauore examen scunta[d] sine cunctatione cunctorum secreta perspicaci intuitu enucleantis ac condigna tunc meritis rependentis . Hec[e] ego Æþelredus regali infula Anglorum populis Cristo allubescente subthonizatus[f] condono cuidam meo ministro talem terram . et cetera . Scripta est hec cartula decursis annis ab incarnatione . Cristi . dcccc . xc . bisque quinis necne septenis indictione . v . hiis fauentibus quorum hic subtus onomata et dignitatum vides officia .
Ego Æþelred regia munificientia fretus hoc datum quod dedi agye crucis signamine perpetualiter confirmo ,
Ego Ælfeh archiepiscopus concessi
Ego Þulfstan archiepiscopus . consensi .

Ego Aþulf episcopus	confaui .
Ego Lyuing episcopus	coniuui .[g]
Ego Godpine episcopus	conpinxi .
Ego Alfpold episcopus	conscripsi .
Ego . Æþelric episcopus	consculpsi .
Ego Ælfhun . episcopus	concaui .[h]
Ego Ælfhelm episcopus	consignaui .
Ego Byrhtpold episcopus	confirmaui .
Ego Æþelpold episcopus	concarraxaui .[i]

et ceteri . clitones . vj . abbates . iiij[or] . comites . iij . patricius vnus . ministri sexdecim .
Ego Þinsye monachus qui hoc testamentum dictitaui atque perscripsi .

[a] Carta . . . septenis . *rubric* [b] *An error for* immo [c] *An error for* mortuis
[d] *An error for* cuncta [e] *? For* hinc [f] *An error for* subthronizatus
[g] *First column of subscriptions ends here* [h] *Second column of subscriptions ends here*
[i] *Third column of subscriptions ends here*

The most notable features of this text, which appears to be a draft or formulary, are the omission of any beneficiary or place-name and the claim that it was drawn up by the monk Wynsige. The elaborate dating clause is probably an attempt to avoid mentioning the millennium, and means 1007. The same formula is used in charters from Evesham and St Albans (S 1664, 912), the latter having other similarities with the present text. The indiction is right for that date and most of the witnesses are consistent with it, the possible exception being Ælfhelm of Dorchester whose successor was, according to the Ramsey History, consecrated in 1006 (*Chronicon Abbatiae Ramesiensis*, ed. W. D. Macray (Rolls Ser., 1886), p. 115).

31

King Æthelred exchanges two and a half hides (cassati) *at Rolleston, Staffordshire, for the vills of Aldsworth and Arlington, Gloucestershire, with Abbot Wulfgeat and the Abbey at Burton.*
A.D. 1008

B. Aberystwyth, N.L.W., Peniarth 390, fo. 182[rv] (pp. 363–4): copy, s. xiii[med]
C. London, British Library, MS. Loans 30, fo. 10[rv]: copy, s. xiii[1]
Ed.: a. Shaw, *Staffordshire*, i. 28
    b. Hart, pp. 211–18
Listed: Sawyer 920
Printed from C with main variants and subscriptions from B

Mutuatio duarum villarum pro villa de Rolueston' .[a]

✠[b] Universorum[c] conditor et creator dominus noster Iesus Cristus seruili forma semetipsum pro nostra redemptione circumtegens . et inter homines Deus homoque uerus conuersatus cunctos fidelcs salutaribus instruit documentis et[d] ad celestia gaudia toto mentis conamine quamtocius properemus taliter omnibus proclamat dicens . Thesaurizate uobis thesauros in celo ubi nec erugo nec tinea exterminat . et ubi fures non effodiunt nec furantur . Hinc compunctus ego Ethelred[e] rex Anglorum et [f]cum substantia[f] michi ab ipso domino ubertim donata celestia mercari cupiens cuidam meo fideli abbati[g] Þvlfgeto cognominato quandam terre particulam cum eo mutuaui . Ille michi dedit duas villas . vna uocatur Ealdesworthe[h] . alia uero Ælfredintun . Quia ualde longe erant a monasterio suo . ideo rogauit obnixis precibus ut aliquam terram ei concederem iuxta monasterium in congruum locum . et ego dedi ei[i] in loco quem solicole vicini æt Roluestun[k] appellant . id est duos cassatos et dimidium . libenter impendo[l] ad monasterium beati Benedicti omniumque[m] sanctorum quod est in villula Byrtuniensis situm . ad usum Dei seruorum eidem loco famulantium inperpetuo confirmo hereditatem . quatinus victum vestitumque atque omnem vtilitatem eis administrandum quamdiu huius uolubilis orbis[n] vergitur rota . Si autem tempore contigerit aliquo[o] quempiam hominum[p] aliquem antiquiorem librum contra istius libri libertatem producere ? pro nichilo computatur . isto per omnia in sua stabilitate permanente atque vigente . Sit autem hec prescripta tellus ab omnibus libera secularibus negociis . cum omnibus ad illam rite pertinentibus in campis . pascuis . pratis . siluis . aquarum[q] cursibus tribus tantum rebus exceptis que legaliter seruantur hactenus . id est expedicione pontis . arcisue . constructione .ʳ Siquis autem quod non optamus hoc nostre munificencie donum peruertere conamine stolido studuerit ⫶ collegio priuatus perpetue felicitatis erumpnam hauriat atrocissime calamitatis mortis nisi ante terminum presumptionem hanc temerariam legali satisfactione emendare studuerit . His metis rus hoc giraturˢ . +þis syndan þa langemera to Roluestune ⫶ Ærest of dufan on hæcce of hæcce on þone greatan þorn of þan þorne to ðan hæg stope æfter hæg stope to dottes hlape of dotdes hlape to þere strete þær on ansidelege . of ansidelege on þa dic . of ðan dice on þan fulan sich of ðan fulan siche on pattiches æces of pattices æces on þan holan gryfe þær ða ealdan broc holan syndan of ðan holan on þan ufer ende balcan of balcan to middel lege . of middel lege to ðan scid hæge æfter scid hæge þpers ofer bracan hyrst þ on mæran broce dune mid broce to þan stanigan forde þe ligeð to eadgares lege of ðan forde to pulffeges hæge andland hæges on þa ofesan æfter ofesan to ðan fulan syce þ on þan broce of ðan broce on stoc legan ford of ðan forde abiðan ofesan þ on ðone dic hæge leofnaðes of ðan dice on þan fulan syce æfter sice on pilebroc dun æfter broce on þan fulan sic þe scot betux tpam lundan æfter sice to cnapanhylle of cnapanhylleᵗ to ðan hæg stope of ðan hæg stope on þa deopan dæle of ðan dæle on dufan . on þa bradan strete æt burtone . anlang stræte to pinstanesgemæra ut ðorh ðone pudu to ðan þorne þer ða þeofes licgan æfter þære mæd eafdan on þ puda a æfter ofesan þ eft on ðan bradan stræte

Acta est autem hecᵘ mutacio anno dominice apparicionis . mᵒ . viijᵒ . indictione . viᵃ . consencientibus hiis testibusʷ .

+Ego Æþelredˣ rex Anglorum hoc donum perpetua ditaui libertate . +Ego Æþelstanʸ filius regis . +Ego Eadmundᶻ filius regis . +Ego Eadredᵃᵃ filius regis . +Ego Eadpigᵇᵇ filius regis . +Ego Eadgarᶜᶜ filius regis . ᵈᵈ

+Ego Ælfheah archiepiscopus	composui .
+Ego Þulstan archiepiscopus	conclusi .
+Ego Leofincg episcopus	consignaui .ᵉᵉ
+Ego Ælfhun episcopus	consensi .
+Ego Æþelric episcopus	condixi .
+Ego Æþelpold episcopus	confirmaui .ᶠᶠ
+Ego Godpine episcopus	acquieui .
+Ego Ælfgar episcopus	adunaui .ᵍᵍ

et ceteri . abbates decem . duces tres . et ministri septem .

ᵃ Rubric; Carta Æþelredi regis de Roluoston' pro Ealdeswyrðe et Alfredeton' anno . mᵒ . viij . rubric B   ᵇ B; chrismon omitted in C   ᶜ B; Uvniuersorum with large coloured initial duplicating the first letter in C   ᵈ Error for ut   ᵉ Æþel- red B   ᶠ · · · ᶠ cum consubstancia B   ᵍ abbate B   ʰ Ealdespyrðe B ᶦ terram omitted   ᵏ Rolfestun B   ˡ inpendo B   ᵐ omnium B ⁿ or'bis B   ᵒ Order corrected from contigerit tempore C; Si autem contigerit alico B   ᵖ Error for hominem   ᑫ aquarumque B   ʳ hactenus et cetera . B ˢ His metis et cetera B; B omits bounds   ᵗ Altered from caapan- C   ᵘ Acta est hec B   ʷ hiis testibus consentientibus . B   ˣ The subscriptions are printed

from B; Ethelred C   *ʸ* Ethelstan C   *ᶻ* Edmund C   *ᵃᵃ* Edred C
ᵇᵇ Edwig C   *ᶜᶜ* Edgar C   *ᵈᵈ* et ceteri archiepiscopi et episcopi . C
ᵉᵉ First column of subscriptions ends here   *ᶠᶠ Second column of subscriptions
ends here*   *ᵍᵍ Third column of subscriptions ends here*

This charter is probably authentic. The formulas are appropriate, the indiction is
right, and the witness-list is consistent with 1008 and includes the ætheling Edgar
who ceased to subscribe that year. Hart, pp. 215–26, points out that the verbs
in the episcopal subscriptions occur in the same order in the foundation charter,
28. The land at Aldsworth and Arlington had been given to Burton Abbey by
Wulfric (see above, p. xxxiii). Rolleston was bequeathed by him to his brother
Ælfhelm and was presumably confiscated by the king in 1006. The abbey did
not keep it for long and it was held T.R.E. by Earl Morcar with an assessment
of 2½ hides, as in this charter (see above, p. xxiv). The bounds are in two parts,
the main estate and a detached part by the Trent. The bounds of the detached
part begin *on þa bradan strete æt burtone*, which is presumably Ryknild Street.
The Trent is not named but the *þorn þer ða þeofes licgan* is shown by the bounds
of Wetmoor (**35**) to have been close to the river. The eastern boundary of the
main estate of Rolleston was then, as now, the River Dove and the south-east
section was probably very similar to the modern boundary for *dottes law* may
be identified with Dodslow on the Tithe Award (S.R.O., S.M.S. 417) at SK 232
267, close to the modern boundary. The bounds return to the Dove by a deep
dale, which can hardly be the shallow valley through which the modern boundary passes to join the river; the valley in which Tutbury stands would fit that
description much better. The large number of boundary points between Dodslow and the return to the Dove clearly indicates that the area described by these
bounds extended a long way west of the present parish of Rolleston. Very few
points can be positively identified, but *ansidelege* is Anslow (and occurs also in
35), the ford which leads *to eadgares lege* presumably lay on a road to Agardsley
and *stoc legan ford* was probably associated with Stockley.

32

King Æthelred grants eight hides (manentes) *at Weston upon
Trent, one hide* (manens) *in Morley, one in Smalley and Kidsley,
one in Crich, and one in Ingleby, Derbyshire, to Morcar*, minister.

A.D. 1009

A. Stafford, William Salt Library, 84/5/41: original, parchment, 160 × 520–530
mm., damaged by folding
Endorsements: (1) by the scribe of the charter: +*Þestunes Landbóc* . (2) in
a hand of s. xiii : *Ethelredus rex Morkare* (3) in a hand of s. xiii : .[. .] *xxᵘˢ* .
(4) in a medieval hand : *XXXI*
B. Aberystwyth, N.L.W., Peniarth 390, fo. 182ᵛ (p. 364): copy of A, s. xiiiᵐᵉᵈ
Ed.: Hart, pp. 219–28
Listed: Sawyer 922
Printed from A with main variants from B and readings from B where A is
damaged

✠ Omnia*ᵃ* que uidentur temporalia sunt et que non uidentur æterna
sunt . Idcirco*ᵇ* terrenis et caducis ęterna et iugiter mansura mercanda

sunt . ut his uisibilibus lucris inuisibilia bona que fine carent domino
Deo auxiliante feliciter adquirantur . Quapropter . ego Æþelredus .
diuina mihi arridente munificentia . inperiali regiminis gentis Anglorum
sceptro p[ ]titus^c . aliquam terre partem quam mihi aeternus cęli
creator et omnium rerum conditor sua bonitate largiendo indulsit .
confero honorabili^d meo ministro . Morkare . id est . viii^{to} . manentes
in loco et circa locum ubi dicitur antiquo uocabulo . Þestun . et . i .
manens in Morleage . et . i . in Smælleage . et in Kidesleage . et . i . in
Cryc^e . et . i . in Englabý . cum omnibus ad se rite pertinentibus pratis^f .
pascuis . campis . siluisque^g ut habeat et possideat . et post se^h cuicumque uoluerit in æternam hereditatem derelinquat^i . Sint^k quoque
prenominati agelluli absoluti et liberi . nullisque humanis seruitiis
subiciantur . exceptis ipsis seruitiis^l quibus insistere quosque^m monet
communis utilitas regni id est expeditio . et arcis pontisque restauratio .
Qui autem hanc nostri decreti xanctionem^n prauo^o molimine mutilare
conatus fuerit certum^p teneat portionem poenarum cum^q angelis apostaticis sé perpetualiter perpessurum non modica^r ; qui uero benigniter
fideliterque huius assercioni cyrografi . fidem áccommodauerit^s ; sanctorum omnium coetui copuletur calcetenus . His itaque confiniis pre-
scripta^t rura cinguntur .
+Ðis syndan þa landgemæru þe lic[.]eð into þestune . þ is ærest of
siðriðe forda [.]n mæres ford . 7 of mæresforda þesta[.]iððarugandic .
7 spa on hina hóh . 7 spa of ðan hó þestan þiððæne holanmere forð into
ceoleardes beorge 7 of ðam beorhge in mæresdic . 7 of mæresdic in
þulfeardes þórn . 7 of þulfeardes þorne in þa grenandíc . andlang þære
dice in þone pytt . 7 of þam pytte in deorpentan in þa myðan . 7 of ðam
ge[m]yðan upp æft' treontan eft on siðriðe ford .^{t} Anno . dominice
incarnationis . millesimo . ix . scripta est . uius^u munificentię singrapha
his^w testibus . consentientibus quorum inferius nomina^x caraxantur .
+Ego Æþelræd rex Anglorum hoc donum libenti animo concessi^y
+Ego Æþelstan filius regis huic^z donationi consensi .
+Ego Eadmund frater predicti clitonis adiuui .
+Ego Eadred libens annui
+Ego Ælfheah archiepiscopus Dorobernie non abnui .
+Ego Þulfstanus Eboracensis archipresul non rennui .
+Ego Godþine episcopus ad libitum regis propria manu conscripsi^{aa} .
+Ego Liuincg episcopus roboraui .^{bb}
+Ego Æþelpold episcopus adquieui .
+Ego Aþulf episcopus subscripsi .^{cc}
+Ego Brih[tþ]ald   episcopus
+Ego Eadnoð   episcopus
+Ego Alfun   episcopus
+Ego Æþelric   episcopus
+Ego Æþelsig   episcopus
+Ego Ælfþald   episcopus

+Ego Godpine	episcopus
+Ego Ælfgær	episcopus
+Ego Ælf's'tan	episcopus
+Ego Aldun	episcopus[dd]
+Ego Germanus	abbas
+Ego Ælf's'ig	abbas
+Ego Þulgar	abbas
+Ego Ælfsig	abbas
+Ego Brihtræd	abbas
+Ego Leofgar	[a]bbas
+Ego Æluere	[ab]bas
+Ego Ælfric	dux
+Ego Leofpine	dux
+Ego Eadric	dux[ee]
+Ego Uhtred	dux
+Ego Æþe'l'mær	minister .
+Ego Æþelric	m̄
+Ego Ægelgær	m̄
+Ego Ælfpine	m̄
+Ego Ulfketel	m̄
+Ego Godpine	m̄
+Ego Siferð	m̄
+Ego Þiðer	m̄
+Ego Æþelpine	m̄[ff]
+Ego Godp[ ]	m̄
+Ego Fredgist	m̄
+Ego Ulf	m̄
+Ego Ælfeh	m̄
+Ego Þulf[r]ic	m̄
+Ego Ulfk[e]tel	m̄
+Ego þurferð	m̄
+Ego Aske[t]el	m̄
+Ego Þulfsig	m̄
+Ego Kata	m̄[gg]
+Ego Þulfstan	m̄
+Ego Asketel	m̄
+Ego Þulfgeat	m̄
+Ego Aþelpold	m̄
+Ego Ælfeh	m̄
+Ego Styr	m̄
+Ego þurbrand	m̄
+Ego Þulfstan	m̄
+Ego Spaue	m̄
+Ego Æþelric	m̄[hh]

[a] Carta Æþelredi regis de Þeston . facta Morkare anno domini . m⁰ . ix⁰ . Kydesleg'

et Cruch . *rubric* B   *b* B; Idc[.]rco A   *c* A *for* potitus; *blank space be-*
tween sceptro *and* aliquam B   *d* B; hono[.]bili A   *e* et in Cryc . i . B
f B; -ib[. . .]ratis A   *g* B; siluis[.] A   *h* B; post [. .] A   *i* et cetera .
ut supra B *in place of* cuicumque . . . derelinquat   *k* Sui B   *l* B; ip[. . .
. . .]uitiis A   *m* B; quo[. .] A   *n* A, B; *spelling for* sanctionem   *o* paruo B
p Read id certum   *q* B; -aru[. .]um A   *r* B *error for* modicam; modica *with
the parchment damaged over the last letter* A   *s Altered from* accommidauerit A
t prescripta . . . eft on siðriðe ford . *omitted* B   *u A spelling for* huius   *w* Huius
munificentia singrapha hiis B   *x* quorum 'hec' nomina B   *y* B; anim[. . . .]cessi A
z hui B   *aa* B; conscrip[]i . A   *bb* B *ends here*: et ceteri episcopi . x .
abbates . vij . duces . iiij^or . et ministri . xx^ti . ix .   *cc The first column of subscriptions ends here*   *dd The second column of subscriptions ends here*   *ee The
third column of subscriptions ends here*   *ff The fourth column of subscriptions
ends here*   *gg The fifth column of subscriptions ends here*   *hh The sixth column
of subscriptions ends here*

Description of A: Three horizontal and five (originally three) vertical folds.
Ruled with a stylus, no bounding lines or prickings visible. Written area 145 ×
515 mm.

The Latin text is in Caroline minuscule with round *r* in *or* and the *cc* form
of *a* in *ra*. Uncial *d* occurs in *anno dominice*. The abbreviation ÷ is used for *est*.
The Old English bounds are in Anglo-Saxon minuscule with both short and
long forms of *s*, the latter infrequently, and with two occurrences of Caroline *a*
(*deorwentan*, *trentan*). The personal and place-names are normally in Anglo-
Saxon minuscule, with several occurrences of *k*, and the titles of many witnesses
are in Caroline minuscule, but there is some confusion, e.g. insular *r* in *rex* and
frater and the Caroline *st* ligature in *westune*. The names of the beneficiary
and, as a witness, his brother, *SIFERÐ*, are in capitals as are the titles *DUX*
and *MINISTER* (the latter normally abbreviated as *M̄*) in the subscriptions.
The chrismon, which is a plain *chi rho*, with loops in the side angles of the *X*,
was apparently written first and occupies the first part of the first three lines.

This charter is in an early-eleventh-century hand. It has a very full list of
witnesses, implying an unusually large assembly which, as Professor Whitelock
suggests, must have been summoned to deal with the crisis of that year. This
exceptionally long witness-list is in favour of its authenticity and so too is the
absence of a bishop of Selsey; Selsey was vacant in 1009 following the death of
Ordbriht which, according to Florence of Worcester, happened in that year.
The only difficulty is the presence of Bishop Ælfstan, otherwise unknown, and
of Bishop Æthelsige. A bishop of that name succeeded Æthelric at Sherborne,
whose last signature is in 1009 and who is a witness in the present charter. It is,
however, not necessary to assume that two bishops of Sherborne witness this
text. We have no contemporary information about the see of Cornwall, where
there is a gap between Ealdred, who last signs in 1002, and Burwold, who appears in 1018, and it is possible that the revival of Lindsey did not end with the
death of Sigeferth, who last appears in 1004. There are no episcopal lists for
these sees at that time and it is therefore possible that Ælfstan and Æthelsige
should be assigned to them. Their only known subscriptions are in this charter
and in 34 and in this respect they may be compared with Ealdhun of Durham
whose only subscription is in the present charter.

The bounds refer to the mouth of the Derwent and the Trent and the
Westune can therefore be identified as Weston upon Trent (*PN Derbyshire*,
pp. 512–13), which must then have extended to the confluence of those rivers,
and included Aston upon Trent and Shardlow which according to DB were
berewicks of Weston (DB, i. 273a). The later ownership of the estates given to
Morcar by this charter confirms its reliability. Weston was held by Earl Ælfgar
T.R.E. with appurtenant land at Smalley and Kidsley as well as the berewicks

of Aston and Shardlow (DB, i. 272b, 273a). The total assessment of this estate
was over 11 carucates. Crich was held T.R.E. by Leofric and Leofnoth who
were Morcar's successors elsewhere (see above, p. xxvi), and with *Scochetorp*
was assessed at ½ carucate (DB, i. 277a). Ingleby was held in DB by Ralph fitz
Hubert and assessed at 1⅛ carucates, but with no pre-Conquest holder named
(DB, i. 277a). As Ralph's *antecessores* for all his Derbyshire estates were Leofric
and Leofnoth, they probably also held this estate T.R.E. There were, in addition, two very small holdings in Ingleby, assessed at 3 bovates and ⅔ bovate
respectively (DB, i. 278a–b). Morley was probably the place where Wulfric held
land which he bequeathed to Burton Abbey (see above, p. xxxii) and which
was assessed at ⅔ carucate and held T.R.E. by Siward (DB, i. 275b), who also
held other estates given to the abbey by Wulfric (see above, pp. xxxii–iii).

33

King Æthelred grants two hides (cassatae) *at Hallam, Derbyshire,*
to Elemod [*? Æthelmod*], minister. A.D. 1011

B. Aberystwyth, N.L.W., Peniarth 390, fos 182ᵛ–183 (pp. 364–5): copy, s.
   xiii^med

Ed.: a. F. Barlow, *Edward the Confessor* (1970), pp. 328–9
     b. Hart, pp. 228–31

Listed: Sawyer 923

Carta Æþelredi regis de Burhalim . anno domini . m° . xi° .ᵃ

✠ᵇ Sunneᶜ vereque bonitatis Deum solum . substantia simplum .
personis triplum ⫶ constare nemini ratione vigentium hesitandum est .
qui sue incircumscripteᵈ diuamiaᵉ maiestatis circumscripta queque quasi
pugillo continet chirali ⫶ cunctaque que sunt eius bonitate bona sunt ⫶
non tamen condita per se ⫶ set quia a summo bono essendi ceperant
formam ⫶ bona sunt . Quam ob causam eiusdem summe bonitatis bona
perpetualiter siquidem permanenda . viuaci mentis intencione iugiter
appetenda sunt ⫶ quibus quippe adeptis ⫶ nichil desiderabilius excellen-
tiusve requiri quibit . Hinc etenim ego Eþelredus tocius rector archosque
Bryttannie ⫶ regalis potentie dignitatibus Dei dapsilitate inpensimaᶠ
fauente preditus opum largitione caducarum transitoriarumque ⫶ bona
haut caduca hautque defectiua adipisci omnimodo exoptans inter
cetera bonorum studia largiendorum quibus me minime deficientis agal-
liasmataᵍ regni adepturum esse spero ⫶ terre particulam quandam duas
videlicet cassatas Elemod ministro gratissimo libens hilarisque impartior
⫶ ob ipsius siquidem indefessi obsequia famulatus . que quidem terra
a gnosticis patrie accolis Burhhalun nuncupatur ⫶ Eandem denique
terram quamdiu spiramine attrahendo uel emittendo frui valeat . tocius
alienus conflictus securus possideat . dumque se vivacis alitum flaminis
amissum ire perspexerit ⫶ arbitrium ei liberum assistat cui successorum
eius . alieno scilicet uel propinquo eandem terram subigat possidendam .
Matronae autem suprascripte tam naturales quam legittimas villas

michi iure decretario assignatas ministro prememorato Elemodo viginti et vnius librarum appensibus[h] aureis michi concessis alacriter condonaui . Itaque hoc nostre largitionis donum in ipsius arbitrio tuta semper valletur libertate cum cunctis ad ipsam rite pertinentibus terram . campis videlicet et cetera . tribus causis exceptis et cetera . Sit ergo terre istius libertas vndique solida et munita . et antiquioris uel iunioris libri quocumque modo prolati nullomodo contradictioni subiaceat . set magis omnibus hostibus deuictis proprie potestatis ditione floreat . Istis terminibus predicta terra circumgirata est et cetera . mº . xiº .

+Ego Æþelred rex tocius Brittannice telluris hanc libertatem confirmaui .

+Ego Ælfheagus Dorobernensis ecclesie archiepiscopus consignaui .

+Ego Þustanus Eboracensis archiepiscopus consensi

+Ego Ælfgyuu collaterana eiusdem regis hoc michi placere professa sum .

+Ego Æþelstanus .	clyto .	confirmaui .[i]
+Ego Eadmund .	clyto .	consignaui .
+Ego Eadred	clyto .	corroboraui .
+Ego Eadpig	clyto .	coniuui .
+Ego Eadpeard	clyto .	consolidaui .
+Ego Ælfhun	episcopus	conquieui
+Ego Æþelpold	episcopus	coniugaui .
+Ego Lyuuingc .	episcopus	communeraui .[k]
+Ego Æþelric	episcopus	consensi .
+Ego Ælfpold	episcopus	conclaui .
+Ego Aþulf	episcopus	confixi .
+Ego Godpine	episcopus	confirmaui .
+Ego Eadnoð	episcopus	coadunaui .
+Ego Ælfmær	episcopus	consolidaui .

et ceteri abbates sex . duces . iiij[or] . et ministri . viginti et tres .

---

[a] Carta . . . xiº . rubric   [b] *The monogram combines* chi rho *with* aw   [c] *Error for* summe   [d] *? Error for* incircumscripta   [e] *Error for* dinamia   [f] *Error for* inpensissima   [g] *Error for* agalliamata. *Dr Lapidge comments: The word in question is Greek* ἀγαλλιάματα (n. pl.), *a word from the Septuagint psalter (Ps. xxxi) meaning something like 'excesses of joy'*   [h] *Dr Lapidge comments: If this is* appensio *for 'weight', the abl. pl. would be* appensionibus   [i] *This and the following six subscriptions form a column*   [k] *This and the following subscriptions form a second column*

As Professor Barlow has pointed out, the reference to *matronae . . . suprascripte* is not justified by the text and shows that this charter has not been copied in full. The witness-list is consistent with the date 1011 and is the last appearance of Ælfwold of Crediton whose successor Eadnoth may have witnessed charters in 1012 unless, as the position of the subscriptions suggests, they belong to Eadnoth of Dorchester (S 926, 927). *Burhhalun* has been identified as Hallam in Derbyshire (*PN Derbyshire*, pp. 466–8) which appears in DB as *Halun* and was assessed at 1 carucate, held T.R.E. by Dunstan (DB, i. 277b). Burton Abbey does not appear to have had any interest there.

F

34

King Æthelred grants five hides (mansae) æt Ufre [*? Mickleover, Derbyshire*], *to Morcar*, minister. A.D. 1011

B. Aberystwyth, N.L.W., Peniarth 390, fo. 183ʳᵛ (pp. 365–6): copy, s. xiiiᵐᵉᵈ
Ed.: Hart, pp. 232–4
Listed: Sawyer 924

Carta Æþelredi regis de Vfra . anno domini . mᵒ . xi ᵒ .ᵃ

✠Domino nostro Iesu Cristo cum patre et flamine sacro omnis essentie machinam genuino naturalis potentie gubernante moderamine omnisᵇ usie creatura que in principio formata formoseque condita videlicet phebea lampas . cinthia firmamentoque celi affixa uel errantia sidera . terrena quoque animalia seu maritima siue aerea . necnon ᶜherbarum vel leguminum atque uirgultorumᶜ ab origine qua esse ceperunt indite sibi nature statuta conditoris non sunt transgressa precepta . set usque defectum sui ea servantia permanent . set heu prohdolor inprouida fragilitas hominum omnibus creaturis prelatior propter preuaricacionem corruens in cecitatem caliginose mortis primam inmortalitatis stolam lugubriter amisit . Idcirco meritam incurrit interᵈ omne genus humanum . regnumque post regnum mobiliter uadit et perniciter recedit . Qua de re ego Eþelred diuina arridente gratia rex cum archana cordis indagatione perhennem gratulationem et tutissimum fulcimentumᵉ cum peculiari donacione quam arcitenens hilariter suis deuotis daturus est insuper et vitam eternam . aliquantulam ruris particulam cum consensu optimatum meorum id est . v . mansas ubi a rurigenis æt Vfre appellatur meo fideli ministro Morcare satis deuote inpendere curaui . ita ut ab omni mundiali censu perpetualiter ditali munificacione libera collocetur . nisi ab expedicione contra hostiles turmas et arcis municione pontisve instructione sicut ab antiquis constitutum est . inter agmina sanctorum eternaliter in celi galaxia exultantium eterne beatitudinis repperiaᶠ tripudia qui nostre donacioni consentiri animum impulerit . Si quis uero non exhorruerit machinari contra nostrum decretum sciat se casurum in profundum auernalis orci baratrum . Anno dominice incarnationis . millesimo . xiᵒ . Hiis testibus consentientibus

+Ego Æþelred rex Anglorum hoc donatiuum dando sub astipulacione multorum firmaui .

+Ego Æþelstan regis filius consensi .

+Ego Eadmund frater eiusdem subscripsi .

+Ego Eadred tercia proles regia adquieui .

+Ego Ælfheh archiepiscopus   corroboraui

+Ego Þulfstanus archiepiscopus annui .

+Ego Adulf pontifex .   adnotaui .ᵍ

+Ego Godwine antistes   non renui .

+Ego Brihtpold episcopus .   non abnui
+Ego Eadnod presul .   consolidaui
+Ego Ælfhun episcopus   confirmaui
+Ego Æþelric pontifex .   consensi
+Ego Æþelsig episcopus   conquieui .[h]
+Ego Ælfpald episcopus   con .
+Ego Godpine   episcopus con
+Ego Ælfgær   episcopus con
+Ego Ælfstan   episcopus con
+Ego Germanus   abbas

et ceteri abbates septem. [i] et ceteri duces . quatuor et ministri . xxx[ta] .

[a] Carta . . . xi⁰ . *rubric* [b] *Blank space for about nine letters follows* omnis. *The missing word might be* deifice [c] . . . [c] *A word, such as* prosapia *or* genera, *governing these genitives, has been omitted* [d] *Error for* iram [e] *A word such as* desiderans, *governing these accusatives, has been omitted* [f] *Error for* repperiat [g] *First column of subscriptions ends here* [h] *Second column of subscriptions ends here* [i] *Third column of subscriptions ends here*

This charter is probably authentic. It is evidence for a very large assembly, similar to that recorded in 32. Many witnesses, including Bishops Æthelsige and Ælfstan, occur in both charters although Lyfing of Wells, Æthelwold of Winchester, and Ealdhun of Durham are missing. Dr Dumville suggests that the misreading of *iram* as *inter* (see note *d*) implies that the exemplar was in eleventh-century script with the *cc* form of *a* in the ligature *ra*, and a normal suspension mark for *m*. The 5 hides were probably at Mickleover which was given to Burton Abbey by William I. The DB assessment was 10 carucates (DB, i. 273a) and the early twelfth-century Burton Surveys assign 4 of these to Mickleover itself and the rest to its berewicks, Little Over 3, Findern 2, and Potlack 1 (*Surveys*, pp. 229–36). There is therefore no agreement between the assessment of the present grant and any part of Mickleover.

35

King Æthelred grants one and a half hides (manses) *at Wetmoor, Staffordshire, to Abbot Wulfgeat and the Abbey at Burton.* A.D. 1012

B. Aberystwyth, N.L.W., Peniarth 390, fo. 183ᵛ (p. 366): copy, s. xiii[med]
C. London, British Library, MS. Loans 30, fos 10ᵛ–11: copy, s. xiii[l]
Ed.: a. Shaw, *Staffordshire*, i. 19–20
  b. Hart, pp. 235–41
Listed: Sawyer 930
Printed from C with main variants and subscriptions from B

Carta de villa de Withmere.[a]

✠[b] Vniuersorum[c] conditor et creator dominus noster Iesus Cristus seruili forma semetipsum pro nostra redempcione circumtegens . et inter homines Deus homoque uerus conuersatus cunctos fideles salutaribus instruit documentis et^d ad celestia gaudia toto mentis conamine quamtocius properemus taliter omnibus proclamat dicens Thesaurizate uobis thesauros in celo . et cetera^e . Hinc compunctus ego Æþelred rex Anglorum et^f cum substancia michi ab ipso domino ubertim donata celestia mercari capio^g ؛ cuidam meo fideli abbati Wlfgeto cognominato quandam terre particulam dedi ei in loco quem solicole vicini Withmere^h appellant . id est vnum mansem et dimidium pro amabili obedientia eiusque placabili pecunia quam michi in sue deuocionis obsequio detulit . id est . lxx^{ta} . libras in auro et argento . Ideo ei libenter inpendo ad monasterium suum quod nominatur sancti Benedicti omniumque sanctorum quod est in villula Byrtuniensi^i situm ad vsum Dei seruorum eidem loco famulantium imperpetuum confirmo hereditate . quatinus victum vestitumque atque omnem utilitatem eis administrandum quamdiu huius uolubilis orbis uergitur rota . Si autem tempore contigerit aliquo quempiam hominem aliquem^k antiquiorem librum contra istius libri libertatem producere ؛ pro nichilo computatur . isto per omnia in sua stabilitate permanente atque vigente . Sit autem hec prescripta tellus ab omnibus libera secularibus negociis cum omnibus ad illam rite pertinentibus . in campis . pascuis . pratis . siluis . aquarumque cursibus tribus tantum rebus exceptis que legaliter seruantur hactenus . id est expedicione pontis arcisue constructione^l . Si quis autem quod non optamus hoc nostre munificentie donum peruertere conaminc stolido studuerit ؛ collegio priuatus perpetue felicitatis erumpnam hauriat atrocissime calamitatis mortis . nisi ante terminum presumptionem hanc temerariam legali satisfactione emendare studuerit .^{m}

Hiis metis rus hoc giratur^n . +þis synt þa landgemære to piþmere . Ærst of trente þær þa ðeofes hangað on middan bere fordes holme . of ðan holme to geriht to þan lepe butan fif lan beheonan of þan landan to þan sice . of þan syce to þan mære þorne uspeardan forstun of þan þorne to an æcer . of an æcere in þone hæge . of ðan hæge ؛ in þæm broce . and long broces . þ̄ cume on þone dic ؛ on ansyðelege . norð æfter dice þ̄ cume on ceolfes crofte . on þone þe ioerneð fram eansyðelege æfter stræte to þan stubbe . of þan stubbe ؛ on þone dic . æfter dice þ̄ on stræte þ̄ yrnð bi ebrocan . of ðan stræte on þone dic . of þan dice ؛ on geriht on þone sich þe yrnð be chese pælle hylle . 7 hunger hylle . æfter syche on geriht on þe ellen þe stundað on pihtmere mære ant stretones . of þan ellan ؛ on þone forð æfte syce þe scoet of þan forde on trentan up æfter trente þ̄ cume þære þe þeofes hengað . ׀ . ant pylltunes landes æcer ant mæd land ؛ healf into pihtmere 7 healf in to roluestune . Acta est autem^o hec^p mea donatio anno ab incarnacione domini nostri Ihesu Cristi^q . m^o . xii^o . indictione uero^r . x^a . Hii testes aderant . qui hanc conscripserunt et consenserunt . et cum signo 'sancte' crucis cristi corroborauerunt et firmauerunt .^{s}

+Ego Æþelred rex Anglorum hanc et cetera^t . +Ego Æþelstan^u filius regis .

+Ego Ælfheh[w]	archiepiscopus	composui .
+Ego Þulfstan	archiepiscopus	consignaui .[x]
+Ego Leofing	episcopus	conclusi
+Ego Ælfhun	episcopus	consensi .[y]
+Ego Æþelric	episcopus	condixi .
+Ego Æþelpold	episcopus	confirmaui .
+Ego Godpine	episcopus .	assensi .[z]
+Ego Ælfgar	episcopus	adquieui .
+Ego Æscpy	episcopus	corroboraui .
+Ego Sigegar	episcopus	addonaui .[aa]

et ceteri abbates . quinque . duces . v[que] . et ministri . quinque .

[a] *Rubric*; Carta Æþelredi regis de Withmere . anno ab incarnatione domini . m⁰ . xij . indictione . x . *rubric* B   [b] B; *chrismon omitted in* C   [c] B; Uvniuersorum *with large coloured initial duplicating the first letter in* C   [d] *Error for* ut   [e] conamine et cetera ut supra in precedenti folio . B   [f] et *omitted* B   [g] *Error for* cupio; substantia et cetera . ut supra . B   [h] vicine Þithmere B   [i] Byrtoniensis B   [k] aliquem *omitted* B   [l] in campis et cetera . tribus exceptis et cetera . B   [m] Si quis quod non optamus et cetera . ut supra . B   [n] Istis metis rus hoc giratur et cetera . B; B *omits bounds*   [o] autem *omitted* B   [p] hec B   [q] domini nostri Ihesu Cristi *omitted* B   [r] uero *omitted* B   [s] aderant qui et cetera . B   [t] *The subscriptions are printed from* B; Ego Æðelred rex Anglorum hanc meam donacionem consensi . et scribere iussi et manuum inpressione signaui . C   [u] Æðelstan C   [w] Ælfheah C   [x] C *ends* et alii quamplures episcopi . abbates . duces . et ministri .   [y] *First column of subscriptions ends here*   [z] *Second column of subscriptions ends here*   [aa] *Third column of subscriptions ends here*

This spurious charter appears to have been based on **31**. The verbal similarities enabled the scribe of Peniarth 390 to omit several passages and replace them with *et cetera ut supra*. He could have omitted more. The episcopal subscriptions are the same as in **31** with the addition of Æscwig, presumably of Dorchester, whose subscriptions stop in 1002, and Sigegar of Wells, whose episcopate ended even before that and whose successor Lyfing also subscribes. Archbishop Ælfheah is included although he had been taken captive in the autumn of 1011 and died in captivity in April 1012. If the witness-list is based on **31** some changes were made, possibly to conceal the connection between the charters; four of the æthelings are left out and the numbers of abbots, ealdormen, and thegns are different.

Wetmoor belonged to Burton Abbey at the time of the Conquest and was then assessed at 1½ hides, as in this charter (DB, i. 248b). The bounds begin and end on the Trent and describe a circuit that approaches Anslow (*eansyðelege*) and is on the east a common boundary with Stretton. Shaw suggested that the place where the thieves hang was commemorated in Gallows Flat and Gallows Lane (Shaw, *Staffordshire*, i. 20). The first letter of *pylltunes* is probably an error for þ, and the reference is to Willington, Derbyshire.

36

King Æthelred grants five hides (cassati) æt Burtune *to Theodulf, his man.* A.D. 1012

B. Aberystwyth, N.L.W., Peniarth 390, fos 183ᵛ–184 (pp. 366–7): copy, s. xiii^med

Ed.: Hart, pp. 241–4

Listed: Sawyer 929

Carta Æþelredi regis de Burtone ab incarnatione domini anno . millesimo . xij .ᵃ

☧ In nomine domini nostri Iesu Cristi . Omnia que hic humanis considerantur obtutibus tam preterita quam etiam presentia necnon futura festinando iugiter de die in diem sine ulla dilatione declinant ad ruinam rapidissimoque cursu annorum cum mensibus temporalia siquidemᵇ tempora fugitiuis incessanter horis properant ad finem . Quapropter dispensante domino omnia regnorum terre regna ego Æþelredus Anglorum videlicet rex sollicita mente cogitando perscrutaui profuturum ac necessarium esseᶜ cum hiis transitoriis ac minime mansuris diuiciis perpetua atque iugiter perseuerantia celorum premia adquirerem . Idcirco tali memoria instructus atque meorum utique antecessorum roboratus exemplis dabo meo fideli homini þeodulfo aliquam terre partem id est . v . cassatos in loco qui uulgari consuetudine dicitur æt Burtune . cum omnibus ad se rite pertinentibus pratis campis terris pascuis siluis . liberaboque illam supradictam terram ab omni seruitute regali preter expedicione et arcis instructione pontisue . ita ut habeat et possideat et post obitum eius cuicumque uoluerit in perpetuam hereditatem derelinquat . Hiis metis et cetera . Si quis huius cupiditatis spiritu inlectus frangere uel irrita facere temptauerit huius priuilegii testimonia ·⁊ sciat se separatum a participacione sanctorum . si quis uero augere uoluerit ·⁊ augeat deus partem illius in iudicio in resurrectione iustorum . Scripta est hec et cetera . millesimo . xij . hiis testibus .

+

+Ego Æþelred rex hanc meam donacionem hoc signo crucis Cristi conformaui .

+Ego Æþelstan filius regis .

+Ego Eadmund frater predicti clitonis adiuui .ᵈ

+Ego Eadred donum regis confirmaui .

+Ego Þulfstan archiepiscopus corroboraui

+Ego Godpine pontifex

+Ego Adulf episcopus hilaris

+Ego Ælfhun	episcopus	non renuiᵉ
+Ego Æþelpold	pontifex .	solidaui
+Ego Byrhtpold	episcopus	muniui
+Ego Ædnoð	presul	confirmaui
+Ego Æþelsige	episcopus	assensum prebui

+Ego Leofing presul . +Ego Ælfgar episcopus . con' +Ego Godpine episcopus . Ego Bruhtpold episcopus et ceteri abbates . vj . duces . iiij^{or} . et ministri . xvj .

^a Carta . . . xij . *rubric*   ^b *Caret mark for an insertion before* tempora   ^c ut *omitted*   ^d *This and the following four subscriptions form a column*   ^e *This and the following four subscriptions form a column with titles and verbs in columns*

This appears to be an authentic charter. The witness-list is consistent with the date and omits Archbishop Ælfheah who was killed on 19 April 1012. The beneficiary has a continental name that was rare in England before the Conquest and he does not appear to subscribe charters. *Burtun* cannot be identified, but it may have been the place bequeathed by Wulfric to Burton Abbey which has been identified as Burton Hastings, Warwickshire, held T.R.E. by Siward and assessed at 4 hides (see above, p. xxxiii).

37

King Æthelred grants two hides (mansae) *at* Ecgintune [? *Eckington, Derbyshire*] *to Morcar*, minister. A.D. 1012

B. Aberystwyth, N.L.W., Peniarth 390, fo. 184 (p. 367): copy, s. xiii^{med}
Ed.: Hart, pp. 244–7
Listed: Sawyer 928

Carta Æþelredi regis de Egentona . anno domini . m° . xij .^a

+Flebilia fortiter detestanda totillantis seculi piacula diris obcene^b horrendeque mortalitatis circumsepta latratibus . non nos propria^c indepte^d pacis securos . set quasi fetide corruptele in voraginem casuros prouocando ammonent vt ea toto mentis conamine cum casibus suis non solum despiciendo sed etiam uelud fastidiosam melancolie nausiam abhominando fugiamus tendentes ad illud euuangelicum . date et dabitur uobis . Qua de re infima quasi peripsema quisquiliarum abiciens superna ad instar preciosorum monilium eligens . animum sempiternis gaudiis^e figens ad nanciscendam melliflue dulcedinis misericordiam . perfruendamque infinite leticie iocunditatem ⸴ ego Æþelredus rex Anglorum per omnipatrantis dexteram que Cristus est tocius Britannie regni [s]olio sublimatus quandam telluris particulam meo fideli ministro Morcero . id est duas mansas in illo loco qui^f solicole æt Ecgintune vocitant libenter tribuo . vt ille eam sine iugo honerosi vectigalis cum pratis . pascuis . siluis . riuulis . omnibusque ad eam vtilitatibus rite pertinentibus libenter ac eternaliter quamdiu uerberanti ocellorum conuolatu . auraque spirabili potiatus^g habeat . et post generalem qui omnibus certus incertusque homunciis^h constat transitum . cuicumque successionis heredi uoluerit condonando derelinquat . et perpetualiter contradat . Predictum siquidem rus hiis terminis circumcinctaⁱ patescit et cetera . Si hoc quod fieri non optamus aliquis tipho supercilii turgens hanc mee

donacionis breuiculam elidere aut infringere conauerit ⁊ sciat se ultima
contionis die classica clangente archangeli salpice . tumulis sponte
dehiscentibus somata diu fessa relinquentibus . omnibus pauefactis
creaturis cum Iuda melius non nato . impiisque contra Cristum con-
fligentibus Iudeis . quia non dictus proditor a satoris prosato filius
perditionis dicitur . eterna dampnatione edacibus innumerabilium tor-
mentorum flammis periturum . Huius namque a^k Deo inspirante atque
inuente^l voluntatis scedula . anno domini incarnationis . mᵒ . xijᵒ .
episcopis . abbatibus ducibus . patrie procuratoribus regia dapsilitate
ouantibus perscripta est . cuius etiam inconcusse firmitatis auctoritas
hiis testibus roborata constat . quorum nomina subtus caracteribus de-
picta annotantur .

+Ego Æþelredus singularis priuilegii ierarchia preditus rex huius in-
diculi fulcimentum cum signo sancte semperque amande crucis corroboraui et subscripsi .

+Ego Æþelstanus cliton consensum prebui figens crucem . +Ego
Eadmund illius supradicti regis filius consensi et subscripsi . +Ego
Þulfstanus Ebor*acensis* ecclesie archiepiscopus consensi . et ceteri
episcopi ⁊ x . abbates ⁊ vij . duces ⁊ iiij^{or} . et ministri   xvij .

ᵃ Carta . . . xij . *rubric*   ᵇ *For* obscene   ᶜ *?Error for* patria (*cf. S* 379)
ᵈ *Glossed* (*s. xiii*) adepte   ᵉ *Read* in sempiternis gaudiis (*cf. S* 379)   ᶠ *Error
for* quem   ᵍ *Error for* potiatur   ʰ *Error for* homunculis   ⁱ *Error for*
circumcinctum (*cf. S* 379)   ᵏ *? Delete* a   ˡ *Error for* iuuante

This is in the style of Athelstan's charters. The closest parallel is a Winchester
charter dated 932 but a similar anathema occurs in a Sherborne text dated 933
(S 417, 423). The dependence on earlier formulas is so great that this charter
must be dismissed as spurious. Hart, pp. 246–7, suggests that this is an authentic
charter, closely modelled on one of Athelstan's. Elsewhere, pp. 27–8, he argues
that in the early part of Æthelred's reign charters were sometimes complete
copies of earlier exemplars. Most of the examples cited as supporting this asser-
tion do not do so and even when the correspondence is very close, as between
S 844 and 855, dated 983 and 984, and S 463, dated 940, there are significant
differences in the subscriptions. The king's subscription in the present charter
is verbally very close to that commonly used by Athelstan and this is a particularly suspicious feature. Dr Dumville has pointed out that the grecizing form
of the nominative *cliton* is not found in charters after 955/6, when it is replaced
by a latinized form *clito*.

This charter purports to be a grant of 2 hides *æt Ecgintune* which has been
identified as Egginton, about four miles north of Burton (*PN Derbys.*, p. 459),
apparently because of their proximity. Burton Abbey never had any claim to
that place; it is not mentioned in Wulfric's will and was held T.R.E. by Toki
and assessed at 4 carucates (DB, i. 276b). The *Eccintun* which Wulfric bequeathed
to Morcar can be identified as Eckington, north of Chesterfield (see pp. xxvi–vii),
and it seems likely that this charter was intended to refer to the latter place. It
may have been drawn up for Morcar to provide a title-deed for an estate that he
had inherited without a charter. **27** implies that Wulfric had lost some of his
charters and **17** and **26** appear to be attempts, presumably made at Burton
Abbey, to make good such deficiencies. Morcar seems to have deposited his
charters at Burton and this one could have been produced there, but it is possible that it was made elsewhere.

38

King Edward grants two hides (territoria) *at* Berghe *to Tofig,* comes. A.D. 1048

B. Aberystwyth, N.L.W., Peniarth 390, fo. 184ᵛ (p. 368): copy, s. xiii^med, with glosses, s. xiii
Ed.: a. F. Barlow, *Edward the Confessor* (1970), pp. 332–3
    b. Hart, pp. 248–52
Listed: Sawyer 1017

Carta sancti Eadwardi regis et confessoris . patroni Westm' . de Berghe . anno domini m° . xlviij° .ᵃ

✠ Adstipulatione siquidem sacri spermatis herilis promulgando intonat buccina mestiferam tremendi examinis ymeram prepeti fore subreptione occursuram glomeratis terrigenumᵇ vniuersalis vbi astabit cuneus ac cunctitonantis almifluo altithroniᶜ clangente diathemateᵈ ᵉac in dieculaᶠ palatinisᵉ raptim collegio addicti contubernialibusᵍ lucicomi nasciscunturʰ poliⁱ ciuilia acta quorum lanx trutinandoᵏ fore probat faustissima quorumque eneruitˡ studia probis actionibus extant classiaᵐ imperpetua ceu cleronomi multabuntur erumpnaⁿ . ac pro talione infandaᵒ gehennalis Stycgie sine meta haurient infernalia . Quapropter ego Eadpeard tocius Albionis basileos mee donationis arte libere fruens quandam telluris particulam . ij . videlicet territoria in loco qui ab incolis Berghe cognominatur cuidam mihi fideli comiti Touig vocitamine in perpetuam hereditatem donant'ᵖ concedo . vt habeat ac possideat quamdiu vitali calore arctusᑫ caluerint . et post vite sue terminum cuicumque sibi libuerit sine aliquo scrupulo in hereditariam libertatem concedat . Tellus autem predictumʳ sit cum omnibus ad eandem rite pertinentibus . campis . pascuis . siluis . aquarum riuulis ab omni mundiali obstaculo liberumˢ . tantum expedicione . pontis arcisve restauracione exceptis . Quod si quispiam hanc nostre donacionis libertatem inuidie face turgens euertere conatus fuerit ⁖ cum Pilato et Iuda Scariothen . Caypha quoque eorumque commanipularibus eternaliter Acherontica combustione trudatur ⁖ nisi ante mortis articulum satisfactione penituerit congrua quod nostre donacionis presumpsit violare quod absit statuta . Hiis nempe metis rus antescriptum circumcingitur . et cetera . Acta est autem hec mea donacio anno ab incarnacione . domini nostri Iesu Cristi . m° . xlviij . indictione . ijᵃ . hiis testibus consentientibus quorum nomina hic inferius karraxanturᵗ

+Ego Eadpeard rex Anglorum cum triumpho sancte crucis hoc donum inmobile corroboraui .

+Ego Eazi archiepiscopus regie roborator donationis agye triumphale crucis signaculum depinxi .

+Ego Ælfric archiepiscopus triumphale tropheum agye crucis impressi .

+Ego Æðelstan episcopus consolidaui .
+Ego Eadnoð   episcopus consummaui .
+Ego Stigand   episcopus   confeci
+Ego Aldred   episcopus   adquieui .
+Ego Duduc   episcopus   subscripsi
+Ego Rodbeard episcopus consensum prebui .
+Ego Ægelpeard   abbas
+Ego Þulfric   abbas
+Ego Ælfpine   abbas[u]
+Ego Leofstan .   abbas
+Ego Leofsig .   abbas
+Ego Earnpig .   abbas
+Ego Ospig .   abbas
+Ego Godpine .   dux
+Ego Leofric .   dux
+Ego Sipard   dux
+Ego Harold   dux
+Ego Beorn .   dux[w]
+Ego Leofpine   minister .
+Ego Tostig   minister
+Ego Ælfstan   minister
+Ego Ælfgar   minister
+Ego Odda .   minister
+Ego Ordgar .   minister
+Ego Ordulf   minister
+Ego Brihtric   minister
+Ego Ælfpine .   minister[x]

[a] Carta . . . xlviij°. *rubric*   [b] *Read* terrigenis; *Dr Lapidge points out that it must agree with* glomeratis, *and must be dative plural dependent upon* occursuram   [c] *Glossed* Dei   [d] *Read* cogente diademate; *marginal gloss* comis id est hilaris benignus   [e · · · e] *Read* in diecula ac palatinis   [f] *Glossed* diurn. .   [g] *Read* adductis contubernalibus   [h] *Read* nanciscuntur   [i] *Read* gaudia   [k] *Glossed* librando   [l] *Glossed* id est sine virtute   [m] *Possibly a grecism* clausia *from* κλαῦσις '*weeping*'   [n] *Glossed* id est heredes condempnabunt et deducent   [o] *Glossed* id est nimia   [p] *Read* donando   [q] *Read* artus   [r] *Read* predicta   [s] *Read* libera   [t] *Glossed* id est scribuntur   [u] *First column of subscriptions ends here*   [w] *Second column of subscriptions ends here*   [x] *Third column of subscriptions ends here*

This extraordinary charter clearly baffled the scribe of Peniarth 390 and his misreadings have further obscured much of its meaning. Dr Lapidge, who is responsible for most of the suggested emendations, has proposed the following reconstruction of the first sentence:

Astipulatione siquidem sacri spermatis,
Since indeed, with the assent of the holy seed (i.e. offspring, Christ),

herilis promulgando intonat buccina
by its act of promulgation the Lord's trumpet announces

mestiferam tremendi examinis ymeram prepeti fore subreptione
that the sad day of the dreaded judgement with swift speed

occursuram glomeratis terrigen⟨is⟩,
is to fall on the assembled earth-dwellers,

universalis ubi astabit cuneus;
when the universal throng shall be present;

ac cunctitonantis almifluo altithroni ⟨cog⟩ente dia⟨d⟩emate
and with the benign power of the lofty-throned thunderer compelling

⟨h⟩ac in diecula,
on that day,

⟨ac⟩ palatinis raptim collegio adductis contubernalibus:
and with the associates of the heavenly court drawn together from all over in an assembly:

⟨illi⟩ lucicomi na⟨n⟩ciscuntur poli ⟨gaudia⟩
those persons attain to the joys of the shining heaven

acta quorum lanx trutinando fore probat faustissima;
whose deeds the balance in weighing approves of as being most blessed;

quorumque eneruit studia probis actionibus,
and those whose endeavours it severs (or 'separates') from good deeds

⟨illis⟩ extant cla⟨u⟩sia imperpetua:
for them there is eternal lamentation:

ceu cleronomi multabuntur erumna ac pro talione
like the heirs (of eternity) they shall be punished with tribulation and for punishment

infanda gehennalis Stycgie sine meta haurient infernalia.
they shall absorb the unspeakable regions of hellish Styx without end.

The glosses, which may be in the hand of the main scribe, are unlikely to have been devised in the thirteenth century and were probably copied from the charter, of which they may have been an original feature: hermeneutic texts were commonly provided with a contemporary gloss.

The unusual difficulty of this text is a strong argument in favour of its authenticity; no post-conquest forger is likely either to have composed it or to have chosen it as a model. It is dated 1048 in the second indiction which began in September of that year. The witness-list is consistent with this date, and includes Leofsige who seems likely to have been abbot of Ely. This would support Miss Harmer's suggestion that he died in 1055, not 1044 (*Writs*, p. 566). Neither the beneficiary Tofig *comes* nor *Berghe* can be identified. Professor Barlow suggests that as no earl of this name is known he was in fact a thegn and the copy is wrong (*Edward the Confessor*, p. 332). The evidence for the division of the earldoms in the reign of Edward the Confessor is too slight to justify such an emendation. Professor Whitelock has pointed out, in a private communication, that the evidence for other eleventh-century earls is sometimes very slight, e.g. Sihtric *dux*, who subscribes two charters in 1026 and 1031 (S 962, 963). She suggests that Tofig may have succeeded Thuri, *comes Mediterraneorum*, who is named in two writs addressed to the shire of Huntingdon but was succeeded there by Earl Siward according to a writ dated 1050–2 (S 997, 1106–7, cf. Harmer, *Writs*, pp. 572, 574). Hart, pp. 251–2, suggests that the beneficiary was Tofig the Proud although admitting elsewhere, p. 361, that he is unlikely to have lived so long. Burton Abbey had no claim to any place with this name. Hart argues that the assessment in *territoria* points to the Danelaw and he hazards the suggestion that it was Bergh Apton in Norfolk.

INDEXES

In these indexes *w* is substituted for *p* of the MSS and *Uu* is alphabetized as *w*. The forms of personal names occurring in the texts are followed as far as possible but, where normalized forms have been used, variants are noted under the first entry of each name. All variants are given except for *Æ, Ae,* and *Ę* in both initial and medial positions and variants between *ð, þ* and *th*; thus *Æþil-* or *Ethil-* would not be noted as variants of *Aeðil-*, but *Æþel-* would. Editorial comments are given in square brackets [ ]. Charters are referred to by their numbers, in bold type; other references are to the pages of the introduction or the commentaries.

1 INDEX OF PERSONAL NAMES

This is an index of names and titles rather than of individuals. References to laymen with the same name and rank are normally grouped together. Ecclesiastics are, as far as possible, distinguished but no attempt is made to identify individuals who held more than one office. Where two or more bishops of a see had the same name, they are distinguished by the numbers that have been conventionally assigned to them.

Ældred, *see* Ealdred
Ældric, *see* Ælfric
Ælfgar (Ælfgær), bishop [of Elmham], **28, 31, 32, 34, 35, 36**
— ealdorman, will of, xx
— earl, xxiv, xxvi, xxix, xxx, xlii–xliii, xlv–xlvi, 12, 26, 63
— *minister*, **12, 14, 28** *bis*, **38**
Ælfgifu (Ælfgyuu), wife of King Æthelred, 33
— wife of Earl Ælfgar, xlii–xliii
— 'of Northampton', daughter of Ealdorman Ælfhelm, xxii, xlii–xliii
— will of, xx
Ælfheah (Ælfæah, -æh, -eah, -eh, -heag, -heh, Elfelh), archbishop of Canterbury, **32, 33**; 69, 71
— archbishop [of Canterbury], **30, 31, 34, 35**
— bishop of Lichfield, **26, 27**
— bishop [of Lichfield or Winchester II], **24, 25**
— bishop of Winchester [I], **4, 10, 12**; 8
— bishop [of Winchester I], 18; *see also* Æthelfled
— bishop of Winchester [II], **26, 27**
— bishop [of Winchester II], **28**
— *dux*, **23**; 20
— *minister*, **12** *bis*, **17, 32** *bis*; xli, 20
Ælfhelm, bishop [of Dorchester], **28, 30**; 58
— *dux*, brother of Wulfric Spot, **28**; xiii, xviii–xvix, xxi, xxii, xxiv, xl, xlii–xliii, xlv, 5, 7, 22, 35, 60

— *minister*, **21, 23**; 34–5
— kinsman of Wulfric Spot, **29**; xviii, xxiii
Ælfhere (Ælfere, Ælfuere), abbot [? of Bath], **32**
— *dux*, **14, 17, 23**; 36
Ælfhun (Ælfhyn, Alfun), bishop [of London], **28, 30, 31, 32, 33, 34, 35, 36**
Ælfled, *see* Æthelflæd
Ælfmær (Ælmær), bishop [of Selsey], 33
— abbot [of Tavistock], **28**
— *minister*, **28**
Ælfnoþ (Ælfnað), *minister*, **17**
— **23**; 2
Ælfred, bishop [of Selsey], **8, 11**; 16
— *minister*, **12, 14, 17**
— **27**
Ælfric (Ældric), archbishop of Canterbury, **26, 27**; xviii–xxi, xxiii
— archbishop [of Canterbury], **28**
— archbishop [of York], **38**
— bishop [of Crediton], 24
— bishop [of Hereford], **4, 10**; 16
— bishop [of Ramsbury I], **10**; 16
— bishop [of Hereford or Ramsbury I], **8, 11**; 14
— priest, xxx
— *dux*, **26, 27, 28, 32**
— *minister*, **12, 17**
— 12
Ælfsige (Ælfsig, -sing, -sin, Elfsige), bishop [of Winchester I], **13, 14, 15, 17**; will of, xxxviii–xxxix

G

2 INDEX OF PLACE-NAMES

3 WORDS AND PERSONAL NAMES USED IN BOUNDARY MARKS

būtan 'outside'. *butan fif lan beheonan* **35**
Ceabbe (pers.n.) *ceabbe broc* **27**
Cēolf (pers.n.) *ceolfes crofte* **35**
Cēolheard (pers.n.) *ceoleardes beorge* **32**
chese ? from **cis* 'gravel'. *chese wælle hylle* **35**
cnapa 'boy, young man, servant'. *cnapanhylle* **31**
croft 'small enclosure'. *hwæte croft* **17**; *ceolfes crofte* **35**
cumb 'valley'. *cumbes heafde, cumbe; andland cumbes* **14**; *cumb welle léa* **27**
cund. cf. Cound, Salop (river n.) *cundes fenn, cundesleage* **11**
dæl 'valley, hollow'. *dæl, andlong dæles* **23**; *deopan dæle* **31**
Dene (pers.n.) *denes broc* **11**
denu 'valley'. *færdene* **17**
dēop 'deep'. *deopan dæle* **31**
dīc 'ditch'. *mærdic* **10**; *dic, gillundes dic* **11**; *dic ende* **17**; *on þa dic; dic hæge leofnaðes* **31**; *rugan dic; mæresdic; grenan díc* **32**; *on þone dic (ter), æfter dice (bis)* **35**
Dott (pers.n.) *dottes hlawe, dotdes* ~ **31**
ende 'end'. *dic ende* **17**; *on þan ufer ende balcan* **31**
Ēadgār (pers.n.) *eadgares lege* **31**
eafdan ? **31**
eald 'old'. *alde wic* **23**; *ealdan broc holan* **31**
Ēanswīth (pers.n.) *ansidelege* **31**; *(e)ansyðelege* **35**
*ēcels 'land added to an estate'. *smæle æcels* **26**
ecg 'edge'. *blacan ecge* **26**
ēg 'island'. *hryxies mæne weig* **26** [from gen. of *risc-ēg* or *riscig-ēg*]
ellen 'elder'. *ellen, ellan* **35**
fær ? 'road, passage, route'. *færdene* **17**
fenn 'fen, marsh'. *cundes fenn* **11**
ford 'ford'. *fulan ford; bradan ford; stanegan fórd* **23**; *sproges forda, stanian forda, wulstanes forda* **26**; *forde* **27**; *stanigan forde; stoc legan ford* **31**; *siðriðe forda; mæres ford* **32**; *bere fordes holme; on ðone forð* **35**
fūl 'dirty'. *fulan broc; fulan ford* **17**; *fulan sich; fulan syce (bis); fulan sic* **31**
gāt 'goat'. *gáte brycge* **26**
gillund ? *gillundes dic* **11**
Godrīc (pers.n.) *godrices lea* **26**
grēat 'thick, bulky'. *greatan þorn* **31**
grēne 'green'. *grenanhylle* **17**; *grene wege* **27**; *grenandíc* **32**
gryfja (Old Norse) 'hole, pit'. *holan gryfe* **31**
hæcc 'gate'. *on hæcce* **31**
hæg 'fence, enclosure'. *scid hæge; to*

wulffeges hæg andland hæges; on ðone dic hæge leofnaðes **31**; *in þone hæge* **35**. See also **hæg stōw**
hæg stōw ? 'hedged path, driveway'. *hæg stowe (bis)* **31**
hēafod 'head'. *cumbes heafde* **14**; *pire broces heafde* **27**
healh 'nook, valley, corner'. *stenges healh*, ~ *heale* **11**; *blacan hale* **26**
hīwan 'household, community'. *hine hylle* **11**; *hina hóh* **32**
hlāw, hlǣw 'tumulus'. *lytlan hlawan*, ~ *lauwan* **27**; *dottes hlawe* **31**
*hlēp 'leap, steep place' ? *to þan lewe* **35**
hnæpp 'bowl'. *swompes (h)næpe* **26**. See also **snæp**
hōh 'spur or ridge of land'. *myra hoh; æðeredes hoh; swines hoh* **23**; *hina hóh, hó* **32**
hol¹ 'hole, hollow'. *ealdan broc holan* **31**
hol² 'hollow, lying or running in a hollow'. *holan broce* **11**; *holgan broc* **26**; *holan gryfe* **31**; *holan mere* **32**
holm 'island'. *bere fordes holme* **35**
hungor 'hunger'. *hunger hylle* **35**
hwǣte 'wheat'. *hwæte croft* **17**
hwīt 'white'. *hwitan mor, witan mor* **11**
hyll 'hill'. *hine hylle*, ~ *hille* **11**; *grenan hylle* **17**; *cnapanhylle* **31**; *chese wælle hylle; hunger hylle* **35**
hyrne 'angle, corner, projection of land'. *stod faldes east hyrnan* **14**
hyrst 'hillock, copse'. *bracan hyrst* **31**
land i, 'strip in an open field'. *butan fif lan beheonan, of þan landan* **35**; ii, 'estate'. *ðrym landgemæren* **17**
lang 'long, tall'. *longan snapan* **27**
lēah 'wood, clearing, meadow, pasture'. *potteres le(a)ge; cundes le(a)ge* **11**; *blacelege; godrices lea* **26**; *cumb welle léa* **27**; *ansidelege; middel lege; eadgares lege; stoc legan ford* **31**; *(e)ansyðelege* **35**
Lēofnōth (pers.n.) *dic hæge leofnaðes* **31**
lind 'lime-tree'. *lind broc* **11**
lundr 'small wood', *twam lundan* **31**; ? *gillundes dic* **11**
lȳtel 'little'. *lytlan ðorn*; ~ *broce* **14**; *lytlan hlawan* **27**
mǣd 'meadow'. *mæd* **31**
mǣne 'common', *hryxies mæne weig* **26**
(ge)mǣre 'boundary'. *mærdic* **10**; *ðrym landgemæran* **17**; *mæran broce* **31**; *winstanesgemæra* **31**; *mæres ford; mæres dic* **32**; *mære þorne* **35**
mearð 'marten, weasel'. *mearðes scage* **26**
mere¹ 'pool'. *mere* **14**; *holan mere* **32**
mere² 'mare'. *myra hoh* **23**
micel 'big'. *michalen ac, mycelen æc* **11**
middan. See **onmiddan**
middel 'middle'. *middel lege* **31**

mōr 'marshland, moor'. *hwitan mor* **11**; *mor; wulfgares more* **26**

(ge)mȳðe 'confluence'. *in ða myðan, of ðam gemyðan* **32**

nearu 'narrow'. *æt þære nearawan sæten* **26**

ofer³ 'over, above, across'. *þwers ofer bracan hyrst* **31**

*ofes 'edge'. *on þa ofesan, æfter ofesan; abiðan ofesan* **31**

onmiddan 'in the middle of'. *on middan bere fordes holme* **35**

pīl 'pile, stake'. *pile broc* **31**

pire ? *pire broc* **11, 27**; *pire wasse* **11** [cf. Ekwall, *English River-Names*, s.v. Pur Brook]

pottere 'potter, pot-maker'. *potteres le(a)ge* **11**

pytt 'pit, hollow'. *pyt(te)* **14**; *pytt* **32**

rēad 'red'. *readan ácon* **27**

risc 'rush' or **riscig** 'rushy'. *hryxies mæne weig* **26** [from gen. of **risc-ēg** or **riscig-ēg**]

rīð 'stream'. *siðriðe forda* **32**

rūh 'rough'. *rugan hlæwe* **14**; *rugan dic* **32**

sǣte² 'house'. *æt þære nearawan sætan* **26**

scaga 'small wood, copse'. *mearðes scage* **26**

sceaddern ? *sce(a)dder(n) þorn* **26**

sceard 'notched, mutilated'. *sceardan beorge* **14**

sc(e)ort 'short'. *sceortanstane* **17**

scīd 'split piece of wood, plank'. *scid hæge* **31**

sīc 'small stream'. **26**; *fulan sich,* ~ *syce* (bis), ~ *sic* **31**; *to þan sice* **35**; *of þan syce, sich, syche* **35**

(ge)sīð 'companion, leader, noble'? *siðriðe forda* **32**

slǣd 'valley, hollow'. *andlang slædes* **17**

smæl 'narrow'. *smæle æcels* **26**

*snæp 'boggy ground'. *longan snapan* **27**

*sprogh(Old Norse) 'brushwood, twigs'? *sproges forda* **6**

stān 'stone'. *stan beorh,* ~ *beorge* **14**; *sceortan stane* **17**

stānig 'stony'. *stanegan fórd* **23**; *stanian forda* **26**; *stanigan forde* **31**

steng 'pole, staff'. *stenges healh* **11**

stocc 'tree-trunk, stump'. *stoc legan ford* **31**

stōdfald 'stud fold'. *stod faldes east hyrnan* **14**

stōw. *See* **hæg stōw**

strǣt 'Roman road, paved road'. *stræte, strete* **17, 26, 27, 31, 35**; *bradan strete* **31**

strēam 'stream, current'. *andlang streames* **14**; *ongean stream* **17**

stybb 'stub, tree-stump'. *þorn styb(be)* **14**; *to þan stubbe* **35**

sūr 'sour'. *sur æppel treo* **26**

swamm 'fungus, mushroom'. *swompes (h)næpe* **26**

swīn 'swine, pig'. *swines hoh* **23**

þēof 'thief'. *to ðan þorne þer ða þeofes licgan* **31**; *þær þa ðeofes hangað* **35**

þorn 'thorn tree'. *þorn styb(be); lytlan ðorn* **14**; *sce(a)dder(n) þorn* **26**; *greatan þorn* **31**; *to ðan þorne þer ða þeofes licgan* **31**; *wulfeardes þórn* **32**; *mære þorne* **35**

þrēo 'three'. *ðrym landgemæran* **17**

þurh 'through'. *ut ðorh ðone wudu* **31**

þwers 'crosswise'. *ðwers ofer ðawuda* **27**; *þwers ofer bracan hyrst* **31**

trēow 'tree'. *berhtelmes treo* **26**; *sur æppel treo* **26**

twēgen 'two'. *twam lundan* **31**

uferan 'upper'. *on þan ufer ende balcan* **31**

usweardan forstun ? **35**

*wæsse 'marsh'. *pirewasse* **11**

wattic(h)es æces ? **31**

weg 'way'. *andlang weges* **17**; *hryxies mæne weig* **26**; *grene wege* **27**

wīc 'dwelling, farm, dairy farm'. *alde wic* **23**

wyll 'well, spring'. *wylle* **17**; *cumb welle léa* **27**; *chese wælle hylle* **35**

wudu 'wood'. *wuda* **27, 31**; *ut ðorh ðone wudu* **31**

Wulfgār (pers.n.) *wulfgares more* **26**

Wulfhēah (pers.n.) *wulffeges hæge* **31**

Wulfheard (pers.n.) *wulfeardes þórn* **32**

Wulfstān (pers.n.) *wulstanes forda* **26**

Wynstān (pers.n.) *winstanesgemæra* **31**

4 LATIN GLOSSARY

The following abbreviations are used: n. = noun; v. = verb; adj. = adjective; adv. = adverb; p.p. = past participle; pret. = preterite.

accola (n.) [**27, 33**]: inhabitant, native dweller

adinventor (n.) [**28**]: inventor, discoverer

agalliama (n., from Greek ἀγαλλίαμα) [**33**]: transport of joy

agellulus (n.) [**23, 32**]: small plot of land

agius (adj., from Greek ἅγιος) [**12, 15, 17, 30, 38**]: holy

agon (n., from Greek ἀγών) [**9**]: *literally* battle, *but here the meaning has been extended, on the analogy of* S 520, *to mean* support for battle, troop-levy

almifluus (adj.) [**38**]: bountiful, benign

aporiatum (p.p. as adj., from *aporiare* (v.)) [**31**]: rejected, discarded

appensa (n., from *appensio*?) [**33**]: weight, measure, amount

architectorius (adj. or possibly n.) [**2, 19**]: creative, creating (*or perhaps simply* the Creator)

archos (n., from Greek ἀρχός [**33**]: ruler

arcipotens (adj.) [**17, 26**]: *originally meant* powerful with a bow (*arcus*), *but through confusion with* arx *came to mean* powerful in protection, mighty bulwark

arcitenens (adj.) [**34**]: *originally meant* bearing a bow (*as in Vergil*, Aen. III. 75), *but by confusion with* arx *came to mean something like* He who rules the heavenly citadel (*this meaning is attested in Anglo-Latin as early as Aldhelm*)

basileos (n., from Greek βασιλεύς) [**21, 22, 38**]: king

beatizo (v.) [**11**]: to endow

brevicula (n.) [**37**]: brief compass

calcetenus (adv.) [**32**]: in the end, finally

carasso (v., pret. *caressi*, from Greek χαράσσω) [**21**]: to write, subscribe (cf. *charaxo*)

cataclisma (n., from Greek κατακλυσμός) [**2**]: flood, inundation

celotenus (adv.) [**9**]: heavenwards, with heavenly aspirations

charaxo (v., ultimately from Greek χαράσσω) [**2, 9, 10, 11, 12, 19, 22, 23, 24, 26, 27, 32, 38**]: to write, endorse, subscribe

charisma (n., from Greek χάρισμα) [**5, 6, 9, 10, 11**]: favour, bounty, grace

chiralis (adj., from Greek χείρ and Latin -*alis*) [**33**]: of the hand, pertaining to the hand

?chrema (n., from Greek χρῆμα) [**8**]: treasure, piece (of gold), money

circumgiro (v.) [**4, 16, 19, 33**]: to bound, enclose, encircle

?classia (n., from Greek κλαῦσις) [**38**]: weeping, lamentation

cleronomus (n., from Greek κληρονόμος) [**20, 24, 38**]: heir

clima (n., from Greek κλίμα) [**2**]: region, latitude

cliton (n., ultimately from Greek κλυτός, 'renowned') [**13**]: prince. *Note that at a certain point* (c. 955/6) *the grecizing form* cliton *gives way in charters to* clito, *which thereafter becomes a normal Anglo-Latin word for* prince [**21, 30, 32, 33, 36, 37**]

collaterana (n.) [**33**]: consort, wife

colon (n., instead of the more normal *colonus*) [**25**]: inhabitant

commanipularis (n.) [**38**]: fellow soldier, comrade

concarraxo (v., ultimately from Greek χαράσσω) [**30**]: to subscribe

cosmus (n., from Greek κόσμος) [**16**]: the world, universe

crepundia (n.pl.) [**9**]: *originally meant* a child's rattle, *but in Anglo-Latin texts from Aldhelm onwards it is employed to mean something like* ornamentation, *and hence* trappings, appurtenances, *as here*

cunctitonans (adj.) [**38**]: all-thundering, *hence* omnipotent

custodite (adv.) [**25**]: carefully

cyrografum (n., from Greek χειρόγραφον) [**32**]: hand-written document, charter

decretarius (adj.) [**33**]: determined by decision

deifice (adv.) [**25**]: divinely

deificus (adj.) [**18, 21**]: divine

dema (n., from Greek δέμας) [**30**]: bodily frame

denichilo (v.) [**8, 9**]: to annul

?diathema (n.) [**38**]: *if the word is derived from Greek* διάθεμα, *it ought to mean* disposition *or the like, but this meaning is inappropriate in context in* 38; *it is therefore a possible corruption of* diadema, royal diadem, *hence* power *by extension*

didasculus (n., from Greek διδάσκαλος) [**13**]: master, teacher; *it was apparently stretched to mean* bishop *in the subscription of Oswulf of Ramsbury in* 13

diecula (n.) [**38**]: the brief space of a day

dinamia (n., from the Greek δύναμις) [**33**]: power, force *discifer* (n.) [3, 23]: steward (cf. OE disc-thegn)

ditalis (adj.) [34]: rich, generous, abundant

divisa (n.) [3, 9]: boundary

enucleo (v.) [30]: to reveal, explain

essentialiter (adv.) [5]: in (divine) essence

ethraliter (adv.) [13]: in the upper sky or aether; *hence* ethereally

eulogium (n., ultimately from Greek εὐλογία) [5, 8, 11, 13]: that which is (finely) expressed, *hence* written document

?evax (n. ?) [13]: *this word in classical Latin was an interjection meaning* hail *or* welcome; *it is found with this meaning in glossaries written in Anglo-Saxon England. But this meaning is completely inappropriate in the subscription to* 13 *of the queen-mother Eadgifu. It might be a corruption of* ava (grandmother), *a title which she uses in subscriptions elsewhere, but against this suggestion is the fact that she was Eadred's mother, not his grandmother*

exenium (n., ultimately from Greek ξείνια) [23]: gift, donation

?eya (interjection?) [6, 8]: *possibly derived from Greek* εἶα, *an interjection meaning* well, now, *and used in these two charters to mean something like Latin* ecce

gabalus (n.) [23, misspelled *sabulus*]: gallows *hence* cross *hence* sign of the cross

galaxia (n., from Greek γαλαξίας, 'the Milky Way') [34]: the heavenly realm

gnosticus (adj., from Greek γνωστικός) [33]: wise, learned. *The adjective* gnosticus *is used as a substantive, learned man, in* 20, 21 *and* 24

herilis (adj.) [38]: of the master, lord

ierarchia (n., from Greek ἱεραρχία) [37]: holy office

Iesualis (adj.) [11]: pertaining to Jesus (cf. S 404)

indeclinabiliter (adv.) [12, 15, 16, 17]: unalterably, unceasingly

indiculus (n.) [37]: document, charter

infulatus (adj.) [3]: adorned

largiflue (adv.) [8]: abundantly, generously

largifluus (adj.) [3, 26]: abundant, generously endowed

largissim (adv.) [4]: generously, abundantly

largitio (n.) [3]: generosity, kindness

literula (n.) [2]: letter (= written character)

lucicomus (adj.) [38]: resplendent, shining

melliflue (adv.) [8]: sweetly, *hence by extension* generously

mestiferus (adj.) [38]: sad, doleful

missito (v.) [25]: to send

monarchia (n., from Greek μοναρχεία) [18]: monarchy

mortiferus (adj.) [28]: deadly, death-bearing

munificatio (n.) [34]: endowment

nominetenus (adv.) [6]: name-wise

omnipatrans (adj.) [37]: all-accomplishing, omnipotent

onoma (n., from Greek ὄνομα) [10, 21, 30]: name

oppido (adv.) [20, 24]: exceedingly, very much

paradigma (n., from Greek παράδειγμα) [8, 13]: example, lesson

patrigena (n.) [2]: estate, citizenry

patulo (adv.) [30]: clearly

peripsema (n., from Greek περίψημα) [21, 37]: off-scouring, rubbish (*a word which owes its currency among draftsmen of Anglo-Latin charters to Aldhelm*)

pernecessarium (adj.) [24]: extremely necessary

philargiria (n., from Greek φιλαργυρία) [5, 6, 23]: love of silver, avarice, covetousness

piscosus (adj.) [5]: abounding in fish

pneuma (n., from Greek πνεῦμα) [28]: (Holy) Spirit

previsor (n.) [2]: overseer

propugnator (n.) [4, 8, 9, 13]: defender

protoplastus (n., from Greek πρωτόπλαστος) [24, 28]: the first created man (Adam), *hence* man *in general*

quisquilia (n.) [37]: waste, rubbish (*a word whose currency among draftsmen of charters is owed to Aldhelm*)

roborator (n.) [38]: supporter

ruricola (n.) [4, 15, 19, 24]: inhabitant of the country

rurigena (n.) [34]: (native) inhabitant of the country

sabulus (n.) [23]: *see* gabalus *above*

sartago (n.) [4, 12]: *lit.* a frying-pan; *by extension*, an instrument of fiery torture, a furnace

satrapa (n.) [8]: *probably a latinization of* OE thegn

scibilis (adj.) [21]: well-known

sigillo (v.) [9, 11]: to seal (a document), *hence simply* to endorse, subscribe

signaculum (n.) [1, 5, 9, 38]: sign, mark, seal

signamen (n.) [30]: sign, mark, seal

silvaticus (adj.) [5]: wood-land

singrapha (n., from Greek συγγραφή [32]: that which is written, *hence*, charter *or* document

solicola (n.) [8, 12, 31, 35, 36]: inhabitant (of the land)

soma (n., from Greek σῶμα) [37]: body, corpse

spatiolus (n.) [30]: little place

sperma (n., from Greek σπέρμα) [38]: seed, offspring

subarro (v.) [3]: to pledge, to endorse

sublevamen (n.) [19]: relief, support

subsigillo (v.) [21]: to seal (a document), to endorse, to subscribe

tauma (n., ultimately from the Greek letter *tau*) [24, 25]: +, the sign of the cross

termen (n., instead of the usual *terminus*) [10]: boundary, limit

terratenus (adv.) [6]: land-wise

terrigena (n.) [25]: inhabitant

theologia (n., from Greek θεολογία) [5]: divinity (*rather than* theology)

theos (n., from Greek θεός) [2, 19]: God

tiphos (n., from Greek τῦφος) [37]: vanity, pride

?trichelaus (n., possibly a corruption of Greek τροχηλάτης) [2]: *used of St. Paul (whose words from* II Cor. V. 16 *are quoted in this context in* 2), *possibly describing him as a* charioteer, *hence* contestant, *on the basis of* I Cor. IX. 24; *but this is a highly conjectural interpretation of an immensely difficult word*

tripudialiter (adv.) [13]: joyously

triviatim (adv.) [20]: publicly, commonly; *hence* far and wide, everywhere

usia (n., from Greek οὐσία) [34]: substance, essence

veneniferus (adj.) [28]: poisonous

ventilatus (adj.) [2]: set in motion, proffered

verbigena (n.) [28]: He who was born of the Word (i.e. Christ)

vocamen (n.) [11, 17, 23, 26]: name

vocitamen (n.) [38]: name

vulgariter (adv.) [16]: commonly

vulgarus (n., instead of *vulgus* or *vulgaris*) [23]: common person

ymera (n., from Greek ἡμέρα) [38]: day

DIPLOMATIC INDEX

An index of *sanctio* clauses, although desirable, is omitted because in the present charters they are so varied that an index would require extensive quotation from the texts, which would be more appropriate in a cumulative index than here.

1 VERBAL INVOCATIONS AND PROEMS

(a) *Invocations*

Annuente altithroni moderatoris imperio **20**

Domino dominorum dominante in secula seculorum **12**

Domino nostro Iesu Cristo cum patre et flamine sacro . . . moderamine **34**

In nomine cosmi salvatoris . . . inmortale **16**

In nomine Dei summi **23**

In nomine Dei summi et altissimi Iesu Cristi **21**

In nomine Domini **29**

In nomine domini Iesu Cristi **3, 15, 17, 26, 36**

Pollente perpetualiter domini nostri Iesu Cristi regno **27**

Regnante imperpetuum domino nostro Iesu Cristo **14**

Regnante Theo inperpetuum architectorio **2**

Superna aspirante gratia **1**

(b) *Proems*

Adstipulatione siquidem sacri spermatis **38**

Cum enim nos liquide **30**

Cum fas licitumque **18**

Cuncta que humanis obtutibus **3**

Cuncta que in hoc seculo **23**

Cunctis catholice conuersantibus certum est **8**

Eterne hereditatis territoria et perpetue prosperitatis priuilegia **4**

Flebilia fortiter detestanda **37**

Huius instabilitas uitae **27**

In principio creauit Deus celum **13**

Manifestum est cunctis **14**

Nihil intulimus in hunc mundum **21**

Nobilitatis mundane fastigium **22**

Omnia que hic humanis considerantur obtutibus **36**

Omnia que uidentur temporalia sunt **32**

Omnibus quibus cristianitatis censuram **17, 26**

Omnis usie creatura **34**
Opere precium constat **2**
Perpetua hereditas **5, 6, 7**
Perpetue prosperitatis priuilegium **9**
Postquam malesuada ueneniferi serpentis suggestio **28**
Prophetica primitus predicacio et apostolica deinceps disceptacio **11**
Quicquid inter seculares **10**
Regna regnorum huius presentis seculi transeunt **12**

Summe vereque bonitatis Deum solum **33**
Universorum conditor et creator **31, 35**

(c) *Combined Invocations and Proems*

Annuente Dei patris ineffabili . . . clementia . . . **25**
Regnante domino nostro Iesu Cristo inperpetuum . . . **24**
Regnante Theo imperpetuum architectorio . . . **19**

2 DISPOSITIVE WORDS

(a) *Past tense*

condonauit **8**
dedi **16, 23, 31, 35**
dedi . . . largiendo donaui **15**
dedit **6, 7**
inpendere curaui **34**
inpenderem **19**
largitus sum **20, 22**
mutuaui **31**
tradens . . . tradidi **2**

(b) *Present tense*

collaudat **13**
concedo **12, 21**
condono **24, 30**
confero **32** (*see also* **8, 9**)
do et concedo **10**
donando concedo **38**

effert et honorat concedens **6, 7**
impartior **33**
impendo **27, 31**
inpendo . . . confirmo **35**
locupletat **11**
(locupletat . . .) concedens **11**
locupletat et honorat concedens **5**
locupletat . . . tribuendo **4**
offero **28**
tribuo **37**

(c) *Future tense*

concedens donabo **3**
conscribens donabo **1**
dabo . . . liberaboque **36**
largiendo . . . concedens perdonabo **25**

(*d*) *No verb*

14, 17, 18, 26

3 ROYAL STYLES

(A) *Dispositive clause*　　　　　　　　　　　　　　(B) *Subscription*

Æthelflæd, Lady of the Mercians

domina Merciorum **1**

Athelstan

rex Anglorum tociusque climatis . . . Cristiane　　　　rex **2, 3**
patrigene preuisor **2**
Angulsaxonum rex **3**
rex Angulsexna and Norþhymbra imperator paganorum　　rex Anglorum **4**
gubernator Brittanorumque propugnator **4**

Eadmund I

rex et rector Angulsæxna **5, 6, 7**　　　　　　　　　rex **5, 6, 7**

Eadred

rex Ængulsæxna ond Norðhymbra imperator paganorum
gubernator Brittonumque propugnator **8**
rex rite Anglorum gloriosissimus rectorque Noþhanhimbra
et paganorum imperator Brittonumque propugnator **9**
Anglorum rex **10**　　　　　　　　　　　　　　　　rex **10**
rex Anglorum **11**　　　　　　　　　　　　　　　　rex Albionis **11**
rex Anglorum gubernator et rector **12**　　　　　　　rex Anglorum **12**
rex Angulsæxna et Norþhimbra imperator　　　　　　　rex tocius Britannie **13**
paganorum gubernator Brettonumque propugnator **13**

Eadwig

rex Anglorum ceterarumque gentium in circuitu
persistentium **14**
rex Anglorum ceterarumque gentium in circuitu
persistentium gubernator et rector **15**
disposicione gentis Angligene et diuersarum
nationum industrius rex **16**
rex Anglorum ac tocius Bryttanicæ telluris
gubernator et rector **17**

rex Anglorum **14, 15, 16,
17**

Eadred

rex Merciorum . . . Albionis monarchiam solus
exercens **18**

rex Anglorum **18**

Eadgar

rex Anglorum **19, 20**
tocius Albionis dei disposicione regni
fastigium optinens **21**
tocius Brittanie basileos **22**
rex Anglorum ceterarumque gentium in
circuitu persistentium gubernator et rector **23**

rex Anglorum **19, 20**
tocius Anglice nationis
basileos **21**
rex **22, 23**

Æthelred

rex et monarchus tocius Albionis **24**
rex et gubernator tocius angliene gentis
aliarumque gentium in circuitu persistentium **25**
rex Anglorum ac tocius Brittanicę telluris
gubernator et rector **26**
rex Anglorum **27, 28, 31, 35, 37**
regali infula Anglorum populis Cristo
allubescente subthronizatus **30**
inperiali regiminis gentis Anglorum
sceptro potitus **32**
tocius rector archosque Bryttanie **33**
rex **34**
Anglorum videlicet rex **36**

rex Anglorum **24, 25, 26,
27, 28, 31, 32, 34, 35**

rex tocius Brittanice telluris **33**
rex **36, 37**

Eadward the Confessor

tocius Albionis basileos **38**

rex Anglorum **38**